Governance and Public M.

Series Editor
Paul Joyce
INLOGOV
University of Birmingham
Birmingham, UK

IIAS Series: Governance and Public Management

International Institute of Administrative Sciences (IIAS)—*Setting the Governance Agenda Worldwide*
Website: http://www.iias-iisa.org
Edited by Paul Joyce

To cover the diversity of its members, the IIAS has set up four sub-entities:

– The EGPA (European Group for Public Administration)
– The IASIA (International Association of Schools and Institutes of Administration)
– The LAGPA (Latin American Group for Public Administration)
– The AGPA (Asian Group for Public Administration)

Governance and Public Management Series
This IIAS series of books on Governance and Public Management has a focus and breadth that reflects the concerns of the International Institute of Administrative Sciences. The Institute, which was set up in 1930, involves academics and governments from all around the world. The Institute's work involves supporting both practitioners and academics, which it does by encouraging the production of relevant knowledge on public governance and public management and by facilitating its dissemination and utilization.

It is the intention of the series to include books that are forward-looking, have an emphasis on theory and practice, are based on sound understanding of empirical reality, and offer ideas and prescriptions for better public governance and public management. This means the books will include not only facts about causes and effects, but also include ideas for actions and strategies that have positive consequences for the future of public governance and management. The books will offer a point of view about responses to the big challenges facing public governance and management over the next decade, such as sustainable development, the climate crisis, technological change and artificial intelligence (A.I.), poverty, social exclusion, international cooperation, and open government.

All books in the series are subject to Palgrave's rigorous peer review process: https://www.palgrave.com/gb/demystifying-peer-review/792492

More information about this series at
http://www.palgrave.com/gp/series/15021

Michiel S. De Vries • Juraj Nemec
David Špaček
Editors

International Trends in Participatory Budgeting

Between Trivial Pursuits and Best Practices

palgrave
macmillan

Editors
Michiel S. De Vries
Institute for Management Research
Radboud University Nijmegen
Nijmegen, The Netherlands

Department of Public Administration
Kaunas Technological University
Kaunas, Lithuania

Department of Public Administration
University of the Free State
Bloemfontein, South Africa

David Špaček
Faculty of Economics and Administration
Masaryk University
Brno, Czech Republic

Juraj Nemec
Faculty of Economics and
Administration
Masaryk University
Brno, Czech Republic

ISSN 2524-728X   ISSN 2524-7298   (electronic)
Governance and Public Management
ISBN 978-3-030-79932-8   ISBN 978-3-030-79930-4   (eBook)
https://doi.org/10.1007/978-3-030-79930-4

Contents

Notes on Contributors

Mstislav Afanasiev Doctor ès economics, is a professor at National Research University, Higher School of Economics (HSE) in Moscow, and chief research fellow at the Institute of Economic Forecasting, Russian Academy of Sciences (Ecfor RAS) in Moscow, Russian Federation. He is the head of HSE research seminar *Modernisation of Public Finance*. He received doctor honoris causa from John Cabot University. He has published almost 140 books and scientific articles on public finance, macroeconomics and corporative finance, including well-known university textbook *Budget and budgetary system*, 6 ed. (2020).

Janina Apostolou is a research assistant and coordinator of an international economics and trade programme at the Hamburg University of Applied Sciences. She is also a PhD candidate at Andrássy University Budapest and is currently completing her dissertation analysing the diffusion of participatory budgeting in Germany from a political economy perspective.

Francesco Badia in Business Administration, is Associate Professor at the University of Bari Aldo Moro, where he teaches Management of Tourism Organizations and Management of Tourism and Cultural Events. His main research interests focus on local governance, participatory mechanisms, management of cultural organisations and cultural heritage, cultural tourism strategies and corporate social responsibility and non-financial disclosure. He has published almost 100 scientific works as books, journal articles (among them *Journal of Management and Governance*,

Sustainability, International Journal of Arts Management), book chapters, and conference proceedings.

Eduard Bakoš is an assistant professor at the Department of Public Economics, Faculty of Economics and Administration, Masaryk University in Brno and consultant of the Institute of Public Administration at the same faculty. Previously, he had worked at the University of Defence, where he lectured on security and crisis management from the perspective of public administration. Currently, he focuses both professionally and pedagogically on public finance, intergovernmental cooperation, and local government. He was involved in several applied projects for various public authorities.

Jože Benčina is Associate Professor of Economics and Public Management in the Faculty of Public Administration at the University of Ljubljana, Slovenia. He is currently the head of the Chair of Economics and Management in the Public Sector at the Faculty of Public Administration.

Slađana Benković is a professor in the Faculty of Organizational Sciences at the University of Belgrade, and the head of the Financial Management and Accounting department. She has published a significant number of papers in international and national conferences, monographs, and journals. She was a scholarship holder of the US and UK governments, and from 2013–2019, she was a member of the Finance Committee of the UB. Benković took part in numerous scientific and research international projects, but her involvement in the process of higher education institutions programme evaluation in Serbia and as an external evaluator of the European HEIs programme should be highlighted.

Arnold Bernaciak is associated professor in the Faculty of Finance and Banking at WSB University in Poznań, Poland. He is the vice-rector of Science. His research interests focus on environmental and ecological economics, sustainable development, and environmental management. He has published almost 100 journal papers, chapters in books and conference papers. He also cooperates with Polish local governments as an expert in the fields of sustainable development and environmental protection strategies. He is a member of the board of the Polish Association of Environmental and Resource Economists.

Emil Boc is an associate professor at Babeș-Bolyai University of Cluj-Napoca, Romania, member of the Department of Political Sciences. He was the prime minister of Romania between 2008 and 2012. He is also Mayor of Cluj-Napoca, with previous mandates for the years 2004–2008 and 2012–present. Emil Boc is also European rapporteur of SEDEC—CoR on "brain drain in EU".

Michiel S. de Vries is Professor of Public Administration, Radboud University Nijmegen, and studied Sociology at the University of Groningen. He worked previously at the University of Amsterdam, Thorbecke Academy in Leeuwarden, and the Free University Amsterdam. He has a PhD in Law (Utrecht University). In 2016 he received a Doctor Honoris Causa in Public Economics from the Masaryk University of Brno. Michiel S. de Vries is Full Professor of Public Administration at the Radboud University of Nijmegen, Distinguished Professor of Public Administration at Kaunas University of Technology, and extraordinary professor at the Free State University in Bloemfontein. He is past president of IASIA and member of the editorial board of numerous journals on public administration. His research concentrates on local government, policy evaluation, policy change and comparative public administration and has resulted in over 300 scholarly publications and over 20 edited volumes and monographs.

Jasmina Džinić is an assistant professor at the Chair of Administrative Science, Faculty of Law, University of Zagreb, Croatia. She teaches several courses in the fields of public administration and public management. She has published more than 40 scientific papers and book chapters, and one book in co-authorship. In 2011, she received the award for the paper *Regulatory bodies and regulation: some problems connected with issuing decrees for law implementation* and in 2015 she was awarded with the NISPAcee Mzia Mikeladze PhD Thesis Award. Her professional field of interest comprises public management, administrative reforms, organisational theory, and public administration education.

Martina Eckardt is full time Professor of Public Finance at Andrássy University Budapest, Hungary, and member of the Otto-Friedrich University Bamberg, Germany. She has been dean at the Department of International Relations (2008–2010) and served as member of the University Council from 2010 to 2018 at Andrássy University Budapest. Her research topics include social policy, law and economics, institutional economics, inter alia. Since 2014 she is board member of the German Law and Economics Association.

Tarso Genro is a lawyer and the president of the New Paradigms Institute (Instituto Novos Paradigmas). He was mayor of Porto Alegre, RS, Federal Deputy, Secretary of the Council for Economic and Social Development of the Presidency of the Republic, Minister of Education, Minister of Justice, Minister of Institutional Relations of the governments of President Luiz Inácio Lula da Silva, the PT's national president, and is the author of several books and articles on law and political theory, such as: "Possible Utopia", "Individual Labor Law", "Contribution to the Criticism of Collective Labor Law", and "'The Future for Setting Up': Democracy and Socialism in the Global Age".

Daniel Klimovský is Associate Professor of Political Science at Comenius University in Bratislava, Slovakia. Besides political science, his background also includes public administration and public policy. His research and teaching activities are focused on public administration as well as political issues linked to sub-national levels. Phenomena of co-creation, citizen engagement, and innovations in decision-making at local level became main areas of his research activities recently. Concerning his international recognition, he has taken part in several important research projects, and published dozens of various publications in twelve languages. He has rich experience in lecturing abroad, and he has closely cooperated with the Council of Europe, Network of Institutes and Schools of Public Administration in Central and Eastern Europe, Regional Studies Association, Social Watch, Open Society Foundation in Slovakia, Government of the Slovak Republic, Association of Towns and Communities of Slovakia, Association of Self-Governing Regions in Slovakia, Office of the Plenipotentiary of the Government for the Development of Civil Society, and so on. In addition, he cooperates with the Science and Research Centre of the Faculty of Economics and Administration, University of Pardubice in the Czech Republic.

Péter Klotz is currently an assistant professor and integrity management specialist at the National University of Budapest, Hungary. He is deputy head of the anti-corruption and integrity development project of the NUPS and at the same time, leader of the integrity advisor postgraduate training course at the University. Péter Klotz conducted several researches in the past in the topics of human resources management, integrity management, and local governments.

Maja Klun is a full time professor in the Faculty of Public Administration, University of Ljubljana. She was a guest lecturer at different universities across Europe. Her main fields of research are public finance and economics of public sector. She publishes in different journals and conference papers. She is co-author and co-editor of scientific monographs as well. From 2009 she is working as vice-dean for the research at the Faculty of Public Administration. She was also deputy of secretary general at EAPAA for a few years.

Artur Roland Kozłowski is WSB Professor with PhD and habilitation in Social Sciences with specialisation of International Relations. He is the head of Law and Security Science Institute and dean of the Department of Economy and Management in Gdynia at WSB University in Gdansk. He is an author of three books of CEE geopolitics and a co-author of two other books—one on Polish and Ukrainian diplomacy and another on higher education in Central Europe. He has also published around 40 scientific articles on CEE in international relations, political systems, development of populism, participatory budget. He is a member of the Congress of Political Economists (US) and the Polish Society for International Studies.

Yuri V. Krivorotko is a Doctor of Economic Sciences, professor, Head of Economics and Accounting at the BIP—University of Law and Social-Information Technologies. He is currently a member of the University Council and Economics and Law faculty. He is also an expert in Public Finance at the NGO "Lev Sapieha Foundation". Krivorotko has authored and co-authored 23 books and published more than 100 articles and working papers. Yuri Krivorotko is an individual member of the Institutes and Schools of Public Administration in Central and Eastern Europe (NISPAcee). He is also CoE expert in local government finance from Belarus on the project of local financial benchmarking (2015–2017). Since September 2017 he holds the position of Bank Independent Director recognised by the National Bank of the Republic of Belarus.

Soňa Kukučková is an assistant professor at the Department of Finance, Faculty of Business and Administration, Mendel University in Brno. She graduated in Finance from the Faculty of National Economy, University of Economics in Bratislava. She received PhD in Economic Policy from Masaryk University in Brno. Then for several years, she has worked for financial institutions (KPMG, Volksbank, and Sberbank) at different positions and focused on finance and accounting. She currently teaches public finance, and her research topics are behavioural economics, public budgets, and local government.

Dan-Tudor Lazăr is a professor at Babeş-Bolyai University of Cluj-Napoca, Romania, member of the Department of Administration and Public Management. He was the prime minister's adviser on economic affairs in the Romanian government between 2009 and 2010, and Secretary of State in the Ministry of Public Finance for the period 2010–2012. Dan-Tudor Lazăr has also been vice-rector for finance, digitalisation and the relation with students at Babeş-Bolyai University of Cluj-Napoca, Romania, starting from 2012.

Miloš Milosavljević is an associate professor at the University of Belgrade. He teaches financial management and accounting. His research interest covers public finance and public administration. Hitherto, he has been involved in a number of international and national projects (funded by Tempus, Erasmus, IPA, SDC, and USAID) as a manager, researcher, or trainer/teacher. The projects cover different topics related to financial management and public finance. He has published several books and monographs, and more than 100 articles in international and national journals and conference proceedings.

Juraj Nemec is full time Professor of Public Finance and Public Management in the Faculty of Economics and Administration at Masaryk University in Brno, Czech Republic, and part time professor in the Faculty of Economics at Matej Bel University in Banska Bystrica, Slovakia, with 38 years' experience in teaching at pre-graduate, graduate and doctoral levels. In 2016 he was elected as the president of the Network of Institutes and Schools of Public Administration in Central and Eastern Europe (NISPAcee). He is the vice-president of the International Association of Schools and Institutes of Administration and the member of the Committee of Experts on Public Administration at United Nations. He has published over 400 books and scientific articles.

Lucie Sedmihradská is an associate professor at the Department of Public Finance, Prague University of Economics and Business. Aside from teaching she has been involved in several local and international research projects focusing on public budgets, local government finance, and inter-municipal cooperation. She has published approximately three dozen journal articles and book chapters and a monograph on municipal budgetary process. She currently serves as elected finance official in one of the Prague city districts.

Nataliya Shash Doctor ès economics, is a full time professor in Financial Management Department at Plekhanov Russian University of Economics in Moscow, Russian Federation. Since 2015, she has been a member of the expert group of the Government of the Russian Federation in the field of improving the efficiency of budget expenditures and improving state programmes. Since 2019, she has been a consultant for the project on improving the efficiency of operations and implementing financial management tools in the public sector of the economy. She is the author of almost 130 books and scientific articles on public finance and macroeconomic development.

Iwona Sobis is an associate professor at the School of Public Administration at the University of Gothenburg in Sweden. Her main professional duties include lecturing and conducting seminars with 1st, 2nd, and 3rd cycle students. Her research from 1995 to 2010 focused on the Western advice to Central and Eastern Europe during transition from socialism to a market economy. Since 2011, she has conducted comparative studies on public reforms, municipal development, local democracy, care for the elderly, and EU's internal migration. She has published 50 research articles, book chapters and books. She is a member of few expert groups on the research proposal review of some European countries and a reviewer of several international scientific journals.

Dmitriy V. Sokol is an associate professor in Corporate Finance Department at the Economic Faculty of Belarus State University, Minsk, Belarus. With that, he is the vice-chairman of the Board of NGO "Lev Sapieha Foundation" (a non-governmental think-tank on problems of local self-government), where he acts as expert in local finance and budgeting issues. Since 2007, he has been actively engaged in analyses of effectiveness of local finance and budgeting in Belarus. He has repeatedly acted as a country and local expert in projects of the Council of Europe and the European Commission. He has more than 60 scientific and methodological publications.

David Špaček is an associate professor at the Department of Public Economics, Faculty of Economics and Administration, Masaryk University, Brno, Czech Republic. He has participated in various national as well as international projects as a member of their research team, project coordinator and project leader. In his research and lecturing, he concentrated on various aspects of public management and public administration—for example public administration reform, e-government and e-participation, quality and performance management and performance appraisal. He has also been involved in consultancy for the European Union and its projects.

Željko Spasenić works as a teaching assistant at the Faculty of Organizational Sciences, University of Belgrade. For two years he has worked as teaching associate at the Faculty of Economics, University of Belgrade, engaged for two courses: Business Economics and Principles of Economics. Afterwards, he pursued banking career in Erste Bank, UniCredit Bank, and Societe Generale Bank as a risk manager responsible for underwriting large corporates, financial institutions, municipalities, real estate, and structured finance deals. He also has experience as ERP consultant with focus on finance and production module of MS NAV. Currently, he is a PhD student at the Faculty of Organizational Sciences, University of Belgrade, in the field of quantitative management.

Mária Murray Svidroňová is Associate Professor of Public Economy and Services at Matej Bel University in Banska Bystrica, Slovakia. Her pedagogical and research activities are focused on the economics and management of the third sector, public and private nonprofit organizations, and civil society. She is particularly interested in social innovation issues in the area of public service provision, for example through co-creation, community building, participatory budgeting, and civic activism. She is active in several international studies and research projects dealing with public service innovation and civic engagement. In cooperation with the Office of the Plenipotentiary of the Government for the Development of Civil Society, she participated in the preparation of legislative changes in the field of financing NGOs. She runs her own civic association. She was the chairperson of the Mayor's Council of Banská Bystrica for non-governmental organizations She is a member of the Accreditation Commission of the Ministry of Education of the Slovak Republic for Specialized Activities in the field of youth work.

List of Figures

List of Tables

The Diffusion of Participatory Budgeting: An Introduction to this Volume—With an Intermezzo by Tarso Genro, the Mayor of Porto Alegre Between 1992 and 1996

Michiel S. de Vries, Juraj Nemec, David Špaček, and Tarso Genro

1.1 INTRODUCTION

As the saying goes, the sequel is never as good as the original and copies always contain flaws. That may be true for films, books, and paintings, but the question is whether it is also a valid remark concerning innovations in

M. S. de Vries
Institute for Management Research, Radboud University Nijmegen, Nijmegen, The Netherlands

Department of Public Administration, Kaunas Technological University, Kaunas, Lithuania

Department of Public Administration, University of the Free State, Bloemfontein, South Africa
e-mail: m.devries@fm.ru.nl

© The Author(s), under exclusive license to Springer Nature Switzerland AG 2022
M. S. De Vries et al. (eds.), *International Trends in Participatory Budgeting*, Governance and Public Management,
https://doi.org/10.1007/978-3-030-79930-4_1

public policymaking. In public policy it might be the reverse, as pilots might contain imperfections to be removed when actors learn more from the first experimental case and the resulting innovative practice is repeated in an improved manner. Participatory budgeting (PB) was such an innovation, starting in Porte Alegre in Brazil as a result of efforts made by the Brazilian Workers' Party at the end of the 1980s. In that city, later referring to itself as the 'Capital of Participatory budgeting', it was seen as the first step from representative democracy towards that of direct democracy, calling PB a case of radically democratising democracy; a practice in which the until then marginalised people from poor neighbourhoods were allowed to deliberate with the municipality how to spend part of its budget. It proved to be a powerful instrument as was seen in the widespread diffusion of PB and becoming sometimes a standard practice in cities all over the world. Table 1.1 gives the number of PB processes in 2019.

Notwithstanding the impressiveness of the number, such figures can be deceiving. Europe seems to be the continent in which PB has spread the widest. However, almost half of those cases are to be found in Poland (1800 cases), which is due to a national law regulation concerning PB. This law from 2018 made PB compulsory in 66 cities and optional for the remainder of local governments. The same applies for South America in

Table 1.1   The spread of participatory budgeting worldwide in 2019

Continent	Number of participatory budgeting cases
Europe	4577–4676
South America	3061–3081
Asia	2773–2775
Africa	955–958
Central America and the Caribbean	134–142
North America	178
Total, 71 countries	11,690–11,825

Source: Authors, based on Dias et al. (2019)

J. Nemec (✉) • D. Špaček
Faculty of Economics and Administration, Masaryk University,
Brno, Czech Republic
e-mail: juraj.nemec@umb.sk; david.spacek@econ.muni.cz

T. Genro
Porto Alegre, Brazil

which Peru is, for similar reasons, frontrunner with 1869 PB processes in local government and 2089 in total, which accounts for two-thirds of all such processes in South America.

Notwithstanding such ambiguities, Table 1.1 shows that PB has, in name, travelled all over the world. Its diffusion was a process well described by Osmany Porto de Oliveira (2017). He argued that in this process of the international diffusion of PB individuals played a crucial role, especially local Brazilian authorities in the beginning and then by international experts (de Oliveira, 2017, p. 6). Its diffusion in Brazil occurred above all through the action of mayors, activists, networks linked to the Partido dos Trabalhadores (PT), the Workers Party, and the action of civil society (de Oliveira, 2017, p. 10). The United Nations (UN), the European Union (EU), and the World Bank have been responsible for the diffusion outside Brazil. They have been fundamental in stimulating cooperation between municipalities with the purpose of spreading PB. A major impetus was experienced when Porto Alegre won the award for 'Best Practice' for Urban Management during the International Conference on UN-Habitat II held in 1996 in Istanbul. In 2000, PB was adopted by a number of municipalities in Europe with France and Spain being the frontrunners.

The introduction of PB in three European countries was well described by Anja Röcke in 2014. She paid specific attention to the developments in Germany, France, and the UK. She concluded that specific actors and factors are crucial in order to start the process of PB: it is necessary to have a clear political will or leadership strategy that deliberately aims at going beyond established practices of citizen participation; a strong power position for implementing these goals, as well as a certain level of administrative and wider political support; and financial resources (for having the possibility, for instance, to use different mobilisation strategies or employ external facilitators for the discussion) (Röcke, 2014, p. 169).

Notwithstanding this knowledge, the question about the quality of sequels and copies remains an important one as the scholarly literature mentions that 'PB is being implemented in very different ways, largely as a result of legal, social, political, and historical traditions that exist in different countries' (Harkins & Escobar, 2015). Concerning Europe, Röcke was critical about the actual participation of participants, their procedural power in monitoring and controlling the process, and the deliberative quality (Röcke, 2014, p. 166).

She is not alone in this criticism. From a critical perspective, many scholars mentioned that such community-based meetings are often dominated by certain groups/people while other groups are [still] marginalised (Fung, 2006; Irvin & Stansbury, 2004; Kuruppu et al., 2016; Lowndes & Wilson, 2001; Musso et al., 2011; Nyamori et al., 2012). Holdo mentioned that 'empirical studies have often been less encouraging for participatory democrats (Baiocchi & Ganuza, 2014). PBs do not necessarily empower civil society to self-organise independently of the government if such ability is lacking at the outset (Holdo, 2016, p. 1). Furthermore, he states that it 'offers opportunities for manipulation. … PB plays a strategic part in partisan power struggles, and therefore does not have empowerment as its primary political goal' (Holdo, 2016, p. 3). Regarding a Sri Lankan case, it was concluded that 'the practice of PB was just a symbolic means of monopolising power and exerting domination and symbolic violence' (Kuruppu et al., 2016); for a case in Laos it was concluded that the PB process had no intrinsic value at all (High, 2009) and for Latin American cases Goldfrank concluded that 'participatory budgeting has not generally led to poverty reduction, more accountability, and participation, or to better municipal government' (Goldfrank, 2007, pp. 94–98). This is rather different from what was concluded about the original case in Porto Alegre. There it was said to have resulted in measurable benefits, including the expansion of access to basic public services such as sewerage systems, water, and paved roads (Moynihan, 2007, p. 68). During the period 1989–1996, the first seven years in which PB was practiced, the proportion of households with access to water services rose from 80% to 98%; the percentage of the population served by the municipal sewerage system increased from 46% to 85%; the number of children enrolled in public schools doubled; and, on average, an additional 30 km of roads were paved every year (Gonçalves, 2014, p. 108). PB directed more investments to regions that were generally poorer (Melgar, 2014, p. 129), and the process fundamentally changed the relationship between the citizens and the state. It was claimed to have improved the functioning of government and to have led to improved public services and infrastructure. 'It changed not just "where" public money was spent (spatially) but also on "what" the money was spent (functionally)' (Calabrese et al., 2020, p. 1385). In Porto Alegre the achievement of substantive goals for poor neighbourhoods was crucial, with secondary effects in improving the relationship between the citizens and the state. This is seen in the intermezzo presented below, in which the mayor of Porto Alegre at the time PB started in that city, Tarso Genro, at our request, talks about the objectives thereof, the procedures followed, the opportunities it offered, and the challenges faced.

Intermezzo: The Political Genesis of Participatory Budgeting
Tarso Genro, Mayor of Porto Alegre between 1992 and 1996

Based on democratic political theory, I discuss the political and institutional policy genesis of Participatory Budgeting (OP). I am doing this as one of the active 'formulators' of its implementation and as a collaborator in diverse academic works, some of them as an interviewee, others as an informal 'consultant.' The hundreds of works about OP have already shown that it can be critically analysed as a victorious democratic experience, with its magnitudes and limits. The present contribution moves in another direction, as it looks for its ideological and political assumptions, until now 'invisible', that are not contained in those researches that contributed to its worldwide recognition.

Both in the celebration of the 200th anniversary of the French Revolution and the destruction of the Berlin Wall, hundreds of intellectuals 'celebrated what would be an eternal marriage of capitalism with human rights, through a democratic and representative way (...), but, after thirty years, the couple finds themselves in the shadow of divorce (Spitz, 2019). I adduce: with its illegitimate children evoking fascism, anti-science, xenophobia, indifference to death and the agony of the excluded and the poor.

In the climate that preceded the implementation of Participatory Budgeting *in Porto Alegre, at the 'end of communism' festivals, the celebrations were not seen by us as though they were signs of a new future for the left, but rather as the start of recovery of a collapsing utopia. We were, therefore, distant from the liberal-democratic optimism expressed right after the historic explosion and were instead closer to being a rebellious orphanage.*

In November 1989, a breakdown of the 'real' experiences of the East and the liberal turning point of the European democratic social contract added to the destruction of the Wall, signalling, however, to the left of the world, the imperative of reflecting on the roots of our socialist ideology. Without an encounter with a past considered to be heroic (which was fading) the present of this past would fall into the void, and the dialogue of the left, on socialism and on the 'de-democratic issue', would lose its meaning.

While I write this text, capitalism is bound up, not with democracy, but with global financial capital, besieged by the coronavirus pan-

(*continued*)

(continued)

demic. The world's poor and miserable remain 'on the margins of life', at the mercy of what capitalism has become after the fall of the Wall: Trump representing the humanist crisis of capitalism and Merkel representing its guilty enlightenment conscience. The spectrum of 'communis' does not hover in any part of the world and the lack of a humanistic (and possible) democratic counterpoint to neoliberalism unleashes market forces to their maximum level of fetishism in the global order.

The city of Porto Alegre was a fertile ground for debate in 1989. The dictatorship's political action, more repressive where attempts at armed struggle were intense, had not defused the left that operated in the region: liberation theology Christians, heterodox and traditional communists, 'autonomists' and social democrats, with their discrete or clandestine organisations, survived. Most of its cadres, then, were already part of the Workers' Party, which intended to build itself as the 'moral reserve' for a left, even if it was generally socialist, ready to recompose the old utopias.

When the 1988 Constitution came into force, whose assembly was agreed upon between the 'consenting' opposition and sectors of the military regime, the left again took on a relevant public role. That was when it put on another outfit and opened itself, successively, to new forms of struggle and organisation. The idea of a socialist revolution, through the different routes that the left proposed in the fight against the military dictatorship, began to collapse, obstructed by the clarity of the democratic political struggle that demands other forms of contention and more sophisticated views to understand the new questions of State and government.

Part of this military left in the neighbourhoods 'infiltrated', along with the city's social movements, defending community demands for basic sanitation, public electricity, day-care centres, improvements in public transportation and infrastructure works, such as paving the streets. In this new period, the left would also revive its influences with the universities and the trade union movement, as well as returning to be present in the representative organisations of the liberal professionals active in the resistance movements against the regime of exception.

In the democratic restoration, whose decisive moment was the promulgation of the Constitution of 88, the left maintained its momentum, to try to radicalise the emerging democracy. It was in this context that

(continued)

(continued)

OP became the common project of a plural left, which emerged from hiding with its more hardened militants but had also already been integrated by young social struggle activists from the early 1980s onwards. Its principal ideas on politics were developed in direct opposition to the traditional parties of that time which were tolerated by the dictatorship and which had also reorganised after the political amnesty in 1979.

In this environment, the government programme of the first Popular Front Nominate (1988) in Porto Alegre was composed and which would prove capable of winning the direct elections for City Hall. This slate had the signatory of this text as a candidate for vice-mayor, under the leadership of bank-unionist Olívio Dutra as candidate for mayor. At the time, Olívio was an avant-garde union leader and had become the most influential figure in the state of Rio Grande do Sul in organising the Workers' Party.

These are the specific conditions in which the 'anti-system' idea of the Participatory Budget arises, through the social and political left, which proposes to encourage an imagined popular participation, but with a form far from what it would be in the future. Our inspiration came from the examples of the Paris Commune, the Soviets, the German Social Democratic Councils, the spontaneous popular plenary sessions of the community movements in the city which had remained alive albeit in a reserved and sometimes clientelist manner during the military dictatorship.

In assuming, in the 1989 elections, commitments to governance 'on the left' through what we called Popular Councils, we initiated a practical movement in search of a model of popular participation and, afterwards, we opened a theoretical debate about the normative form of our project, which was still undefined. The discussion, which travelled extensively through the plural bases of the PT, was not internalised by the other left-wing parties, indifferent to a movement that began with little chance of becoming a national and world example.

The practical movement was naturally supported in community movements (organised or in nucleation), which allowed it not to have to start from 'zero' and encouraged us to capture the energy of the existing community struggle which had survived the authoritarianism of

(continued)

(continued)

the military regime. We proposed new forms of organisation to communities for their valorisation before the State, assuming the commitment that they would have a privileged impact on the composition of the public budget so that their demands would be met.

In the ongoing elaborations we defended direct democracy, idealised by traditional conceptions of the left, which saw the institutions and the political spaces of democracy as spaces of struggle, refusing to be endowed with a 'universal value.' In the process of its implementation, direct democracy became, however, a democratic instrument of public management, integrated into the ongoing legal order, pushing its limits, but truly reorganising the institutional life of the city.

The normative model that was perfected would come from a peculiar form of understanding of public law which proposed to constitute through a dialogue with the General Council of the OP an internal regulation which in turn would regulate the operation of the OP in a negotiated way with its regional city councils. This form of regulation was agreed upon with the elected government and therefore governed a political-legal contract of local scope, as of a non-state public right, agreed upon by the political delegation via electoral vote and the regional councils of the OP.

This contract, in order to 'work', would have to be respected by governments that, by ideological conception, assimilated democratic radicalisation and understood that the production of the budget 'should go down' to the lower classes.

The next moment would be the objectification of a fraction of the Social State at the local level, not as the preliminary moment of a socialist project as we unrealistically wanted. The democratic conciliation that had won in Brazilian society, with the Constitution of 88, recommended that we put aside the most immediate illusions and absorb entirely the new democratic political process, the result of the conciliation that had removed us from the dictatorship.

Here, that which has been formulated by Boaventura de Souza Santos is a good fit for understanding our itinerary: 'The problem of democracy in non-hegemonic conceptions is closely linked to the recognition that democracy is not a mere accident or a simple work of institutional engi-

(*continued*)

(continued)

neering. Democracy constitutes a new historical grammar. This is not the case, as in Barrington Moore Jr., of thinking about the structural determinations for the constitution of this new grammar. It is about realising that democracy is a socio-historical form and that such forms are not determinable by natural laws' (Boaventura de Sousa Santos, 2002).

In the debate on how to compose the Budget, the question of participation that had gone through electoral dissent was now presented as a concrete question of governance, and this need for governance would have a decisive influence on the concept of popular participation that we inaugurated. It would, in fact, turn to the democratisation of local political management (in the city), and no longer to the 'subversion' of formal state institutions. This political and theoretical formulation effort for the new times, in which we would no longer be in systematic opposition to the military regime and its governments, occupied our revolutionary imaginary and called us to the real, ongoing policy, originating from the controlled 'opening' that became an open road from the Social Constitution of 88 onwards.

In our first two governments in the city (1989–1992; 1993–1996), we faced issues that would influence the format of OP in Porto Alegre, giving the city a worldwide projection, not only before the leftist governments, but with all of the governments that bet on some level of innovation in the liberal-representative agenda in the local environment. This innovation was brought about by the political restructuring of city management, at the municipal level, through the absorption of direct democracy combined and integrated into representative democracy.

The process carried out there promoted a meeting in that space between different social groups that crossed the city's class structure, at a specific moment of 'non-revolutionary conjuncture', when 'the OP of the capital of Rio Grande do Sul in 1989–2004 became the experience that best illustrated a radical-democratic solution in the direction of a political pedagogy of self-emancipation' (Marques, 2005).

The evolution of the number of demands in our first three governments (Olívio Dutra, Tarso Genro and Raul Pont) clearly demonstrates the degree of confidence that the process had acquired in the city's poorest communities and in its lower middle classes; the demands had

(continued)

(continued)

evolved 87.71% since the beginning of the OP in 1990, having started with 230 demands reaching 440 in 12 years. The demands were met, totally or partially, by the government, with the execution of each budget in this period.

The final 'baseline' dilemma, which would involve the nature of a left-wing government, within a new legal order which opened spaces for a combination of direct and representative democracy would be the following: would the workers and their allies, having been elected to Government by democratic means, govern the city only for the workers and the excluded or did they govern for 'the whole city?'

Would the inversion of the hierarchy in public investments, prioritising the lower income classes, be enough to characterise a leftist government within the city? However, the axial theme to be answered was more complex; the workers govern for the whole city, but how to transparently privilege the needs of the 'low' in the public budget? It was a question then of establishing regulated budgetary privileges, based on the weight of the direct participation of the communities in the discussion of the public budget, which would be absorbable by the local legislative power, as an organ of the political representation that voted on the budget and transformed it into a legal norm.

This transparent budget privilege is what would drive contractual regulation, between government and councils through the OP's internal regulations, and its consequent success with the popular classes. As investments in public works and investments in health and education appeared as real fruits of popular decision in the lives of the communities, confidence in the march of direct democracy articulated with the electoral delegation was visibly increasing.

This view of management, as a task of the left, implied the formation of a new 'ruling group', implicit or agreed upon within the Workers' Party and the government itself, to expand its support. The conscious institution of a direct democracy, as 'seed of a new State', allowed a process of popular participation combined with respect for political representation.

After 16 years in force by the PT governments, which reorganised the city of Porto Alegre, OP gradually weakened and lost its decision-making power, without being fully dismantled, until its liquidation in

(continued)

(continued)

2020 by the extreme right-wing city government. Such liquidation took place under the indifference or the applause of the local media oligopoly, which perceived the OP as harmful to its influence in the formation of opinion and had always acted in defence of the 'business' vision of public management, with the State being 'managed' as a private company.

In our first and second governments (between 89 and 96), traditional communist parties and the parties that had configured themselves as being from the 'popular' field (workers, above all), did not only sympathise with the forms of direct participation that according to them competed with parliamentary representation in the City Council (Municipal Legislative Power), as well as because, in their view, they empowered the Workers' Party among the city's most popular strata.

In the winning perspective in our country, in which 'place would become a privileged space, (to) make the relationship between government and society more practical', Castells' vision made perfect sense; 'the municipality (…) is the state organ most permeable to a political representation of the dominated classes (…). It was this (view), in opposition to the left, that gave municipal policy its avant-garde character in the long permeability of the left's march through democratic institutions' (Castells, 1980, p. 1269; Larangeira, 1996).

The successive centrist and right-wing governments, which succeeded one another in Porto Alegre, gradually broke with that political contract that granted reliability to the OP, as this relevant information reports: 'in 1989, there were 13 municipalities that adopted the policy of participation in the budget. In 1993, 36 cities adopted the policy; in 1997 (the year that expanded the implementation of OP in medium and small cities) 103 cities; in 2001, 177 cities; in 2005, 203 municipalities; in 2007, 353 municipalities; in 2009, 437 cities; and finally, in 2014, 482 cities had adopted OP in the 26 states of Brazil. In 2017, according to a survey by the Municipal Planning Secretariat of the prefecture of Rio Grande (then the coordinating city of the BR OP Network), only 120 municipalities adopted this policy, and of these, only 24 are in full operation' (encurtador.com.br/dpxEL).

The degradation of OP, until its political death in the hands of the extreme 'managerial' right, is also clear in these data:

(continued)

(continued)

> Over the years it has been found that more than half (a number ranging from 53.2% to 69%) of people think that they 'always or almost always' make decisions about works and services. However, in the last two years of the survey (2005 and 2009), there was a considerable reduction in the perception of 'always or almost always' deciding, while in the same period, the answers 'never' or 'sometimes' had grown to about one-third—'never' went from 0.6 in 1998 to 3.8 in 2009; and 'sometimes' went from 23.8 in 1998 to 32.4 in 2009. Based on this information, it is concluded that opinion regarding decision-making power has become more pessimistic. (encurtador.com.br/kl189)

In Olívio Dutra's government, already at the state level (between 1999–2003), the Participatory Budgeting system was instituted with relative success, although its wear and tear was already underway and resistance in the state parliament was extraordinarily strong, since the participatory political methods of OP strongly reduced the power of oligarchies to control the budget.

Based on this experience of the Olívio Government, in the second government (2011–2015), already as a Popular Front in Rio Grande do Sul and with strong communist participation, with the Governor who writes this text, we formulated a new participatory system, sustained in the OP, thus narrated by one of the leaders of this new experience: 'The State System of Popular and Citizen Participation of Rio Grande do Sul (2011–2014) was instituted by the state government in 2011, aiming to articulate, in a systemic way, different social participation forums. The System brought together ongoing experiences in the state, namely Popular Consultation and the Regional Development Councils (COREDES), supported by State Law instituted by the Alceu Collares Government (1991–1995); the rescue of the Economic and Social Development Council forums and the Participatory Budget itself; and the institution of new ones, the Digital Office and the Office of Mayors.'

Among its guidelines, the System proposed to guarantee direct citizen participation, in person or digitally, in the elaboration, monitoring and evaluation of policies; transversality in its executions, and the promotion of a qualified and systematic dialogue with society.

(continued)

(continued)

Thus, the objective was not limited to the legitimation of government policies, but also the opening of new channels, from which government actions could be debated, concerted and decided upon by society. The interdependence between the spaces of participation, without removing their autonomy, sought to integrate three conceptual dimensions: (i) participation of society in the formulation of strategic policies and in the composition of the budget and investment; (ii) democratisation of public management in the state deliberative process; (iii) interaction between government and issues sensitive to society through new information and communication technologies.

The vocation of each forum component of the System ensured the diversity, breadth and transversality of participation and policies managed at different levels. The multifaceted and dynamic profile enabled the permanent participatory process, from the voting of the annual budget, in the OP plenary sessions, to the formulation of concerted policies at the CDES, through the debates promoted by the Digital Office. The annual calendar of activities allowed for the continuous participation of society in management, the monitoring of the implementation of public policies, the review of strategic planning, and the treatment of conjunctural issues.

In 2013, in an effort to improve the System, the Government determined, through a Guideline Note signed by the Governor, that:

> [...] this process must combine the different dimensions of participation that make up the System, ranging from debates with representations of civil society, held at the CDES on management and strategies, through meetings with debates on development held in the regions, for the present and direct participation of citizens in the debates on the budget, for the dialogue carried out through the virtual mechanisms until reaching universal voting. [...]. The combination of all these instruments, in a consistent and organic manner, is the basis of our Popular and Citizen Participation System. (NOTE GUIDELINE N° 21, March 2013)

The new guideline was not fully fulfilled, among other reasons, as the System was interrupted by the government that succeeded the Tarso Genro administration, condemning this unprecedented experience to temporal encapsulation and, in the end, its melancholic extinction.

(continued)

(continued)

Some results presented by three of its main forums materialise the objectives sought by the guidelines that instituted the Participation System. The balance of the four years of activities of the Council of Economic and Social Development of the State of Rio Grande do Sul (CDES RS) presented the realisation of 24 meetings of the entire Council; 19 Thematic Chambers; 35 Thematic Dialogues; 23 Regional Dialogues; new national and international seminars; two Concertation Letters; 60 Concertation reports and recommendations to the governor. Of these, 192 proposals agreed upon by the 90 councillors representing civil society *were met or processed, totally or partially by the state government (Rio Grande Do Sul, 2014). Of the five participation tools promoted by the Digital Office— Governor Asks; Governor Responds, Government Listens; Keeping an Eye on Public Works; and Dialogues in Network—only in fifteen editions of the 'Government Listens' were there more than 700,000 interactions (https://issuu.com/uira/docs/balanco-gabinetedigital-2011a2014.). In 2014, the State OP registered the participation of more than 1.3 million citizens in voting on investment priorities for the 2015 budget. As participants in the regional hearings: 6101; participants in municipal assemblies: 79,120; participants in digital voting: 255,751; participants in the face-to-face vote: 1,059,842; total: 1,315,593 voters (https://www.estado. rs.gov.br/estado-registra-a-maior-votacao-da-participacao-popular-no-orcamento). The participation system, more than a technical innovation for public management, was certainly a new 'democratic management technology.'*

The experience of the OP in Porto Alegre, which has diversified around the world, was a generous political experience of State management that intended to share (and did) the political responsibilities for the management of public resources, paid by the contributor to the public power. Its importance was attested to by the resistance it raised in the most conservative sectors of society, which had always handled the public budget primarily to meet their interests and who always understood the State, in its most concrete nerve, as money, as a private apparatus for its exclusive control. Yet, the OP is not a lost experience, nor is it the beginning of a revolution. In a future perspective, however, if liberal-representative democracy is recovered as a political universe of common experience, this OP experience will be considered a landmark of reformist daring within the order.

This book delves into the question of whether the many follow-ups in what is called 'participatory budgeting' deserve the same positive qualifications as were given to the developments in Porto Alegre. Did something change and what was it that changed in the practice thereof when PB was implemented in cities outside of Latin America? Were improvements or deteriorations seen?

We distinguish four indicators for the aforementioned hypothesis that sequels often imply a deteriorating practice, namely that the definition changed of what PB means, that the broader goals or purposes of PB change over time; that the way in which PB is organised changes; and that the substance of public participation changed when it spread all over the world. For instance, with the diffusion of PB around Brazil, the amount of money involved, the part of the total municipal budget on which the citizens could deliberate, decreased sharply (Röcke, 2014). Of importance, is that analyses of the developments on the '*what it is about*', the substance of PB processes, nearly stop after the practice emigrated from Brazil. In the scholarly literature, there is little attention to the evolution in the substance of PB outside of Brazil.

1.2 REVERSING THE MAIN AND SIDE-EFFECTS

When PB started in Porto Alegre in 1989, the basic idea was to involve previously marginalised groups in society in the decision-making about the spending of a municipal budget through extensive deliberation. PB started when the leftist workers party (Partido dos Trabalhadores) came into power in Porto Alegre. Its idea was to give disadvantaged groups the possibility to take part in municipal politics, to have actual deliberation with them, and to let them vote on where to spend the money and how to spend it. In particular, it intended to provide opportunities for those citizens from poor districts, for people from ethnic minorities, and for women, to provide arguments and to prioritise the allocation of the money available in the municipal budget. The prime goal was that this would have redistributive effects with more public investments in the poor districts, presumably resulting in an overall rise in the human development in the city (cf. Abers, 1996, 1998, 2000; Avritzer, 2006; Baiocchi et al., 2006). In Porto Alegre, 200 reals per capita were at stake when the process started off (Cabannes & Delgado, 2015). Up to 2004, citizens controlled 100% of the capital investment budget through PB, this being the funds remaining after all maintenance and administrative costs (Calisto Friant, 2019).

The goals were largely achieved. By 2006, almost 20% of all the residents had participated at some point of time in the process of PB (Calisto Friant, 2019, p. 86). Crucial in this type of PB is the centrality of the social dimension in terms of actually transferring power to the marginalised concerning the spending of the municipal budget in order to achieve a redistribution of funds to their long-term social and economic advantage.

When the innovative practice spread to other cities, first within Brazil, then to other countries in Latin America, and then to countries outside this continent, something strange happened. The main intended effects and the unintended side-effects of PB changed places. The main effects became secondary and the unintended side-effects became major goals of PB. Already in 1993 Berry concluded that a prominent effect of PB is that people participating become *more knowledgeable, more tolerant, more efficacious*, and *more confident in government*. No matter the importance thereof, this was seen as just a side-effect in the original. The same remark can be made regarding the following effects mentioned in the existing scholarly literature. For the World Bank, PB is an instrument to improve local institutions and is associated with the principles of *'good governance'*, transparency, *empowerment, and accountability* (de Oliveira, 2017, p. 149; Shah, 2007), and for the United Nations, PB was a legitimate policy to *promote the Millennium Development Objectives, improve public management* of local collectives and fight against poverty (Shah, 2007, p. 137).

PB is said to be able to create a *stronger* civil society, *improve* transparency, *lead to greater public accountability*, and *allocate resources more effectively* (Jaramillo & Alcázar, 2017; Touchton et al., 2019; Wampler, 2007). In 2006, Goldfrank emphasised the *democratic participation* and the need for transparency in the process and outcome of PBs. Montambeault talks about the *redefinition of democratic citizenship* through PB processes, one where participants *'learn'* to become citizen-agents through their participation in these so-called *schools of democracy* (Montambeault, 2016, p. 283). PB is also argued to be rather attractive for citizens compared to other participatory initiatives like (e-)consultations because it is not as abstract and therefore it seems that citizens are more motivated to be engaged with local governments (Royo et al., 2020).

In 2007, Miller claimed that PB 'could enhance the *legitimacy* of municipal decision-making. When participants are willing and able to combine cooperation and contestation, they may condition the use of deliberation as a means of legitimisation.' Kuo and Chen argued that PB has the positive effects of *two-way communication* and *collective discussion*, that it is significant in that it points to things that the public sector does not see, and has the effect that the proposals that come out from PB tend to be more refined because they have gone through several rounds of discussion, and complements representative democracy at a community level (Kuo et al., 2020, pp. 136–137). Wampler (2007) further pointed out that PB needs to go or actually goes hand in hand with (1) *educating* members of the public to see beyond their specific, short-term projects to focus on more general long-term planning needs of the community; (2) *understanding* that government remains the primary actor as the provider of funds and in making sure promises are kept; and (3) understanding that there are some broader issues that may need the *involvement* of the federal or state government and solving these types of concerns may not be realised in one budget cycle (see also Gordon et al., 2017).

PB was seen as a mediating instrument between particular groups of citizens and the city management (Miller & O'Leary, 2007). Cohen et al. argued that PB ensures that people have a fundamental right to have a say in decisions that affect them. PB would improve *effectiveness*: when the decision-making process includes people affected by an issue, improve the *quality of the decisions* and their *implementation*; and *nurture democratic capabilities and agency* among participants (Cohen et al., 2015, p. 6). The expected citizenship education involved in PB is expected to *cultivate engaged, skilled, and knowledgeable citizens* that actively participate in civic and social life in their communities. Baiocchi and Lerner claim that 'enhanced citizen monitoring and oversight can make for better and more *legitimate governance*. For progressive administrators in particular, PB opens new doors for legitimating redistributive politics' (Baiocchi & Lerner, 2007, p. 8). Others have also argued that PB results in greater legitimacy of investment decisions, due to the inclusion of citizens in determining investment priorities; greater further *participation, engagement, education*, and increased *civic responsibility*: achieving greater transparency in public expenditure, encouraging accountability and responsibility of politicians; serving as an instrument for social innovation and having positive effects on the *quality of deliberation* and *democracy* and *social capital* (Cabannes, 2004; Koonings, 2004; Rios & Rios Insua, 2008; Rose et al., 2010). Boukhris et al. argue that citizens' engagement is considered as one of the important dimensions for the development of *smart cities* and increases citizens' engagement, citizens' confidence in their society, their political knowledge, as well as their citizenship. It goes through initiatives that allow groups of citizens to communicate with the authorities to participate in decision-making processes and to form new groups with common interests (Sæbø et al., 2008). International monetary organisations such as the World Bank and other bilateral development agencies, for instance, the United States Agency for International Development (USAID), are involved in disseminating this form of budgeting in the local governments of less-developed countries (LDCs) with rhetoric, amongst others, democratising democracy, eradicating corruption and clientelism, and uplifting the quality of life of the most deprived (Speer, 2012). Researchers in public administration have envisaged PB as a central element in fostering the deliberate or participatory form of democracy (Ebdon & Franklin, 2006; Kuruppu et al., 2016; Michels, 2011; Musso et al., 2011).

Sintomer et al. (2013) talk about the effect on the improvement of communication between citizens and policymakers, and the *dynamisation of the local social fabric* (p. 16); the *linkage between the main organised structures of society*, which facilitates social consensus around certain aspects of public policies (p. 19); the *social consensus* through the mediation of interests, values, and demands for recognition by the various factions in society (p. 20); and the idea of *community empowerment* and *community development* (p. 2; Röcke, 2014). Talpin added that PB could contribute to defining the norms of good behaviour (Talpin, 2011, p. 67).

Anwar Shah writes in his book on the topic that PB is a tool for *educating, engaging*, and *empowering citizens* and strengthening demand for *good governance*. The enhanced transparency and *accountability* that PB creates can help reduce government inefficiency and *curb clientelism, patronage, and corruption*. (p. 1); it would be an important tool for *improving service delivery* to communities (p. 10) and creates opportunities for *engaging, educating, and empowering citizens*, which can foster a more *vibrant* civil society. Participatory budgeting also helps to promote transparency, which has the potential to *reduce government inefficiencies* and corruption. Because most citizens who participate have low incomes and low levels of formal education, participatory budgeting offers citizens from historically excluded groups the opportunity to make choices that will *affect how their government acts*. Put simply, participatory budgeting programmes provide poor and historically excluded citizens with *access to important* decision-making venues (p. 21).

All the goals mentioned above in *italics* are of utmost importance. There is no doubt about it. However, reviewing the vast amount of literature, it seems that a kind of goal displacement has taken place. The substance of PB, that is, the redistribution of a significant part of the municipal funds through actual deliberation with previously marginalised groups, has lost importance compared to achieving effects that were originally seen as side-effects. This is most clearly seen in the procedural modelling of PB by Sintomer et al. They see PB as a process allowing the participation of non-elected citizens in the conception and/or allocation of public finances. They add five criteria: (1) the financial and/or budgetary dimension must be discussed; PB involves dealing with the problem of limited resources; (2) the city level has to be involved, or a (decentralised) district with an elected body and some power over administration (the neighbourhood level is not enough); (3) it has to be a repeated process (one meeting or one referendum on financial issues does not constitute an example of PB); (4) the process must include some form of public deliberation within the framework of specific meetings/forums (the opening of administrative meetings or classical representative instances to 'normal' citizens is not PB); (5) some accountability on the output is required (Sintomer et al., 2008).

In this definition of PB, the process does not need to involve an actual transfer of powers concerning the budget; the process does not need to include marginalised groups; the amount of money involved can vary; and a redistribution of funds is immaterial. This can all vary, resulting in six possible forms of PB, namely democratic participation, democratic proximity, participative modernisation, multi-stakeholder participation, neo-corporatism, and community development (Sintomer et al., 2013). They differ in terms of intensity, scale, normative devices, technique, technology, and ideas (de Oliveira, 2017, p. 40). In the first distinguished form non-elected inhabitants (and eventually their delegates, who are invested with a 'semi-imperative mandate') do have de facto decision-making powers, although de jure the final political decision remains in the hands of elected representatives (p. 14). In the proximity democracy form, only those citizens or organisations are involved that are trusted and have been 'cherry-picked' by the administration and are 'grounded in informal rules and leaves civil society with only marginal autonomy' (p. 17). In the third model, 'participative modernisation', there is only consultation and this addresses mainly managerial issues and the modernisation of service delivery. It is not about neighbourhood issues, social policies, or marginalised groups (p. 17). In the fourth model, multi-stakeholder participation, in which the non-organised citizens are excluded, are replaced by private enterprises, NGOs, and local government. In the neo-corporatism model, the citizens have completely disappeared, and are replaced by 'those who matter', that is, organised groups like NGOs, trade unions and professionals' associations, social groups (the elderly, immigrant groups, and so on), and various local institutions/agencies. Only in the last model, called 'community development', do the origins as developed in Brazil re-appear. It includes clear procedural rules and a relatively high quality of deliberation. The most active participants tend to be the upper fraction of the working class, involved in running the community associations. In this model, the role of NGOs is often decisive, especially when they advocate the rights of disadvantaged or marginalised groups (Sintomer et al., 2013, p. 20).

1.3   Back to Basics: The Substance of Participatory Budgeting

Above we reviewed what is already known about PB, its origin in Porto Alegre (Abers, 2000; Aragonès & Sánchez-Pagés, 2009; Baiocchi et al., 2006), its diffusion worldwide (Dias et al., 2019), the determinative actors and factors for this diffusion (de Oliveira, 2017), the originally unintended side-effects attributed to PB, subsequently becoming main effects, how it could be organised (Cabannes & Delgado, 2015; Citizenlab, 2019; Sintomer et al., 2013); and the challenges involved (Shah, 2007). What is striking is that analyses of what is actually going on in processes of PB, what it is actually about, and how citizens benefit from such processes are limited to a few critical case studies (Goldfrank, 2007; High, 2009; Kuruppu et al., 2016; Röcke, 2014). That is what this book is about.

We asked the contributors of this book to describe the practice as it evolved in their country, focusing on what is substantially at stake concerning the budget and issues involved, the actual participation, the way such processes are organised and administered, and the outcomes of such processes.

The first question to be answered is whether the international developments in the goals of PB had any impact on what is at stake in such processes. Did the goal displacement in PB have any impact on the contents of these processes? If having such processes as such is judged to be more important than any output and outcomes, this might impact on the significance of the substantial aspects of such processes. This is indicated by the part of the budget on which citizens are allowed to have their say, the number of citizens involved in the process, and the extent to which their involvement has resulted in a real change in the public expenditures. This could imply that municipalities opted for such a small percentage of the budget being open for PB, which it transformed into a trivial pursuit with hardly anything but the process itself at stake. A second indicator is given in the way in which municipalities in different countries design processes under the flag of PB. Who is involved and who is not? How do governments design the process? How do the political representatives react to the outcomes of such processes? If the process is more important than the outcomes, it might result in local councils not adopting the proposals resulting from the PB process and simply putting them aside. Again, it is a question of whether such PB is a significant phenomenon or has just become a hoax.

Through answering these questions for the practices in PB in countries especially in Central and Eastern Europe, this volume intends to provide more insight on the significance of such processes, to give recommendations to improve them and to add to the theoretical understanding of such democratic practices. The next chapters provide information about the development of PB in 12 countries: Germany, Sweden, Poland, Hungary, Romania, Belorussia, the Czech Republic, Slovakia, Slovenia, Serbia, Croatia, and Russia. Arguments for choosing this region are that countries in this region are still black boxes of which hardly anything is known concerning these developments and that at the national level the Central European countries involved are often said to be democratically backsliding (cf. de Vries & Sobis, 2020). For instance, an explanation is needed for the weird observation that in the country blamed most for such backsliding, Poland, the development towards direct democracy in the form of PB at the municipal level is most visible compared to other countries in Europe.

As editors, we asked the authors of the country chapters to address, at least in part, the following five questions:

1. First, about the developments in PB in their countries: Why and when PB started in the country and at what governmental level; how many municipalities/regional governments experimented with PB; whether PB processes were on-time only experiments or repeated for several years?
2. Second, about the budget at stake, addressing especially the percentage of the municipal budget open for PB, whether it was about spending additional money or about austerity measures, whether it

was already specified beforehand what policy areas were involved or whether the participants could opt for the destination of that budget?

3. Third, about the participation, addressing the rules/selection criteria used for being eligible as a participant; characteristics of the participants, how were they selected, and whether they were adequately informed/educated/trained, and how many residents did indeed participate.

4. Fourth, about the procedure, addressing whether and how ICT instruments were used, how the PB is organised and administered, whether deliberation and voting were involved, how decisions were made, and whether the outcomes were really implemented.

5. Fifth, about the outcomes, addressing whether the political representatives (councillors/aldermen) accepted the outcomes of the PB, whether the outcome did actually make a change in the contents of the budget, whether the participants were satisfied, and what lessons have been learned?

The country studies serve as the base for the synthesis, to be presented in the final chapter. The concluding chapter summarises the worst and best practices, causes and effects of (successful or unsuccessful) PB, with a focus on transitionary countries with the goal to establish the process characteristics that are responsible for best practices and process characteristics that result in trivial pursuits, that is, symbolic PB.

The preparation of this volume is the joint IASIA (working group Public Sector Governance, Leadership, and Management) and NISPAcee (working group Public Finance and Public Financial Management) activity and received support from a project of the Czech Science Foundation (GA19-06020S): Alternative service delivery arrangements.

REFERENCES

Abers, R. (1996). From ideas to practice – The Partido dos Trabalhadores and participatory governance in Brazil. *Latin American Perspectives, 23*(4), 35–53.

Abers, R. (1998). From clientelism to cooperation: Local government, participatory policy, and civic organizing in Porto Alegre, Brazil. *Politics & Society, 26*(4), 511–539.

Abers, R. N. (2000). *Inventing local democracy: Grassroots politics in Brazil*. Lynne Rienner. https://www.rienner.com/title/Inventing_Local_Democracy_Grassroots_Politics_in_Brazil

Aragonès, E., & Sánchez-Pagés, S. (2009). A theory of participatory democracy based on the real case of Porto Alegre. *European Economic Review, 53*(1), 56–72. https://doi.org/10.1016/j.euroecorev.2008.09.006

Avritzer, L. (2006). New public spheres in Brazil: Local democracy and deliberative politics. *International Journal of Urban and Regional Research, 30*(3), 623–637. https://doi.org/10.1111/j.1468-2427.2006.00692.x

Baiocchi, G., & Ganuza, E. (2014). Participatory budgeting as if emancipation mattered. *Politics & Society, 42*(1), 29–50. https://doi.org/10.1177/0032329213512978

Baiocchi, G., Heller, P., Chaudhuri, S., & Silva, M. K. (2006). *Evaluating empowerment: Participatory budgeting in Brazilian municipalities* (pp. 95–128). The World Bank. https://nyuscholars.nyu.edu/en/publications/evaluating-empowerment-participatory-budgeting-in-brazilian-munic

Baiocchi, G., & Lerner, J. (2007). Could participatory budgeting work in the United States? *The Good Society, 16*(1), 8–13. https://www.jstor.org/stable/20711245?seq=1#metadata_info_tab_contents

Boaventura de Sousa Santos. (2002). *Democratizar a democracia: os caminhos da democracia participativa.* https://books.google.cz/books?id=fZyFAAAAMAAJ&source=gbs_book_other_versions

Cabannes, Y. (2004). Participatory budgeting: A significant contribution to participatory democracy. *Environment and Urbanization, 16*(1), 27–46. https://doi.org/10.1177/095624780401600104

Cabannes, Y., & Delgado, C. (2015). Another city is possible! Alternatives to the city as a commodity | Environment & Urbanization. In *Participatory budgeting, Dossier N° 1.* Creative Common. https://www.environmentandurbanization.org/another-city-possible-alternatives-city-commodity

Calabrese, T., Williams, D., & Gupta, A. (2020). Does participatory budgeting alter public spending? Evidence from New York City. *Administration & Society, 52*(9), 1382–1409. https://doi.org/10.1177/0095399720912548

Calisto Friant, M. (2019). Deliberating for sustainability: Lessons from the Porto Alegre experiment with participatory budgeting. *International Journal of Urban Sustainable Development, 11*(1), 81–99. https://doi.org/10.1080/19463138.2019.1570219

Castells, M. (1980). *The economic crisis and American society.* New Jersey: Princeton University Press.

Citizenlab. (2019). *The beginner's guide to participatory budgeting.* https://www.citizenlab.co/ebooks-en/the-beginners-guide-to-participatory-budgeting

Cohen, M., Schugurensky, D., & Wiek, A. (2015). Citizenship education through participatory budgeting: The case of bioscience high school in Phoenix, Arizona. *Curriculum and Teaching, 30*(2), 5–26. https://doi.org/10.7459/ct/30.2.02

de Oliveira, O. P. (2017). *International policy diffusion and participatory budgeting—Ambassadors of participation, international institutions and transnational networks.* Palgrave Macmillan. https://doi.org/10.1007/978-3-319-43337-0

de Vries, M. S., & Sobis, I. (2020). Bracketing democracy: A comparison of frames used to demarcate democracy and its application to developments in Poland. *East European Politics and Societies: And Cultures,* 088832542096709. https://doi.org/10.1177/0888325420967092

Dias, N., Enríquez, S., & Júlio, S. (2019). *Participatory budgeting World Atlas.* https://www.pbatlas.net/world.html#

Ebdon, C., & Franklin, A. L. (2006). Citizen participation in budgeting theory. *Public Administration Review,* 66(3), 437–447. https://doi.org/10.1111/j.1540-6210.2006.00600.x

Fung, A. (2006). Varieties of participation in complex governance. *Public Administration Review,* 66(Collaborative Public Management), 66–75.

Goldfrank, B. (2007). Lessons from Latin American experience in participatory budgeting. *Participatory Budgeting, 143*(Mar.), 91–126.

Gonçalves, S. (2014). The effects of participatory budgeting on municipal expenditures and infant mortality in Brazil. *World Development, 53,* 94–110. https://doi.org/10.1016/j.worlddev.2013.01.009

Gordon, V., Osgood, J. L., & Boden, D. (2017). The role of citizen participation and the use of social media platforms in the participatory budgeting process. *International Journal of Public Administration, 40*(1), 65–76. https://doi.org/10.1080/01900692.2015.1072215

Harkins, C., & Escobar, O. (2015). *Participatory budgeting in Scotland: An overview of strategic design choices and principles for effective delivery.* Glasgow Centre for Population Health and What Works Scotland, December.

High, H. (2009). The road to nowhere? Poverty and policy in the south of Laos. *Focaal, 53,* 75–88. https://doi.org/10.3167/fcl.2009.530105

Holdo, M. (2016). Reasons of power: Explaining non-cooptation in participatory budgeting. *International Journal of Urban and Regional Research, 40*(2), 378–394. https://doi.org/10.1111/1468-2427.12378

Irvin, R. A., & Stansbury, J. (2004). Citizen participation in decision making: Is it worth the effort? *Public Administration Review, 64*(1), 55–65. https://doi.org/10.1111/j.1540-6210.2004.00346.x

Jaramillo, M., & Alcázar, L. (2017). Does participatory budgeting have an effect on the quality of public services? The case of Peru's water and sanitation sector. In *Improving access and quality of public services in Latin America* (pp. 105–136). Palgrave Macmillan US. https://doi.org/10.1057/978-1-137-59344-3_4

Koonings, K. (2004). Strengthening citizenship in Brazil's democracy: Local participatory governance in Porto Alegre. *Bulletin of Latin American Research, 23*(1), 79–99. https://www.jstor.org/stable/27733620?seq=1#metadata_info_tab_contents

Kuo, N., Chen, T., & Su, T. (2020). A new tool for urban governance or just rhetoric? The case of participatory budgeting in Taipei City. *Australian Journal of Social Issues, 55*(2), 125–140. https://doi.org/10.1002/ajs4.110

Kuruppu, C., Adhikari, P., Gunarathna, V., Ambalangodage, D., Perera, P., & Karunarathna, C. (2016). Participatory budgeting in a Sri Lankan urban council: A practice of power and domination. *Critical Perspectives on Accounting, 41*, 1–17. https://doi.org/10.1016/j.cpa.2016.01.002

Larangeira, Sônia M. G. (1996). Gestão Pública e Participação, a experiência do orçamento participativo em Porto Alegre. *São Paulo em perspectiva, 10*(3), 129–137.

Lowndes, V., & Wilson, D. (2001). Social capital and local governance: Exploring the institutional design variable. *Political Studies, 49*(4), 629–647. https://doi.org/10.1111/1467-9248.00334

Marques, L. (2005). *Governo Lula: Social-Liberal Ou Social-Reformista?*. Porto Alegre: Veraz.

Melgar, T. R. (2014). A time of closure? Participatory budgeting in Porto Alegre, Brazil, after the workers' party era. *Journal of Latin American Studies, 46*(1), 121–149. https://doi.org/10.1017/S0022216X13001582

Michels, A. (2011). Innovations in democratic governance: How does citizen participation contribute to a better democracy? *International Review of Administrative Sciences, 77*(2), 275–293. https://doi.org/10.1177/0020852311399851

Miller, P., & O'Leary, T. (2007). Mediating instruments and making markets: Capital budgeting, science and the economy. *Accounting, Organizations and Society, 32*(7–8), 701–734. https://doi.org/10.1016/j.aos.2007.02.003

Montambeault, F. (2016). Participatory citizenship in the making? The multiple citizenship trajectories of participatory budgeting participants in Brazil. *Journal of Civil Society, 12*(3), 282–298. https://doi.org/10.1080/17448689.2016.1213508

Moynihan, D. (2007). Citizen participation in budgeting: Prospects for developing countries—GSDRC. In A. Shah (Ed.), *Participatory budgeting* (pp. 55–87). The World Bank.

Musso, J., Weare, C., Bryer, T., & Cooper, T. L. (2011). Toward "strong democracy" in global cities? Social capital building, theory-driven reform, and the Los Angeles neighborhood council experience. *Public Administration Review, 71*(1), 102–111. https://doi.org/10.1111/j.1540-6210.2010.02311.x

Nyamori, R. O., Lawrence, S. R., & Perera, H. B. (2012). Revitalising local democracy: A social capital analysis in the context of a New Zealand local authority. *Critical Perspectives on Accounting, 23*(7–8), 572–594. https://doi.org/10.1016/j.cpa.2012.04.004

Rios, J., & Rios Insua, D. (2008). A framework for participatory budget elaboration support. *Journal of the Operational Research Society, 59*(2), 203–212. https://doi.org/10.1057/palgrave.jors.2602501

Röcke, A. (2014). Framing citizen participation: Participatory budgeting in France, Germany and the United Kingdom. In *Framing citizen participation: Participatory budgeting in France, Germany and the United Kingdom*. Palgrave Macmillan. https://doi.org/10.1057/9781137326669

Rose, J., Rios, J., & Lippa, B. (2010). Technology support for participatory budgeting. *International Journal of Electronic Governance, 3*(1), 3–24. https://doi.org/10.1504/IJEG.2010.032728

Royo, S., Pina, V., & Garcia-Rayado, J. (2020). Decide Madrid: A critical analysis of an award-winning e-participation initiative. *Sustainability (Switzerland), 12*(4). https://doi.org/10.3390/su12041674

Sæbø, Ø., Rose, J., & Skiftenes Flak, L. (2008). The shape of eParticipation: Characterizing an emerging research area. *Government Information Quarterly, 25*(3), 400–428. https://doi.org/10.1016/j.giq.2007.04.007

Shah, A. (2007). *Participatory budgeting*. The World Bank.

Sintomer, Y., Herzberg, C., Allegretti, G., Röcke, A., & Alves, M. L. (2013). Participatory budgeting worldwide. In *Dialog Global* (Issue 25).

Sintomer, Y., Herzberg, C., & Röcke, A. (2008). Participatory budgeting in Europe: Potentials and challenges. *International Journal of Urban and Regional Research, 32*(1), 164–178. https://doi.org/10.1111/j.1468-2427.2008.00777.x

Speer, J. (2012). Participatory governance reform: A good strategy for increasing government responsiveness and improving public services?. *World Development, 40*(12), 2379–2398.

Spitz, J.-F. (2019). *Capitalismo democrático O fim de uma exceção histórica?* | *Nueva Sociedad*. https://nuso.org/articulo/capitalismo-democratico/

Talpin, J. (2011). *Schools of democracy: How ordinary citizens (sometimes) become competent in participatory budgeting institutions*. Colchester: ECPR Press.

Touchton, M., Wampler, B., & Peixoto, T. (2019). Of governance and revenue: Participatory institutions and tax compliance in Brazil. *Policy Research Working Paper No. 8797*. World Bank, Washington, DC. https://doi.org/10.1596/1813-9450-8797

Wampler, B. (2007). *Participatory budgeting in Brazil: Contestation, cooperation, and accountability*. Penn State Press. https://www.psupress.org/books/titles/978-0-271-03252-8.html

Participatory Budgeting in Germany: Increasing Transparency in Times of Fiscal Stress

Janina Apostolou and Martina Eckardt

2.1 Introduction

Participatory budgeting (PB) is one of the most popular democratic innovations of recent times. It developed in a number of Brazilian municipalities from the 1990s on. From there, it spread to other countries including Germany. The primary goals of the first PB processes were to combat corruption, to decrease social injustice, and to include citizens in the political process. However, as the idea of PB spread across the world, different concepts of PB evolved with different goals and process designs. This

J. Apostolou (✉)
Hamburg University of Applied Sciences, Hamburg, Germany
e-mail: janina.apostolou@haw-hamburg.de

M. Eckardt
Andrássy University Budapest, Budapest, Hungary
e-mail: martina.eckardt@andrassyuni.hu

holds also for German PB processes where a rather consultative approach prevails as this chapter shows.

Based on a global comparative study of PB processes, Herzberg et al. (2014, p. 15) distinguish the following ideal types of PB processes: grass-roots democracy, participatory democracy, participatory modernisation, multi-stakeholder participation, neo-corporatism, and community development. These types of PB vary in terms of socio-political context, goals, rules and procedures of participation, dynamics of collective action, and the relationship between conventional politics and participatory procedures. Some models like 'participatory democracy' support the empowerment of the citizenry by actually shifting decision-making power. For example, in Brazil outcomes of PB processes are legally binding. Other models like 'participatory modernisation' do not transfer any decision-making power from elected officials to citizens, as is the case in Germany. New Public Management strategies and cultures are at the origin of this type of PB. This holds also for Germany, where PB processes were first adopted at the end of the 1990s in an environment in which the state administration started to modernise itself for the sake of greater efficiency and legitimacy.

German PB processes follow in terms of goal and design the best practice example of PB processes implemented in the city of Christchurch in New Zealand, which won a prize for citizen-friendly modernisation in 1993 (Herzberg et al., 2014, p. 9). Thus, in contrast to countries where PB is an instrument of direct democracy, in Germany it has a mainly consultative character and its outcome is not legally binding (Herzberg et al., 2014, p. 116). Its goals are primarily to inform citizens about a municipality's finances to increase transparency as well as to further citizens' interest in municipal politics.

In the following, we show how such a mainly consultative PB design evolved in Germany and analyse what is known about its effects and what its challenges are. The next section gives an overview of the diffusion of PB processes against the institutional background in Germany, while Sect. 2.3 discusses the major design elements of PB processes in Germany and the impact they have. Section 2.4 looks at the available evidence on the outcomes of PB processes including an own econometric analysis on the motivation for adopting PB processes by German municipalities. Section 2.5 summarises and concludes with an outlook on further research questions.

2.2   Institutional Background and Diffusion of Participatory Budgeting Processes in Germany

The institutional background of German PB processes is defined by Germany being a federal state with a three-level structure of government. Beneath the federal level, there are 16 Länder (the federal states) which also have important legislative competences. At the lowest level, there are 11,014 municipalities (Statistisches Bundesamt, 2019, p. 29).[1] Each of the 16 Länder has its own constitutional rules laid down in its municipal code (Kommunalverfassung) of how the municipality within its jurisdiction is structured, what its competences and tasks are, what the budgetary process looks like and how non-elected citizens are involved in decision-making at the municipal level. These rules also allow for introducing PB at the municipal level by a formal decision of a city council, for example.

The decision-making power in regard to the municipal budget lies with the elected representatives of a municipality. This holds for PB processes as well as for other forms of direct democratic decision-making. Over the last decades, all Länder incorporated in their constitutions more or less far-reaching legal instruments for direct participation of citizens, such as referenda and petitions, both at the state as well as at the municipal level (Mehr Demokratie e.V., 2020). Furthermore, they introduced other consultative participatory procedures, like round tables, civic forums, mediation procedures, and planning cells (Herzberg, 2008, p. 81). However, these direct democratic tools serve mainly as a means to enhance the functioning of representative institutions through the creation of stronger links between elected politicians and the citizenry (Banner, 1999, p. 145). The political culture remains nevertheless characterised as that of a representative democracy, so no profound institutional modification occurred. Therefore, in Germany, direct democratic instruments are not as far-reaching as in other countries like Switzerland, where citizens can vote directly on public expenditure and taxation issues at the municipal and/or state level (Feld & Kirchgässner, 2005, 2007; Kirchgässner, 2013). In contrast to that, in all German municipal constitutions the budget as a whole is exempted from being a subject of direct participatory actions. Furthermore, municipal councils effectively decide only on a small proportion of the budget since a large share is determined by mandatory municipal tasks that are assigned to the local level by the federal or state

---

[1] For more on the German municipal level, see (Zimmermann & Döring, 2019).

level (Zimmermann & Döring, 2019). Thus, participation by citizens is in most cases designed as being merely consultative. It is not intended to change the division of power between elected representatives and citizens.

Against this institutional background, PB was strongly promoted by non-governmental organisations in Germany at the end of the 1990s to promote municipal modernisation. In 1998, the network 'Kommunen der Zukunft' ('Municipalities of the Future', own translation), where the Bertelsmann Foundation, the Hans Böckler Foundation, and the Kommunale Gemeinschaftsstelle für Verwaltungsmanagement had joined forces, promoted the adoption of PB (Günther, 2007). They offered to support the first-time adoption of PB processes and looked for municipalities that were interested in taking part in a pilot project introducing PB. In 2003, a nationwide PB network was launched by the 'Service Agency Communities in One World'. It operates together with the Federal Agency for Civic Education. Within this network, regular network meetings are organised and a directory, as well as reports of municipalities and cities that have implemented or intend to implement PB processes, are published.[2]

The diffusion of PB processes started rather slowly in 1998 with Mönchweiler (2997 inhabitants in 2018) which was the first municipality that adopted PB. Further PB processes emerged between 2000 and 2004 with the support of the initiative 'Kommunaler Bürgerhaushalt' ('Municipal PB', own translation), which was founded jointly by the Bertelsmann Foundation and the state of Nordrhein-Westfalen. Cities and municipalities in Nordrhein-Westfalen got the opportunity to apply for support in implementing PB processes. Consequently, PB processes were introduced in the cities of Hamm, Vlotho, Emsdetten, Castrop-Rauxel, Hilden, and Monheim. The aim of the initiative was to gain insight into the factors that are decisive for the successful implementation of PB in order to derive general recommendations for further promoting PB processes (Bertelsmann Stiftung/ Ministry of the Interior NRW 2004). Hilden is often cited as a best practice example as PB has already become an integral part of the political culture there and has been carried out consistently since 2002. In 2005 with the Berlin district of Lichtenberg (258,000 inhabitants in 2018) the first larger German city introduced a PB process, followed by Hamburg in 2006. However, the PB process only consisted of an internet discussion during which citizens were involved in drawing up the budget for the year 2006.

---

[2] For further information, see www.buergerhaushalt.org.

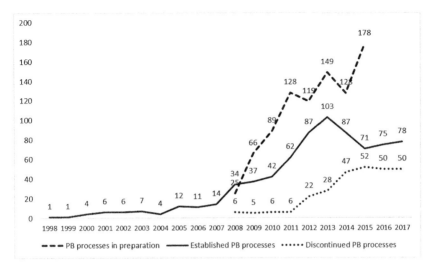

Fig. 2.1 German municipalities with PB processes (1998–2017). (Source: Own composition based on own research and data from Franzke & Kleger, 2010; Günther, 2007; Herzberg, 2009; Ruesch & Ermert, 2014; Ruesch & Wagner, 2014; Sintomer et al., 2010; Vorwerk & Gonçalves, 2018)

With Potsdam, Köln, and Leipzig other larger cities followed in adopting PB processes.

Figure 2.1 shows the development of the number of municipalities with PB processes between 1998 and 2017, distinguishing between the number of established PB processes, those in preparation, and those discontinued.[3,4] The number of PB processes increased over time, however, not uniformly. Established PB processes showed a very slow increase and reached a peak in 2013 with a total of 103 PB processes, followed by a drop of about 30% in the following two years. Thereafter the number stabilised at a slightly higher level. PB processes in preparation comprise municipalities that have considered adopting a PB process without having

[3] Note that there is no official register of PB in Germany. In the following, we use the most recently available data from different sources and only proven cases are named. Therefore, inconsistencies in the compilation of data are inevitable and therefore this data set contains only approximate values for the total number of PB processes in Germany.

[4] There is a rich literature on what should be counted as an established PB process; see for a widely used definition (Sintomer et al., 2008, p. 164, 2010, p. 18).

implemented it yet, in addition to municipalities that employ a pre-form of a PB process such as municipalities that launched a website with structured information on the budget. The number of such municipalities showed a continuous upward trend despite some minor fluctuations between 2012 and 2015. Together with established PB, therefore there is an overall upward movement in the adoption of PB processes in Germany. Nevertheless, also the number of municipalities with discontinued PB processes witnessed a continuous increase between 2008 and 2017. However, at any point in time, their number was lower than the number of established PB processes. Many of the municipalities that have decided not to repeat PB processes did this due to lack of participation by citizens (Bundeszentrale für Politische Bildung, 2018, p. 11).

Figure 2.2 presents the share of municipalities that ever had a PB process adopted according to size class. While municipalities with 25,000–100,000 inhabitants dominated, smaller municipalities with less than 25,000 inhabitants accounted for a third of all PB process, and larger municipalities for a quarter.

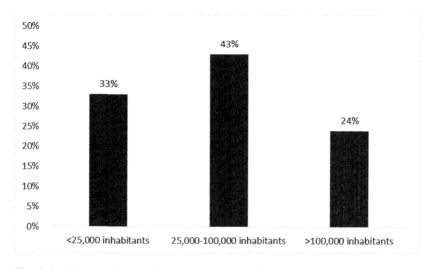

Fig. 2.2 PB according to the size of municipalities (2012–2018). (Source: Own composition based on open data downloaded from 'List of municipalities' on www.buergerhaushalt.org/en/list (last access 02/09/2020))

2.3 The Design of Participatory Budgeting Processes in Germany

In Germany, a relatively homogenous design of PB processes emerged because of the dominant role which foundations and networks of NGOs played in promoting the introduction of PB. However, the initiative to implement a PB process rests with the political agents at the municipal level. These may be from different political parties. In fact, PB processes in Germany are a non-partisan project, not a left-wing phenomenon like in France, Spain, or Italy. Parties both from the left and from the right of the political spectrum act as initiators of PB processes (Sintomer et al., 2010, p. 51).

After the decision of the competent municipal agents to adopt a PB process, a three-stage process of information, consultation, and accountability follows (Holtkamp, 2008, p. 223; Schneider, 2018, pp. 93–96). The information phase is of particular importance in German PB processes since their main goal is to create fiscal transparency. Information on the municipal budget is distributed by a variety of media, like brochures, the Internet, and through press releases. It details the expenses and revenues of the municipality. For a sample of 128 municipalities with PB processes in the period of 2008–2014, Apostolou (2014) found that municipalities mostly divided the budget into different sections. The first section usually provided information about the tasks of the municipality and explained the difference between mandatory and voluntary tasks since only the latter can be objects of a PB process. Another section showed the main sources of revenue for the municipal budget and its expenditure categories. Usually, future investment plans of the municipality or the debt level in the case of indebted municipalities were also included. In the latter case, there was also detailed information on the development of the debt, its main drivers, and refinancing mechanisms.

During the consultation stage, citizens are invited to debate about the budget, make proposals to it, and perhaps decide on it. There are different types of PB processes. Surveys are more like an opinion poll regarding the planned municipal budget. *Vorschlags-PB* processes ask citizens to suggest modifications of the regular municipal budget. In contrast to that, a *Bürgerbudget* allocates a fixed amount of money to citizens who then can submit proposals for what services that money should be spent. Table 2.1 shows that between 2014 and 2017 surveys played only a negligible role, while *Vorschlags-PB* processes dominated. However, *Bürgerbudgets* quickly

Table 2.1   Type of PB processes (2014–2017)

	2014	2015	2016	2017
Survey	2%	4%	4%	3%
Vorschlags-PB	83%	75%	67%	56%
Bürgerbudget	15%	21%	29%	41%
N	95	72	75	78

Source: Own calculation according to Bundeszentrale für Politische Bildung (2018, p. 9)

gained in importance during the last years. It resulted from the specific legal framework in Germany where the budget as a whole is exempted from direct participatory processes.

In PB processes, citizens are asked to make spending or cutting proposals or both. In Germany, between 2012 and 2018, out of 182 PB over 70% asked citizens to make both suggestions for spending as well as for cutting decisions, while 10% merely asked citizens to make spending suggestions. About one fifth, however, inquired solely about austerity measures.[5] Apostolou (2014) found that usually citizens had the opportunity to submit proposals, often on an interactive platform so that participants could comment on each other's proposals and rate them.

The ways offered to citizens to communicate in a PB process differ widely. Although town hall meetings are still important, information and communication technology (ICT) nowadays play a predominant role as a channel for PB. Figure 2.3 presents which channels were used in PB processes between 2012 and 2018. ICT played a predominant role since in 97% of all PB processes citizen involvement was web-based. In contrast to that, only 3% of PB processes used no ICT instruments at all. Furthermore, slightly over a quarter of all PB processes were conducted exclusively via the Internet, while another 13% used complex multi-media channels. From a number of empirical examples, it follows that the online channel is the one that was used most frequently by participating citizens. For example, in Cologne, 98% of the participants used the website to take part in the PB process (Taubert et al., 2011). Also, for Frankfurt, an evaluation showed that 77% of all proposals in the research sample were made online. Among the top 30 proposals, 9 out of 10 were handed in online (Geißel et al., 2013).

---

[5] Own calculation based on open data downloaded from 'List of processes' on www.buergerhaushalt.org/en/list (last access 02/09/2020).

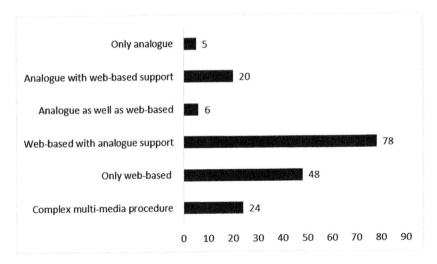

Fig. 2.3 Channels for participating in PB processes (2012–2018, $n = 181$). (Source: Own calculation based on open data downloaded from 'List of processes' on www.buergerhaushalt.org/en/list, last access (02/09/2020))

The participation possibilities for citizens and thus the impact citizens have on the budget also differ widely. This strongly depends on the kind of participation rules that citizens are granted in the PB process. It may range from the weakest form of (1) just giving feedback to proposals of the budget initiated by the municipal authorities over (2) making own proposals for changes to the budget to the strongest form of (3) deciding on which measures should be realised in a given budget. Figure 2.4 illustrates that 54% of PB processes enabled citizens to make proposals, with another 32% to give both feedback and make proposals. In only 4% of PB processes, citizens had the right to decide on the budget draft, while another 5% provided mixed forms of participation. This clearly states that German PB processes at the municipal level are mainly an instrument for consultation, not of direct democratic co-determination.

The final accountability stage refers to the way in which the municipal council deals with the results of the PB process. Since in Germany there is no legal right for citizens to co-determine the municipal budget by PB, it depends on the decision of the mayor and/or the municipal council whether the results of a PB process are implemented or not. In ideal

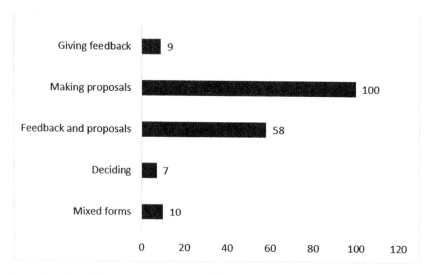

Fig. 2.4 Participation options granted in PB processes (2012–2018, n = 184). (Source: Own calculation based on open data downloaded from 'List of processes' on www.buergerhaushalt.org/en/list (last access 02/09/2020))

circumstances, the administration would check the proposals for feasibility, the effect on the budget, and so on. Then those that meet certain criteria would be implemented by the competent decision-making actors, like the city council. In any case, there should be some feedback given to citizens on the results of a PB process. In many cases, this part of the process is documented online, like in Münster (Stadtverwaltung Münster, 2020). After examination, the administration passed on the revised best-ranked proposals to the council that included them in the budget discussions. The council finally passed a resolution regarding the implementation of the proposals. However, the way of how the feedback is given varies widely between municipalities as Fig. 2.5 indicates. In approximately 40% of the PB processes at least information on the implementation of the results were collected, while in only 16% of the cases detailed monitoring took place. However, one-third of the PB processes did not receive any particular follow-up monitoring.

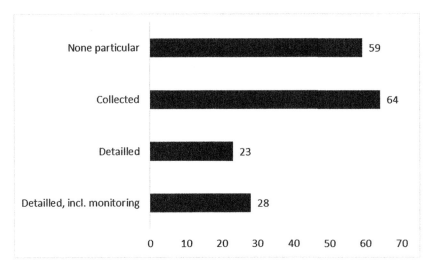

Fig. 2.5 Accountability (2012–2018, n = 174). (Source: Own calculation based on open data downloaded from 'List of processes' on www.buergerhaushalt.org/en/list (last access 02/09/2020))

2.4 EVALUATION OF PARTICIPATORY BUDGETING PROCESSES IN GERMANY

Empirical evidence about the impact of PB processes in Germany is still scarce. Most case studies evaluate PB processes for individual cities such as Cologne or Frankfurt. Thus, they allow only for few general conclusions regarding the design, adoption, or impact of PB processes in Germany (Geißel et al., 2013; Kersting et al., 2013; Klages & Daramus, 2007; Taubert et al., 2011). One is that participants are rather homogenous in their socioeconomic characteristics. They do not encompass the diversity of citizens in a municipality. Usually, a certain stratum of society dominates participation in PB processes. These are males between 36 and 50 years of age who are characterised by a high level of education and occupational status. Moreover, citizens who have lived for a comparatively long time in a municipality are also more likely to engage in a PB process (Günther, 2007, pp. 99–103; Masser et al., 2013, pp. 89–92).

Given the rate of participation by citizens in PB processes, Bundeszentrale für Politische Bildung (2018, p. 11) reports the following figures for four municipalities: Ketzin/Havel 24% (or 1680 participating inhabitants),

Kleinmachnow 11% (or 2200 participating inhabitants), Stuttgart 9% (or 54,000 participating inhabitants), and Potsdam 7% (or 11,900 participating inhabitants). In international terms, this shows quite a strong rate of participation by citizens, although most PB processes had a rather low participation rate.

Schneider (2018) analysed which factors influence participation rates of citizens in PB processes using different large-N datasets. Firstly, he examined from a sociological perspective what motivates citizens to take part in a PB process. He found the following three factors to be important on the individual level: having an internalised norm for participation, being a member in a voluntary association, and showing strong trust in the municipal institutions. Secondly, Schneider analysed which characteristics at the municipal level explain participation in PB processes. He used aggregate data to discover potential relationships between the institutional design of a PB process, its local structural and socioeconomic context, the political and financial situation of the municipality, and participation rates. The results of his regression analysis show a negative effect of the share of people on welfare on the participation rate, a positive effect of the usage of the Internet, and huge differences between Eastern and Western Germany, with the participation rate being much larger in Eastern Germany.

With regard to its political impact, no larger socio-political effects exerted by PB processes in Germany have been found, which is in contrast to other countries, like Brazil for example. Furthermore, direct political effects have been reported to be also rather small (Boulding & Wampler, 2010; Nylen, 2003; Touchton & Wampler, 2014). Neunecker (2016) conducted a detailed analysis of the impact of PB processes on municipal policies by using data from 13 German municipalities that had employed PB processes in 2011. She performed a quantitative evaluation of the 839 top-listed proposals in those PB processes and the corresponding formal council decisions of the selected municipalities. She also conducted a standardised written survey of local council members as well as in-depth guideline-based interviews with local politicians and budget experts in five selected cities. Her empirical analysis reveals that only in rare cases the submitted proposals were actually implemented. Neunecker argues that the low impact of PB on municipal policies follows from the complexity of the municipal political process and the resulting tendency of municipal decision-makers to follow draft resolutions prepared by the administration rather than suggestions made by citizens in PB processes. All in all, the empirical findings suggest that in most cases, PB processes have no or only very small effects on political and financial outcomes in a municipality.

Therefore, the question remains why municipalities nevertheless adopt PB processes. One explanation might be that the decision to adopt a PB process is to find legitimacy for upcoming austerity measures. In Germany, many municipalities in financial distress have adopted PB and even a special type of PB called 'Sparhaushalte', which means saving budgets, has evolved. Furthermore, in Germany PB processes focus on making the financial situation transparent. Following the assumptions of public choice theory, policymakers have an incentive to involve citizens in budgetary decisions in times of financial crisis both to garner sympathy for their positions and for the painful cuts necessary. To test for the potential impact of the budgetary situation for adopting PB, we use an explorative cluster analysis and a confirmative mean value test. Our dataset consists of 2951 German municipalities for the period between 2006 and 2014.[6] Municipalities that only discuss the introduction of a PB process or hand out information about it are considered as having adopted a PB process. The reason for that is that municipalities that consider introducing PB face similar circumstances like the ones that already do employ PB. According to this, 5% of the municipalities in our dataset ran a PB process in the given period, although the majority of municipalities did not employ PB processes.

To explore for subgroups of municipalities with common characteristics, we performed K-means clustering analysis. It allows identifying which municipalities are alike or not and thus can be categorised in different groups. The results in Table 2.2 show that the observations in our sample can indeed be divided in two clusters with cluster 1 including those municipalities with a PB process and cluster 2 those without one. The values for the variables population, overall balance, debt, as well as personnel expenditure and social expenditure are much higher for municipalities that employ or think about employing PB (cluster 1) than for those without PB (cluster 2).

The cluster analysis strongly supports the hypothesis that 'the worse the fiscal health of a municipality, the more likely it is to adopt a PB process'.

---

[6] Data for PB adoption come from own research and (Bundeszentrale für Politische Bildung, 2018; Franzke & Kleger, 2010; Herzberg, 2009; Ruesch & Ermert, 2014, p. 3; Ruesch & Wagner, 2014, p. 288; Sintomer et al., 2010). Budgetary data come from the Bertelsmann Foundation. Within the project 'Wegweiser Kommune', the (Bertelsmann Foundation, n.d.) gathers and publishes data on all German municipalities with at least 5000 inhabitants.

Table 2.2   Cluster analysis of PB adoption (per capita)

Cluster	PB	Population	Overall balance (in Euro)	Debt (in Euro)	Income tax (in Euro)	Personnel expenditure (in Euro)	Social expenditure (in Euro)
1	1	123,000	-110.4	3566	934.5	884.2	219.8
2	0	24,867	-22.1	1691	828.4	502.2	32.7
Total	0.04	28,337	-25.2	1757	832.1	515.7	39.3

Source: Own calculations

Table 2.3   Mean value comparison of municipalities with and without PB (in Euro per capita)

		Population	Overall balance	Debt	Income tax	Personnel expenditure	Social expenditure
PB	Mean	151,918	-74	3438	324	869	179
	SD	387,951	272	2269	129	405	245
	Min	5859	-2110	0	33	221	-86
	Max	3,501,872	779	12,183	1087	2773	1436
	N	440	405	307	433	182	405
No-PB	Mean	18,969	-21	1605	330	499	21
	SD	42,241	356	1793	134	321	83
	Min	4643	-7476	0	4	0	-186
	Max	1,378,176	7344	40,922	1279	3275	1222
	N	11,364	10,947	6699	11,216	4982	10,936
T-value		-7.2[a]	3.8[b]	-13.95[a]	0.95	-12.2[a]	-12.97[a]

Source: Own calculations
[a]99% level of significance
[b]95% level of significance

To test for it, a mean value test is employed. Table 2.3 presents the statistics for the size of the municipalities and different budgetary variables. T-values presented in the bottom line of Table 2.3 suggest that the differences in mean values are statistically significant for the variables population, overall balance, debt, personnel expenditure, and social expenditure. Municipalities that have adopted PB processes were significantly larger and had significantly larger average debt per capita, personnel expenditure per capita, and social expenditure per capita compared to the group of municipalities that had not implemented PB processes. In addition, the group of municipalities with PB had a more negative overall balance and larger budget deficits than no-PB municipalities. These results support our hypothesis. They indicate that a more difficult financial situation characterises municipalities that have adopted PB compared to those that have no-PB processes.

Based on this dataset, Apostolou (forthcoming) performs logistic panel regression. According to her analysis, the following factors positively affect the adoption of PB by municipalities in Germany: debt per capita, population size, geographical proximity, and innovation climate.

2.5   SUMMARY AND OUTLOOK

This chapter analysed the evolution of German PB processes that were first introduced at the end of the 1990s to support modernising public administration at the municipal level. The main goal of PB in Germany is to achieve more transparency in public finances. PB processes are adopted as an instrument to inform citizens about the local budget and to consult them about budgetary decisions at the municipal level. PB processes thus have a mere consultative character. This is also enforced by the institutional framework since budgetary matters are prohibited to be subject to direct democratic means in all 16 German states by their respective constitutions. Accordingly, PB processes do not shift decision-making power from elected officials to citizens.

Nevertheless, since 1998, a growing number of German municipalities have experimented with PB, with 78 PB processes being established in 2017 and 180 being considered by other municipalities to be introduced. As PB in Germany had been promoted in its beginning by several foundations and NGOs that favoured it to be modelled according to the PB process developed in Christchurch/New Zealand, a rather homogenous process design evolved. It includes the stages of information, consultation, and accountability. Major emphasis is on the information and consultation phases while the degree of accountability by the municipalities as regards to the outcome of a PB process is usually rather low.

Although empirical evidence on the outcomes of PB processes in Germany is very limited, a well-established fact is that that citizens' willingness to take part in PB processes are rather low, despite some outstanding exceptions. In addition, there is even some indication that in most cases proposals resulting from such PB processes are not implemented at all by the respective municipalities. This is clearly a backdrop of the mainly consultative character of PB processes in Germany. So, the question arises why PB processes are still implemented despite their limited effects. Following from explorative cluster analysis and confirmative mean value analysis, we find that municipalities with financial difficulties are more likely to adopt a PB process.

Thus, even if the actual impact of PB processes in Germany is small, they nevertheless meet the goal of increasing transparency regarding the financial situation of a municipality. Over time, this could create fiscal awareness about municipal finances and make citizens more educated in the field of public finances. PB processes at the municipal level are well suited to practice democratic deliberation as to the allocation of limited budgetary means for conflicting uses.

A promising way to further this development is by changes in the PB design which aim at increasing participation rates. One approach is to give citizens a real say in PB processes by including a fixed amount of money in the PB over which participants decide on how to spend it. In fact, the rapid increase in established PB processes that include this option shows that a growing number of municipalities realised that this modification in the PB design might intensify and stabilise citizens' interest in municipal finances and politics over time.

Another interesting approach might be to better target PB processes with other direct democratic means at the municipal level, like referenda and petitions. These direct democratic instruments, which have been introduced in all municipal codes by the 16 German Länder during the last 20 years, have become quite popular. They are often about issues that are at the core of municipal policymaking and that directly affect citizens' everyday life, like public transport, housing policy, climate protection, and different aspects of social policy (schooling, senior citizens, etc.). Although budgetary matters are excluded by law from such referenda and petitions, they nevertheless also affect municipal budgets. So far, however, there is no research on the relationship between PB processes and such other direct democratic tools for citizen involvement at the municipal level. It thus seems a promising point for further research to analyse whether PB and such tools are complementary or rather substitutes or whether they perform entirely separate functions. Since their continuous practice shows a lively interest in municipal participation by citizens, resulting from a strong democratic culture in Germany, better integration of these two types of instruments could increase the impact of direct citizen involvement for better policymaking at the municipal level.

References

Apostolou, J. (2014). E-participation: The case of online-based participatory budgeting processes in Germany. *Central and Eastern European E-Gov Days 2014: E-Government: Driver or Stumbling Block for European Integration. Conference Proceedings*, 183–197.

Apostolou, J. (forthcoming). *Municipal finances and adoption of participatory budgeting in Germany—An empirical analysis of adoption patterns from a political economy perspective.*

Banner, G. (1999). Die drei Demokratien der Bürgerkommune. In H. H. Arnim (Ed.), *Adäquate Institu-tionen—Voraussetzungen für eine "gute" und bürgernahe Politik* (pp. 133–162). Speyer.

Bertelsmann Foundation. (n.d.). *Essen—Finanzen—2016–2018—Statistische Daten.* Retrieved April 27, 2021, from https://www.wegweiser-kommune.de/statistik/essen+finanzen+2016-2018+tabelle

Boulding, C., & Wampler, B. (2010). Voice, votes, and resources: Evaluating the effect of participatory democracy on well-being. *World Development, 38*(1), 125–135. https://doi.org/10.1016/j.worlddev.2009.05.002

Bundeszentrale für Politische Bildung. (2018). *9. Statusbericht. Bürgerhaushalt in Deutschland (2014–2017).* https://www.buergerhaushalt.org/sites/default/files/9._Statusbericht_Buergerhaushalt.pdf

Feld, L. P., & Kirchgässner, G. (2005). Sustainable fiscal policy in a federal system: Switzerland as an example. In *Contemporary Switzerland* (pp. 281–296). Palgrave Macmillan UK. https://doi.org/10.1057/9780230523586_13

Feld, L. P., & Kirchgässner, G. (2007). On the economic efficiency of direct democracy. In *Direct democracy in Europe* (pp. 108–124). VS Verlag für Sozialwissenschaften. https://doi.org/10.1007/978-3-531-90579-2_9

Franzke, J., & Kleger, H. (2010). *Bürgerhaushalte: Chancen und Grenzen.* Sigma. https://www.amazon.de/B%C3%BCrgerhaushalte-Chancen-Grenzen-Jochen-Franzke/dp/383607236X

Geißel, B., Kolleck, A., & Neunecker, M. (2013). *Projektbericht "Wissenschaftliche Begleitung und Evaluation des Frankfurter Bürgerhaushaltes 2013".* http://www.fb03.uni-frankfurt.de/46461594/Buergerhaushalt-Frankfurt%2D%2D-Evaluationsbericht_Final.pdf

Günther, A. (2007). *Der Bürgerhaushalt: Bestandsaufnahme—Erkenntnisse—Bewertung.* Boorberg. https://books.google.cz/books/about/Der_Bürgerhaushalt.html?id=-bv2HgAACAAJ&redir_esc=y

Herzberg, C. (2008). *Der Bürgerhaushalt in Europa—Europäische Kommunen auf dem Weg zur Solidarkommune?*

Herzberg, C. (2009). *Von der Bürger- zur Solidarkommune: Lokale Demokratie in Zeiten der Globalisierung.* VSA.

Herzberg, C., Sintomer, Y., Allegretti, G., Röcke, A., & Alves, M. L. (2014). Vom Süden lernen: Bürgerhaushalte weltweit—eine Einladung zur globalen Kooperation. In *Dialog Global Nr. 25*. Engagement Global/Servicestelle Kommunen in der Einen Welt.

Holtkamp, L. (2008). Kommunale Konkordanz—und Konkurrenzdemokratie: Parteien und Bürgermeister in der repräsentativen Demokratie. In *Kommunale Konkordanz- und Konkurrenzdemokratie*. Springer VS. https://doi.org/10.1007/978-3-531-90811-3_1

Kersting, N., Busse, S., & Schneider, S. H. (2013). *Evaluationsbericht Bürgerhaushalt Jena*. Westfälische Wilhelms-Universität Münster.

Kirchgässner, G. (2013). Fiscal institutions at the cantonal level in Switzerland. *Swiss Journal of Economics and Statistics, 149*(2), 139–166. https://doi.org/10.1007/BF03399386

Klages, H., & Daramus, C. (2007). *Bürgerhaushalt Berlin Lichtenberg: Partizipative Haushaltsplanaufstellung, entscheidung und kontrolle im Bezirk Lichtenberg von Berlin; begleitende Evaluation des ersten Durchlaufs*. Deutsches Forschungsinstitut für öffentliche Verwaltung.

Masser, K., Pistoia, A., & Nitzsche, P. (2013). *Bürgerbeteiligung und Web 2.0. Potentiale und Risiken webgestützter Bürgerhaushalte*. VS Springer.

Mehr Demokratie e.V. (2020). *Bürgerbegehrensbericht 2020*. https://www.mehr-demokratie.de/fileadmin/pdf/2020-09-28_Bu__rgerbegehrensbericht_Web.pdf

Neunecker, M. (2016). Partizipation trifft Repräsentation. In *Partizipation trifft Repräsentation*. Springer Fachmedien Wiesbaden. https://doi.org/10.1007/978-3-658-13071-8

Nylen, W. R. (2003). Participatory democracy versus elitist democracy: Lessons from Brazil. In *Participatory democracy versus elitist democracy: Lessons from Brazil*. Palgrave Macmillan. https://doi.org/10.1057/9781403980304

Ruesch, M., & Ermert, J. (2014). *7. Statusbericht des Portals Buergerhaushalt.org. Juni 2014*. Bundeszentrale für Politische Bildung.

Ruesch, M., & Wagner, M. (2014). Participatory budgeting in Germany—Citizens as consultants. *Hope for democracy—25 years of participatory budgeting worldwide*, May, 287–298.

Schneider, S. H. (2018). *Bürgerhaushalte in Deutschland: Individuelle und kontextuelle Einflussfaktoren der Beteiligung*. Springer VS. https://www.amazon.de/B%C3%BCrgerhaushalte-Deutschland-Individuelle-kontextuelle-Einflussfaktoren/dp/3658190299

Sintomer, Y., Herzberg, C., & Röcke, A. (2008). Participatory budgeting in Europe: Potentials and challenges. *International Journal of Urban and Regional Research, 32*(1), 164–178. https://doi.org/10.1111/j.1468-2427.2008.00777.x

Sintomer, Y., Herzberg, C., & Röcke, A. (2010). *Der Bürgerhaushalt in Europa— eine realistische Utopie? Zwischen Partizipativer Demokratie, Verwaltungsmodernisierung und sozialer Gerechtigkeit.* VS Verlag.

Stadtverwaltung Münster. (2020). *Bürgerhaushalt Münster, Münsters Haushalt.*

Statistisches Bundesamt. (2019). *Statistisches Jahrbuch.* Deutschland Und Internationales 2019. www.destatis.de/DE/Themen/Querschnitt/Jahrbuch/statistisches-jahrbuch-2019-dl.pdf?__blob=publi-cationFile

Taubert, N., Krohn, W., & Knobloch, T. (2011). *Evaluierung des Kölner Bürgerhaushalts.* Kassel University Press.

Touchton, M., & Wampler, B. (2014). Improving social well-being through new democratic institutions. *Comparative Political Studies, 47*(10), 1442–1469. https://doi.org/10.1177/0010414013512601

Vorwerk, V., & Gonçalves, M. (2018). *9. Statusbericht des Portals Buergerhaushalt. org.* Bundeszentrale für Politische Bildung.

Zimmermann, H., & Döring, T. (2019). *Kommunalfinanzen—Eine Einführung in die finanzwissenschaftliche Analyse der kommunalen Finanzwirtschaft* (4th ed.). Schriften zur öffentlichen Verwaltung und öffentlichen Wirtschaft.

CHAPTER 3

Participatory Budgeting in Italy: A Phoenix Rising from the Ashes

Francesco Badia

3.1 Introduction

The evolution of the public sector scenario in the last decades has produced growing attention from the public regarding the use of public resources. Consequently, the debate on public management shifted to the proposal of management tools and processes that can promote both the sustainability of public policies and community participation.

The application of this idea is represented by the general concept of participatory governance (Edwards, 2001; Fung & Wright, 2001; Grote & Gbikpi, 2002). Participatory governance (PG) is put into effect when a community becomes the central subject of public policies through the promotion of tools of direct democratic participation. This perspective goes beyond the traditional concepts of transparency and accountability, which have already been present and widespread in public management

F. Badia (✉)
Department of Economics, Management and Business Law,
University of Bari Aldo Moro, Bari, Italy
e-mail: francesco.badia@uniba.it

© The Author(s), under exclusive license to Springer Nature
Switzerland AG 2022
M. S. De Vries et al. (eds.), *International Trends in Participatory Budgeting*, Governance and Public Management,
https://doi.org/10.1007/978-3-030-79930-4_3

47

studies (Almquist et al., 2013; Jenkins & Gray, 1993; Romzek & Dubnick, 1987). From the PG perspective, stakeholders should not only be the recipients of transparent and accountable information by public bodies but also the central subjects of governmental decision-making processes.

In this context, participatory budgeting (PB) is a tool of great interest because it can be considered to be one of the most advanced tools to reconcile deliberative and representative democracy by carrying out processes of civic engagement in an effective way, such as in the pioneering experience of Porto Alegre in the 1980–1990s (Bovaird, 2007; Cabannes, 2004; Sousa Santos, 1998). However, PB has also been subjected to some criticisms that have highlighted how this instrument is too often tied to politics, making this more of a political flag rather than an effective tool to support the effectiveness of public policies (Goldfrank & Schneider, 2006).

In Italy, PB attracted considerable interest in the first decade of the current century and has been adopted in numerous cases by local authorities (Badia et al., 2014; Russo, 2013) but mainly by municipalities, which are the most widespread type of local authority in the peninsula (just under 8000). The literature on the state of the Italian situation has highlighted some difficulties in applying the paths of PG and the adoption of the PB in Italy (Bartocci et al., 2016), but an analysis that seeks to update these circumstances showing the evolutionary trends of the application of PB in Italy is useful.

Moreover, the developing crisis due to the COVID-19 pandemic presents a new challenge for the application of PB because this crisis had a potential double impact on PG practices. On the one hand, due to the necessity of social distancing, meetings and face-to-face activities became more difficult. On the other hand, a new prioritisation of societal needs assumes a central role, and communities ask for direct involvement in these choices.

Starting from these observations, this chapter proposes research on the presence, evolution, main contents, development of the processes and relevant outcomes of PB in Italy, with a specific reference to the last decade and the recent impact of the COVID-19 crisis. The analysis was based on the practices of PB in Italy collected through the Internet and through direct contact with these realities to understand the concrete applications as well as the founding reasons of PB experiences in Italian municipalities. The analysis includes the whole national territory as a reference and identifies 136 PB experiences active between 2015 and 2020 as well as the direct participation of 30 of these experiences in this research.

The chapter is structured as follows. In the next section, the evolutionary profiles of PG in Italy are analysed. This section offers a basic view of the Italian administrative system and the legislative rules for promoting direct participation in the public sector. The presence of the practices of PB, its evolution in the first 15 years of the century and the main or prevailing characteristics of its application are also discussed.

The subsequent section presents the specific results of the empirical analysis developed through the evolution of the diffusion of PB in the last five years and the direct contact with PB experiences in Italy along with the presentation of the research method as well as the findings of the investigation regarding the background, contents, processes and outcomes of the analysed PB experiences. This part is developed coherently with the research project of this book and respecting the common framework adopted in the other chapters. The final section focuses on the discussion of the empirical results and the conclusions of the work.

3.2 Evolutionary Profiles of Participatory Governance in Italy

The administrative structure of Italy is grounded on different levels of government based on article 114 of the Constitution of the Italian Republic: state, regions, provinces and metropolitan cities and municipalities. Under the state, Italy has 20 regions, 107 provinces, and metropolitan cities and about 8000 municipalities (precisely 7903 at the beginning of 2021, but this number has been gradually decreasing for some years due to some merger processes and will likely decrease further).

The Italian Constitution, promulgated in 1948 at the end of the Second World War, allowed for the development of a democratic system, which is now well rooted in the culture of the country. The division between the fundamental powers of the state is protected. In particular, the executive power is based on a relationship of trust with the legislative power exercised by the Parliament (composed of two chambers with equal powers), which is directly elected by the citizens. Recently, in 2006 and 2016, referendums were proposed to modify this system, which were rejected by the Italian population. The last significant change to the system of relations established by the Constitution dates back to 2001, and it revised the system of powers attributed to the state and regions, with a greater attribution to the latter.

Among the most relevant problems concerning the functioning of the country, the main aspect concerns the imbalance between the regions of northern (more developed) and southern Italy (less developed) in terms of wealth per capita and quality of services and infrastructures, as already pointed out almost three decades ago by Putnam et al. (1994), but without the situation having improved in recent years. Another problem that has emerged in recent decades concerns the low level of trust of the population towards the political class and has been on a downward path that began with the so-called crisis of the 'First Republic' following the Tangentopoli corruption scandal (Kickert, 2011; Waters, 1994). Further development has occurred in the last decade with the rise of new parties, sometimes defined as 'populist' (D'Alimonte, 2019; Pirro & van Kessel, 2018) in conjunction with the effects of the financial crisis of 2008, which strongly affected Italy.

In the Italian administrative system, the municipality represents the nearest administrative level to the citizen. Its main functions include urban planning, public order and safety, local roads and public transport, management of buildings and public works, social housing, waste cycle management, management of meteorological emergencies and natural disasters, public parks, school services for children, trade regulation, tourism promotion, social assistance services, registry and marital status services and museums, libraries and other local cultural services. Each municipality enjoys statutory autonomy and has its resources, partly derived from the state budget but partly deriving from autonomous taxes regulated in any case by national laws.

In this sense, the municipal context can be said to be the most fertile place to activate forms of participation, representing the most suitable environment for building an effective relationship between political representatives and citizens (Badia, 2012). In the matter of communication between public administration and citizens, the legislative decree 33 of 2013 had an important impact as it provided for numerous obligations of publicity, transparency and dissemination of information by public administrations, thus promoting communication flows to citizens and ensuring transparency and accessibility to documents and procedures.

Consistent with the trends in the rest of the world, in Italy, there has been the introduction of laws and rules regarding the promotion of PG, especially at the municipal level. These measures took place in particular from the regional legislative level (legislative interventions in this field can be mentioned in the Regions of Tuscany, Lazio, Emilia-Romagna, Umbria,

Puglia, Sicily and Marche). These regional laws, implemented between 2007 and 2020, have attempted to promote participatory logic and tools in a more precise manner, in some cases with the provision of specific funding for the implementation of PG practices. Therefore, in the last 20 years after Italy recorded the first case of PB in Europe in 1994 in the municipality of Grottammare (Bartocci et al., 2016), several municipalities have embarked on the path of such participatory processes.

In this context, the use of PB has been viewed as a valid method with a political-social value to strengthen the bond between political administrators and citizens. According to the scholars who dealt with analysing the applications of PB in the first decade of the century in Italy (Russo, 2013), this tool seemed to be used more as a technique for creating a participatory awareness than as a tool for the collective approval of political choices. Other authors (Sintomer et al., 2012) found that although the first Italian experiences in Europe were among the closest to the pioneering model of Porto Alegre, over time, they became fragmented and diversified, characterised by profound fragility and volatility with a low capacity to last over time.

By analysing the trend in the number of experiences of PB which peaked in 2008 but then decreased following the global financial crisis, Bartocci et al. (2016) noted that public finance may have played a deterrent role in experimenting with new practices. In truth, austerity policies could and should stimulate the search for innovative tools with a view to providing greater legitimacy for citizens. According to the authors, in light of direct interviews with political and managerial figures involved in PG, in some cases the public administrators have considered PB a 'luxury' to be afforded in favourable conditions and not so appropriate in times of difficulty (Bartocci et al., 2016).

Another highly interesting element of this study is that in the majority of cases, the patronage of the PB initiative is political with the identification of the initiative by a party or sometimes even by a single political figure. This likely implies a greater fragility of the instrument because the processes tend to be poorly internalised or at least not very formalised. Finally, in the experiences analysed by the authors from 2000 to 2015 (Bartocci et al., 2016), a more consultative use of PB emerges with little propensity to define or to explain in advance the budget of available resources and a specific reference target of the process.

3.3   Participatory Budgeting in Italy in 2015–2020

3.3.1   Research Method

Because the research cited so far is from a few years ago, this work aims to update the data available, particularly the data presented by Bartocci et al. (2016), which provided a picture of the dissemination of participatory budgeting in Italy up to 2015. This research aims to estimate the number of PB experiences in Italy from 2015 to 2020 through a survey conducted mainly on the Internet. To facilitate a comparison with the data collected from previous research, the same survey approach was maintained to identify the number of cases of PB. The search for information was conducted mainly online using the three internet search engines: Google, Yahoo and Bing.

Similar to what was stated in the cited research by Bartocci et al. (2016, p. 43), although we are aware that this method can result in an incomplete definition of the phenomenon, this research can approximate the total number of PB experiences. One reason is that the Internet is now the main communication tool of public administrations, particularly in Italy in light of the aforementioned legislative decree 33 of 2013 on transparency. Moreover, it seems reasonable to assume that PB was promoted on the institutional sites of the municipalities to give adequate publicity and information to the population. In this research, all the paths or experiences that referred to the use of the term 'Participatory Budgeting' have been considered beyond the specific content adopted.

The study led to the identification of 136 PB experiences between 2015 and 2020 that were active for at least one of these years. The study also made it possible to identify the duration of each participatory path and consequently the average duration. Once the cases were identified, each municipality was asked to respond to a research interview to investigate how PB had been implemented. Thirty subjects involved in the identified PB implementation processes participated in this phase of the research. Due to the development of this phase of direct contact with the municipalities involved in the PB processes, in addition to the diffusion aspect, three other aspects have been investigated, which are consistent with the methodological approach of this book: background, contents, processes and outcomes.

Regarding the background of PB, the research investigated whether the evolution of theories and practices at an international and/or national level had an impact on the participatory processes examined. Furthermore, the aim was to define the main origin of the start of the PB path (political, technical, from the community, etc.). Finally, to grasp even the most current aspects, the last question investigated was whether the ongoing emergency due to COVID-19 has had any effects on participatory processes.

Concerning the contents and the processes, an initial in-depth analysis was enabled through examining the situation of all 136 identified municipalities and concerned the subject of the participatory process. A second aspect was studied through direct contact with the subjects involved in the PB processes and concerned the part of the budget about which citizens are allowed to have a say. Finally, the analysis of the dynamics related to the process concerned the number of citizens involved in the process and the kind or categories of recipients of the participatory processes.

Regarding the aspects linked to the outcome of the PB process, the first question concerned whether PB had any real impact on the management of the municipal budget and the related decision-making or was not significant. The subjects involved in the survey were encouraged to provide examples where possible of concrete positive results obtained from the experience of PB. Furthermore, beyond the impact on the management of the municipal budget, the survey analysed whether there was any significant impact from the point of view of promoting a culture of participation. The final question investigated related to how the political representatives reacted to the outcomes of such processes.

3.3.2   Findings Concerning Diffusion

The study led to the identification of 136 PB practices active in at least one year between 2015 and 2020. The situation for each year can be deduced from the following chart, where the number of identified experiences of this research is combined with the cases presented by the research of Bartocci et al. (2016) for the years from 2001 to 2014 (Fig. 3.1).

The data on the individual years have been constructed taking into account PB processes existing in each year. PB is not always linked to a single budget year. In some cases, a different path is carried out. For example, there may be PB that has a two-year process or one that spans two accounting years. In these cases, because PB was active in both years, PB was considered for both years.

The chart illustrates that the practice of PB had progressive growth in the early years of the century reaching a peak of 125 concurrent

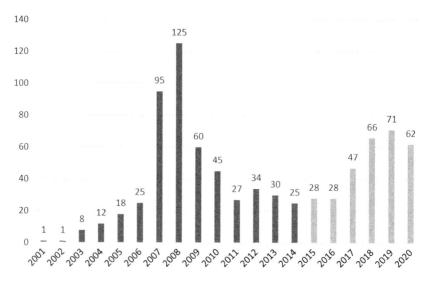

Fig. 3.1 PB diffusion in the Italian municipalities (2001–2020). (Source: author, based on Bartocci et al. (2016) and own data)

experiences in 2008, which remains the year with the greatest number of cases. From that year, which also coincides with the outbreak of the financial crisis, a gradual decline in experience emerges until 2011, the year in which the values return to the levels of five years earlier. A few years of rather stable results with low values followed between 2012 and 2016 while, starting from 2017, a growth path emerges, which stops in 2020, the year of the eruption of the COVID-19 pandemic.

The analysis of this trend, therefore, highlights that at least from an initial evidence profile, two growth peaks can be observed in 2008 and 2019, that is immediately before the outbreak of the two most critical events of the recent years: the financial crisis of 2008 and the pandemic crisis of 2020–2021. A more in-depth study of the link between a crisis and a trend in the use of PB can certainly be the focus of a follow-up on this initial analysis along with following the trend of PB experiences in the coming years to assess whether there may be comparable effects of the first and second crisis.

This part of the research also allows for determining the average duration of PB experiences detected by the survey: the value that emerges is of an average duration of 2.24 years. Moreover, of the 136 cases detected, 45

(33.09%) lasted only one year, a value with an important decrease compared to the data analysed by Bartocci et al. (2016), where 133 of 261 PB experiences lasted only one year and were no longer repeated (therefore equal to 50.96%). This appears to be a highly interesting finding because it reveals that in addition to progressive growth in PB experiences, there is also growth in their consolidation as a practice that is no longer so occasional or sporadic for municipalities.

3.3.3 Findings Concerning the Background

The findings concerning the background include three aspects of investigation:

1. Influence of the evolution of theories and practices at international and national levels on PB practices in Italy.
2. The main source for the start of the PB path (political, technical, from the community, etc.).
3. Effects of the COVID-19 pandemic on the participatory processes.

The analysis of these points is inferred, as previously observed, from research interviews conducted with the 30 municipal representatives of participatory policies who participated in the survey. Concerning the first point, relating to the influence of the evolution of national and international theories and practices, the majority of those involved (18 of 30) claimed to have been inspired by other national or international experiences regarding the practices. In particular, among them, 16 declared the use of at least one national reference or source of inspiration and four of an international one.

Concerning the second point, relating to the origin of the participatory process, the possibility was given to choose between four possible options: pushed by the political component of the local administration, pushed by the managerial component of the local administration, pushed by public opinion and access to public funds. On this point, the answers are clear: in all 30 cases examined, the political component of the municipality was decisive for the initiation of participatory processes. The technical component was fundamental in two cases: the thrust of public opinion in three and the possibility of accessing public funds in five. The data can be considered reliable because based on the circumstance that only 11 respondents played or claimed a political role in the development of participatory processes, the majority of respondents had a technical function (in 72% of cases with an internal job position in the municipality).

Finally, for the third point, the effect of the COVID-19 pandemic on participatory processes, a large majority of respondents (25), noted the effects of the COVID-19 crisis on participatory policies. The results are shown in Table 3.1.

Therefore, fundamentally, the COVID-19 crisis has harmed participatory policies in the immediate time frame. In some cases, the process was simply cancelled (and these data are consistent with what has been observed at a general level). In other cases, the participation was moved exclusively online (and in some of these cases, the respondents found that the quality of the participation decreased in this way). In still other cases, the process, although not stopped, slowed down or became more complicated.

It is interesting that a respondent subject instead noted an increase in participation favoured, according to him, by the fact that 'perhaps people had more time to get information and present projects or to vote on projects. Although this situation is limited to only one case, similar considerations come from other responses: the COVID-19 crisis has led people to feel the need for greater dialogue between citizens and administration. In some cases, during the pandemic and even in periods of lockdown, local administrations, taking advantage of the opportunities offered by new technologies and a growing awareness of their use by the average user, have attempted to activate channels of dialogue and participation, rediscovering or enhancing initiatives already underway or previously planned. There have been slowdowns, but it seems that even in the most negative cases, the foundations have been laid to be able to resume, as soon as the

Table 3.1 List of the effects of the COVID-19 crisis on PB

Effects of the COVID-19 crisis on PB	
Cancellation of the process in course	8 cases
Process slowed down or made more difficult	8 cases
Move to online procedures	8 cases
Greater participation in the PB process	1 case
Total answers	25

Source: author's elaboration

context conditions allow, the path of active participation that has already been undertaken.

3.3.4 Findings Concerning the Contents and the Processes

Concerning the contents and the processes, the following three aspects have been analysed:

1. The subject of PB (referred to all 136 identified municipalities).
2. The part of the budget about which citizens are allowed to have their say, investigated for the 30 participants in the research interviews.
3. The number of citizens involved in the process and the kind or categories of recipients of the participatory processes, analysed again with the 30 respondents.

Regarding the first aspect, especially in recent years, the proposals of PB in Italy considered multiple contents without a specific reference to particular areas. The most frequent modality in these cases was to give the citizens the possibility to carry out proposals of any nature linked to possible intervention and funding from the municipality. Besides, there have been a certain number of participatory paths focused on thematic areas. In these cases, the most frequent objects of attention were the management of public parks, the organisation of public spaces, very often aimed at sports activities, activities for children and young people and the creation of tourist and territorial promotion routes.

Regarding the second point, only a small percentage of the municipality's overall budget is dedicated to PB. By applying the arithmetical average of all the values collected, a value equal to 0.76% is obtained. Regarding the 30 situations analysed, those in which the detected percentage is equal to or greater than 1% are 10, that is a third of the total. The question that was asked here referred only to the latest data available, but the municipalities that have reported not only these data but also the trend in recent years have highlighted how the percentage tends to increase over time, although the values are still quite low.

Regarding the analysis of the final aspect, for which it is possible to obtain an average percentage calculated by the means of the ratio between the number of participants (if on multiple editions according to an average value) and the overall population, the figure that emerges is equal to 7.5%

of the population. This data does not appear to be negligible, although to better understand its value, it would be necessary to compare it with its future development in the coming years. Another interesting aspect that emerged is that in the vast majority of cases, involvement in the PB process was aimed at the entire population. In some cases, especially in larger cities, even city users were involved, meaning those who are permanently in the territory of the municipality for study or work reasons. The exceptions concerning the whole community consideration basically concern specific attention on the younger generations: in some municipalities, the BP was addressed to schools, families and/or younger generations.

3.3.5   *Findings Concerning the Outcomes*

The questions regarding the effective outcomes of PB in the studied experiences included three profiles of analysis:

1. PB impact on the municipal decision-making process or at least the promotion of a participatory culture.
2. Possible examples of concrete positive results obtained from the experience of PB.
3. Reactions of political representatives to the outcomes of such processes.

Regarding the first point, from the 30 responses, it was found that in the vast majority of cases (24/30), there were no significant impacts due to the limited number of resources allocated. In this way PB has had little influence on the overall decision-making process of the institution. In the remaining six cases, mostly detected in medium and large cities, where even a small share of the municipality's budget still represents an important figure of expenditure in absolute value, PB has instead become a relevant process in influencing decision-making processes. On the other hand, considering the impact of PB on the promotion of a culture of participation, the statistics are reversed for the previous answer: in this case, a positive impact was detected in 26 cases of 30, which represents a very positive result from the point of view of the development of the principles linked to civic engagement.

The responses provided by the municipalities about possible concrete examples of positive impacts of PB are numerous and significant. A deepening of this part of the research could be the object of further development of this work. Among the most relevant aspects, there are three profiles of interest. The first concerns the ability to concretise the proposals received from citizens through the PB platform into projects effectively implemented. The second profile concerns the creation of a new sense of trust on the part of citizens towards the institutions, while the third considers the development of a new sense of community-based feelings of collaboration and sharing.

Regarding the reaction of the political component of the administration to PB processes, a subdivision of the answers obtained according to whether they came from a technician or a politician seems appropriate. The technicians who participated in the research substantially confirmed what emerged in the previous part on the origin of the PB: the politicians were the proponents of the PB processes, and therefore, after promoting them, they generally supported them. However, the politicians who tend to respond highlighted that in some cases there has been a clash between majority and opposition forces, which in some situations has been at the origin of the subsequent abandonment of the PB experience, such as in the case of a change in the government majority. Some respondents belonging to small municipalities pointed out that a sort of unanimous consensus has been created among all political forces on the participatory path, especially if already rooted in some editions of PB.

3.4 Conclusions

This article has first illustrated the steps of PB at the beginning of the century and has shown that a phase of constant development was followed by a rapid decline in the use of the tool. During this phase, some application limits of the instrument emerged, such as an excessive link with politics and a scarce ability to make the process last.

A few years later, beginning from about the middle of the last decade, there has instead been a change in the trend, recognisable in a return of attention to participatory policies, fuelled on the one hand by an awareness of political class and on the other hand by the positive feedback of some successful experiences, the example of which is spreading to the rest of Italy. The number of municipalities that have adopted PB has begun to increase again, and the degree of the continuity of these practices has also intensified consistently.

In this new diffusion, the political class itself has played a central role, with the role of the conscious and proactive protagonist of this new course of participation in Italy. This result, therefore, seems to overturn what was observed regarding the experiences of PB in the first decade of the century, where the impact of politics on participatory processes had been negative because it had led to an excessive personalisation of the tool and had compromised its durability, increasing its fragility and vulnerability.

Another element for which the research has shown a progressive increase in the impact of policies linked to PB is that the proposals are growing concerning all the activities and services of the administration and are therefore not limited to some thematic areas. The percentage share of the overall budget of the local authorities that involve PB is usually less than 1% of the total, although some signs of an increase in recent years have been detected. The population participation figure stands at around 7.5%, and the involvement in PB policies has almost always been aimed at the entire population.

Nevertheless, even in light of the small figures allocated to PB, the impacts on decision-making processes do not appear particularly significant. If the overall spending policies of the municipalities are considered, a majority has recorded a significant growth of the culture of participation due to PB. In particular, this new culture of participation has contributed on the one hand to the improvement of the sense of trust of citizens towards their local administrators and, on the other hand, to the birth of a new community spirit based on feelings of collaboration and sharing.

The set of circumstances outlined regarding the experience of applying PB in Italy in recent years suggest that PB can be considered a phenomenon similar to that of the phoenix rising from the ashes and that of the pandemic crisis, which has inevitably led to a small decrease in the use of this practice, could instead further strengthen the will and awareness in the use of this tool, as directly observed in some specific cases.

REFERENCES

Almquist, R., Grossi, G., van Helden, G. J., & Reichard, C. (2013). Public sector governance and accountability. *Critical Perspectives on Accounting, 24*(7–8), 479–487. Academic Press. https://doi.org/10.1016/j.cpa.2012.11.005

Badia, F. (2012). *Il sistema di controllo relazionale nelle reti di aziende pubbliche.* Giuffrè. https://www.ibs.it/sistema-di-controllo-relazionale-nelle-libro-francesco-badia/e/9788814169304

Badia, F., Borin, E., & Donato, F. (2014). Co-governing public value in local authorities. In *Studies in public and non-profit governance* (Vol. 3, pp. 269–289).

Emerald Group Publishing Ltd. https://doi.org/10.1108/S2051-66302 0140000003011

Bartocci, L., Grossi, G., Natalizi, D., & Romizi, S. (2016). Lo stato dell'arte del bilancio partecipativo in Italia. *Azienda Pubblica, 29*(1), 37–58. http://www.aziendapubblica.it/articolo_digital/dettaglio/luca-bartocci-giuseppe-grossi-daniele-natalizi/lo-stato-dellarte-del-bilancio-partecipativo-in-italia-azp_2016_1_37_58-34926.html

Bovaird, T. (2007). Beyond engagement and participation: User and community coproduction of public services. *Public Administration Review, 67*(5), 846–860. https://doi.org/10.1111/j.1540-6210.2007.00773.x

Cabannes, Y. (2004). Participatory budgeting: A significant contribution to participatory democracy. *Environment and Urbanization, 16*(1), 27–46. https://doi.org/10.1177/095624780401600104

D'Alimonte, R. (2019). How the populists won in Italy. *Journal of Democracy, 30*(1), 114–127. https://www.journalofdemocracy.org/articles/how-the-populists-won-in-italy/

Edwards, M. (2001). Participatory governance into the future: Roles of the government and community sectors. *Australian Journal of Public Administration, 60*(3), 78–88. https://doi.org/10.1111/1467-8500.00226

Fung, A., & Wright, E. O. (2001). Deepening democracy: Innovations in empowered participatory governance. *Politics & Society, 29*(1), 5–41. https://doi.org/10.1177/0032329201029001002

Goldfrank, B., & Schneider, A. (2006). Competitive institution building: The PT and participatory budgeting in Rio Grande Do Sul. *Latin American Politics and Society, 48*(3), 1–31. https://www.jstor.org/stable/4490476?seq=1#metadata_info_tab_contents

Grote, J., & Gbikpi, B. (2002). *Participatory governance—Political and societal implications.* Springer VS. https://www.springer.com/gp/book/9783810032379

Jenkins, B., & Gray, A. (1993). Codes of accountability in the new public sector. *Accounting, Auditing & Accountability Journal, 6*(3), 52–67. https://doi.org/10.1108/09513579310042560

Kickert, W. (2011). Distinctiveness of administrative reform in Greece, Italy, Portugal and Spain. Common characteristics of context, administrations and reforms. *Public Administration, 89*(3), 801–818. https://doi.org/10.1111/j.1467-9299.2010.01862.x

Pirro, A. L., & van Kessel, S. (2018). Populist Eurosceptic trajectories in Italy and the Netherlands during the European crises. *Politics, 38*(3), 327–343. https://doi.org/10.1177/0263395718769511

Putnam, R. D., Leonardi, R., & Nonetti, R. Y. (1994). *Making democracy work.* Princeton University Press. https://doi.org/10.2307/j.ctt7s8r7

Romzek, B. S., & Dubnick, M. J. (1987). Accountability in the public sector: Lessons from the challenger tragedy. *Public Administration Review, 47*(3), 227. https://doi.org/10.2307/975901

Russo, S. (2013). Public governance e partecipazione dei cittadini al processo allocativo dei Comuni. *Azienda Pubblica: Teoria e Problemi Di Management*, 61–88.

Sintomer, Y., Herzberg, C., Röcke, A., & Allegretti, G. (2012). Transnational models of citizen participation: The case of participatory budgeting. *Journal of Deliberative Democracy, 8*(2). https://doi.org/10.16997/jdd.141

Sousa Santos, B. de. (1998). Participatory budgeting in Porto Alegre: Toward a redistributive democracy. *Politics & Society, 26*(4), 461–510. https://doi.org/10.1177/0032329298026004003

Waters, S. (1994). 'Tangentopoli' and the emergence of a new political order in Italy. *West European Politics, 17*(1), 169–182. https://doi.org/10.1080/01402389408425006

CHAPTER 4

Participatory Budgeting in Sweden

Iwona Sobis

4.1 Introduction

Participatory budgeting (PB) is one of many forms of public involvement in a process of democratic deliberation and decision-making on how a part of the money from a municipal budget ought to be allocated. The inspiration came from Porto Alegre in Brasilia, which experimented with this democratic innovation between 1989 and 2003 and the idea became fashionable across the world, promising an improvement of local participative democracy, guarantying citizen engagement and involvement in local matters everywhere. Research conducted by (Sintomer et al., 2008) showed that PB was applied by poor countries as well as by rich ones and with a success. For that reason, even the large international organizations like the World Bank, OECD, or EU have promoted this new institution over the years.

It is not surprising that Sweden was also under such influence especially when various public reforms conducted in the spirit of New Public Management (NPM) gradually undermined citizens' trust in the rightness

I. Sobis (✉)
School of Public Administration, Gothenburg University, Gothenburg, Sweden
e-mail: iwona.sobis@spa.gu.se

© The Author(s), under exclusive license to Springer Nature Switzerland AG 2022
M. S. De Vries et al. (eds.), *International Trends in Participatory Budgeting*, Governance and Public Management,
https://doi.org/10.1007/978-3-030-79930-4_4

of decisions made by local politicians or their way in exercising power. Sweden is the third biggest country in the EU with an area about 450,295 square kilometers, a total population 10,327,589 as of December 2019 of which about 2,634,967 inhabitants (25.5%) have a foreign background (SCB, 2020). Stockholm is the capital city with a population of 974,073. Other large cities are Göteborg with a population of 579,281, Malmö with a population of 344,166, and Uppsala with 230,767 residents. Larger towns (approximately 31 municipalities) have about 50,000–200,000 inhabitants. In contrast, the population of the 10 smallest municipalities varies from 2809 in the Åsele Municipality (Västerbottens län/county) to 2451 inhabitants in the Bjurholm Municipality (Västerbottens län/county) (Ekonomifakta, 2020). The Swedish local self-government has a long tradition secured by the Constitution and the Local Government Act (1991: 900) (Sveriges Riksdag, 1991) with subsequent amendments that constitute an integral part of democratic government. Sweden has also ratified the European Charter of Local Self-Government. According to the Local Government Act (1991: 900), local self-government at the local and regional level is exercised by municipalities, respectively county councils, with a clear division of competences. The municipality is responsible for childcare amenities and preschools, primary and secondary schooling, care services for the elderly, recreational and cultural activities, but also for water supply and sewerage, rescue services, and refuse disposal. On the other hand, county councils take responsibility for health and medical services, public transport, and regional cultural institutions (Larsson & Back, 2008; Petersson, 2010; Sveriges Kommuner och Regioner (SKR), 2020a). The country is divided into 21 counties and 290 municipalities. In every county (in Swedish: län) there are several municipalities. Gotland is an exception because the functions of the county council and municipality are performed by the same organization (SKR, 2020a).

Sintomer et al. (2008) emphasize that citizen participation at the local level usually depends on the previously used methods and systems to activate public involvement, which is also confirmed by the Swedish Association of Local Authorities and Regions (SALAR) on their home page (SKR, 2020b). SALAR is the country's largest employer organization, signing key collective agreements for almost 1.2 million employees in municipalities and regions. This Association promotes and supports the introduction of PB in the Swedish municipalities and county councils to strengthen local democracy (SKL, 2011, p. 18). According to SALAR, Sweden has a long tradition of "citizen dialog"; thus, PB became the next innovative step in creating opportunities for citizens to participate in local decision-making.

This chapter is based on work by the Svenska Offentliga Utredningar—SOU (Swedish Public Investigations) ordered by the central government and was part of the legislative process preparing new regulations; the previous empirical studies conducted on this topic; the reports and public documents from SALAR: and the documents and relevant information collected from the municipality Facebook and the homepages of those municipalities which introduced PB in their agenda.

Active work with PB started with the engagement of SALAR disseminating the idea among the local self-governments although only a few municipalities were tempted to experiment with it. A very small number of empirical studies were conducted concerning pilot projects conducted in the municipalities of Avesta, Haninge, Uddevalla, and Örebro between 2007 and 2011 (Adolfsson et al., 2012; Demediuk et al., 2012). Since then, not many new studies have been published. This chapter therefore presents what is known about PB in Sweden during the period 2007–2020.

Below, the focus is on the description of the Swedish PB model, its origin and development, the rules for citizen participation, the principles for the steering organization and administration of PB, and the outcomes.

4.2   THE SWEDISH MODEL

The aim of participatory budgeting in Sweden was to invite citizens into the local decision-making process by planning together how funds from municipal taxes ought to be allocated to different areas. The Swedish model of PB was based on (1) the experiences of the most successful countries in the world, (2) international research about PB, and (3) Sweden's own pilot projects in Avesta, Haninge, Uddevalla, and Örebro conducted during the period of 2007–2011. In view of the fact that all the implemented PB projects were perceived by research as successful (Adolfsson et al., 2012; Demediuk et al., 2012) SALAR consequently continued financial support to other municipalities open to experimenting with PB. The model was adapted to the country's historical origin of the tradition of public involvement in decision-making, and the Swedish understanding of a citizen's role in PB. Five criteria for PB, recommended by the EU, were also incorporated into the Swedish model:

- The process must contain budget/resource dimensions,
- Citizens apply at a level governed by a political assembly such as council or committee,
- Participatory budgeting is repeated over time,
- It includes participation processes for citizens in forums or in councils,
- The municipality or county council shall be responsible for the results of implementation and provide feedback to citizens (SKL, 2011, p. 8).

The current PB model represents the simplification of a complex context. It was adapted to the different geographical, demographic, and cultural conditions of the municipalities. The Swedish model of PB was based on citizen dialogue and SALAR's ten-year-work with municipalities to develop it (SKL, 2011, p. 8). The aim was to offer citizens opportunities to prioritize part of a municipal budget. According to the Swedish PB model, local self-government is expected to:

- Develop criteria for participatory budgeting,
- Advertise it in a community,
- Create opportunities for idea generation, in which citizens make suggestions on what should be done,
- Process the proposals based on criteria,
- Citizens should vote on proposals,
- Politicians should make the decision on the proposals,
- Carry out the chosen proposal(s),
- Follow up on a result (SKL, 2019a)

In 2019, SALAR published Participatory Budgeting—A worldwide model for democratic influence, (Medborgarbudget—En världsomspännande modell för demokratisk inflytande), in which the Swedish PB model was presented in the details to inspire municipalities, and county councils to experiment and develop it further.

4.3   About the Participatory Budgeting in Sweden

4.3.1   The Origin of Participatory Budgeting

SOU 2000:1 on *En uthållig demokrati (A sustainable democracy)* raised the issue of local democracy for the first-time following Sweden joining the EU in 1995. Local democracy was broadly discussed, and the state was under the pressure of conversion. Local self-government became the subject of significant changes because citizen participation in decision-making was perceived both as a right and as a duty. According to this report, the extension of participatory democracy was understood as the reinforcement of deliberative democracy at the local level (p. 22). This report explained that the Swedish political system, similar to other EU member states, represented flexible multi-level governance with several levels and competences. Each of them had fundamentally different democratic values but cooperation and interactions between the EU, national state, county/region, and the municipality were expected to be productive. Independently of the fact that the Swedish municipalities enjoyed a high level of autonomy, it was still the state that set boundaries for local self-government. Other levels of multi-level governance, like the EU or county/region, also had something to say and they influenced the emergence of PB in the Swedish municipalities. Sweden was expected to share the EU common values and norms, and follow EU recommendations, among others to give citizens' the opportunity to participate in public deliberations and decision-making at an early stage:

> The work of asserting democracy does not only apply in relation to the Swedish state's work with the EU and the conditions in Swedish society. It must also apply vis-à-vis the EU institutions and relations within the Union as a whole. Where public power is exercised, opportunities for transparency must also be asserted and citizens' opportunities for participation, influence, and participation must be promoted. (SOU 2000:1, p. 121)

The same SOU-report tells us:

> Citizens must be given greater opportunities to participate and exert influence, and in this way to experience participation in local politics. We need to break the concentration of power held by a few elected officials and executive officials, the thinning of the parties, and above all, the sense of alienation and political inequality of many citizens. (SOU 2000:1, p. 156)

The Swedish municipalities were expected to propose various forms of public involvement in local matters. Decentralization should secure that the state had ceded its power to citizens, citizens' groups, associations, and companies. Various forms of local participative democracy should take care of their joint affairs. It was a question about the citizens' relationship with a municipality in line with the conviction that the greater independence the municipalities gain from the state, the better conditions for meaningful local political participation (SOU 2000:1, p. 157). In this context, PB was perceived as a chance to "democratize democracy". SALAR explains:

> The starting point is also the various conventions and goals that Sweden as a nation has signed and which in many cases are implemented at the local level. The need to involve citizens is clearly stated in the Agenda 2030 goals, in the Conventions on Human Rights, in the Public Health Goals for Sweden, in the democracy goals taken by the Riksdag to achieve a sustainable society. (SKL, 2019a, p. 12)

From the SALAR report (SKL, 2019a) it appears that Sweden has a long tradition of cooperation between local government, trade and industry, civil society, NGOs, and inhabitants. It has always been this way, thus public participation in local matters is nothing new.

The second report SOU 2001:48 on *Att vara med på riktigt (To be part of it for real)* was based, among others, on a Democracy Inquiry advocating the increase of citizens' involvement in local decision-making. The central government recommended and supported the use of citizen dialogue and other democracy experiments at the local level. The delegation of democracy resulted in county councils/regions, municipalities, local organizations or associations being able to apply for financial resources for various democracy projects, which were continued even later on. In SOU 2016:5 on *Låt fler forma framtiden! (Let shape the future more!)* we can read:

> (...) the Municipal Democracy Committee's report contained several proposals aimed at increasing the civic influence between the elections, including the citizens' right to propose and open meetings in proxies. The Committee also stressed the importance of dialogue and consultation before deciding on a local level and recommended that municipalities and county councils should set up and support citizens' panels and youth councils. These tools were considered particularly important for citizens who were outside party politics. (SOU 2016:5, p. 391)

Citizen dialogue and public consultations dominated open informative meetings, meetings in an open space, meetings with special groups of inhabitants, or dialogues with citizens via social media like Facebook,

Blogs, and Discussion Forums on the Internet. Those forms of deliberative democracy have increased over time and were aimed at obtaining citizens' opinions on specific issues, activating or involving citizens in
democratic decision-making processes or they just increased the citizens'
political confidence in complex political problems and promoting their
own municipality (SOU 2016: 5, p. 392). PB was promoted as the alternative consultation form in relation to other forms of citizen dialogue that
"differs from the ordinary citizens' dialogue in the sense that the decision-
making power, in whole or in part, is handed over to the citizens" (SOU
2016:5, p. 395).

4.3.2   The Pilot Projects of PB in Sweden

The first pilot PB projects supported by SALAR started in four municipalities in 2007: Avesta, Haninge, Uddevalla, and Örebro. These projects
were seen as "micro-local participation", "consultation on public finances",
or "funds at the local level" (SKL, 2011, p. 21). In the micro-local participation, citizens from a neighborhood or a specific group of inhabitants
engaged in a specific theme. They discussed what should be done in the
local community. In the consultation on public finances, citizens were
involved in budget priorities. In the funds at the local level, people living
in a neighborhood shared common responsibility for the neighborhood.
Not one of these PB projects was perceived as an ideal model of PB but
rather as a mixed form, dependent on the local conditions.

Adolfsson et al. (2012) and Demediuk et al. (2012) conducted the first
empirical studies about PB in Sweden. Their research concerned the
municipalities of Haninge, Uddevalla, and Örebro. PB was introduced to
create those services demanded by citizens. The aim was to increase contact between the citizens and the local self-government. Adolfsson et al.
(2012) explain:

> In this context, the municipality can be seen as an actor, who is a service
> provider and thus strives to make better decisions by providing citizens with
> good ideas. It can also be seen as a democratic player who is looking for ways
> to better contacts and thus better society and governance. (p. 8)

The Municipalities of Haninge, Uddevalla, and Örebro invested a very
small amount of money for PB from the municipal budgets. The local
authorities wanted to minimize the economic and political risks. At the

same time, they did their best to receive attention from the mass-media by spreading the idea about PB to other municipalities. Adolfsson et al. (2012) and Demediuk et al. (2012) admitted that the concept of "participatory budgeting" or "budget of citizens" was not popular in Sweden. Instead, the concepts of "civic initiatives", "civil dialogue", and "public consultation" have emerged and become fashionable. Citizens could participate in citizens' web panels, consultations, reference groups, information meetings, café dialogues, workshops, open space meetings, advice, and dialogue forums. The PB project conducted in the Municipality of Avesta during the period of 2007–2010 was the exception (SKL 2011, p. 26; SOU 2016:5, p. 395). Carlsson (2014) showed that the municipal budget of Avesta was available on the municipality website. The citizens could prioritize from among all the expenditure items. Carlsson asserts that such a form of PB contributed to increased citizen participation in decision-making but also diminished political equality (Carlsson 2014; SOU 2016:5, p. 395). This form of PB was not repeated, neither in Avesta nor in other Swedish municipalities.

The first experiments with PB led to the government deciding to appoint a special investigator on July 17, 2014. The aim was to prepare proposals for measures to increase and broaden citizen participation in local decision-making in the frame of representative democracy. In SOU 2016:5 we can read:

> (…) in Sweden, the participatory budget has been used to a limited extent. In the few Swedish municipalities that have used the method, the areas that citizens have decided to touch on such as the upgrading of parks, the inclusion of school pupils in various environmental projects, dialogue process and security enhancing measures. (p. 395)

In Sweden, the tradition is that pilot projects have a decisive importance for eventual continuation of the same activities in the future. However, Adolfsson et al. (2012), Demediuk et al. (2012), and Carlsson (2014) showed that although the first pilot projects were successful, recognized by the public, and contributed to an increase in citizen participation, the continuation of such processes has reluctantly gone in Sweden. According to the data collected from SALAR and the homepages of municipalities, only 12 out of 290 municipalities introduced a total of 33 projects of PB between 2007 and 2020. The introduction of PB in Sweden should be divided into two phases: (1) the years 2007–2015 and (2) the years 2016–2020. During the first phase of 2007–2015, the Municipalities of Avesta, Haninge, Uddevalla, Örebro, and Upplands Väsby were experimenting with 11 PB projects but these municipalities never repeated any PB project after 2015. During the second phase of 2016–2020, another group of municipalities, including Göteborg, Nässjö, Stockholm, Torsby, Trelleborg, Uppsala, and Åre started a pilot with PB. They have conducted 22 PB projects, of which 7 are not yet finished, for example, in Trelleborg and Uppsala; their PB projects should be finished in 2021 or 2023. The municipalities participating in the second phase are expected to repeat their PB projects at least three times, to evaluate them, and learn from the outcomes. SALAR provides support during the launch process and networking between municipalities (SKL, 2019b). For a full composition of all PBs in Sweden, see Appendix.

SALAR's latest effort to increase citizen participation in local decision-making has been to establish a network of municipalities for the period 2019–2022 to develop PB in line with the model of democratic and social sustainability. The municipalities of Uppsala and Trelleborg are already in this network. It is interesting that currently, the concept of PB seems to be shaded in official rhetoric; no one is talking about participatory budgeting but about citizen dialogue. SALAR provides support through the organization of network meetings, education, international experience exchange, and method development. Moreover, they have invited Professor Giovanni Allegretti from the University of Coimbra in Portugal, who works all over the world and supports the development of PB. The expectation is that he may provide some pragmatic idea to the Swedish authority on how to broaden this initiative at the local level.

4.3.3   Amounts of Money for Participatory Budgeting in the Frame of Total Municipal Budget

It is impossible to indicate the percentage of the total budget in the PB experiments. The amount of money ascribed to PB varies from municipality to municipality. It can be 175,000 SEK but also 131,000,000 SEK (See: Appendix). This variation is due to the municipality's economic situation, local needs, and the local authorities' courage to test PB. To provide a better understanding of the allocation of financial resources for PB we can observe the PB project on improvement of local infrastructure, for example, development of local squares or parks. According to collected data, it differed from 120,000,000 SEK in Trelleborg for "Development of various stages of the Upper and Urban Parks Quarter" (Trelleborgs kommun, 06-06-2020) to 400,000 SEK per project in the Haninge Municipality for "Eskil Park" and the "Park-Our-Path" in Jordbro (SKL, 2011, p. 28; Appendix) or 500,000 SEK in Torsby for "Tingsbus Park". In the case of the Avesta Municipality, the local self-government ascribed 5,000,000 SEK for "Center of Avesta—Little square" and "Dream Park of Avesta" (SKL 2011, p. 23; Torsby Kommun, 2018; Appendix).

The most frequent topic for PB was the development of the smaller planning areas or countryside, for example, in the Municipalities of Nässjö and Uppsala (Nässjö kommun, 2019; Uppsala kommun, 2020). Some examples of PB were aiming at creating various ideas dealing with security through meetings between people, for example, in the Municipalities of Göteborg, the authorities assigned from 400,000 SEK to 500,000 SEK for different districts. The differences were due probably to the number of citizens living and working in a district (Göteborgs Stad, 2020; Nässjö kommun, 2019; Stockholms stad, 2018). Uddevalla used PB for the environmental development of two schools, 250,000 SEK per school, and for safe walks organized by local officials 175,000 SEK per district (Uddevalla kommun, 2017). In the Municipality of Örebro, the PB project was addressed to young people and was about the creation of a spontaneous sports ground with artificial grass for football and basketball. As a bonus the project played an educational function. The young participants gained knowledge about the municipality's budget work and an understanding of the resources needed to make investments. For this purpose, two compulsory schools and young people from a Leisure Centre received more than SEK 800,000 from the investment budget to conduct this project in real life. About 150 pupils attended (Dialogguiden, 2017a).

From the collected data it does not appear that any additional money was used to support the PB pilot projects. The only exceptions in this regard are the Municipalities of Avesta and Haninge (SKL, 2011).

4.3.4   *Participatory Budgeting Policy Area and Opportunities for Repetition*

Reading only the major topics of PB, it can be ascertained that this institution does not have any specific policy area in Sweden. The first phase of PB pilot projects in Avesta, Haninge, Uddevalla, and Örebro were addressed almost exclusively to the young people and focused on the development of parks, squares, bridges, sport, traffic, cultural events, or the school environment. In the second phase of PB launching, the projects concerned the development of districts, rural areas, as well as cultural efforts aimed at bringing people together. This diversity of the PB projects can probably be explained that some initiatives were launched by city councils, whereas inhabitants sometimes took the initiative into their own hands and decided which tasks should be given priority.

According to the collected data, it seems that the PB projects were repeated, but they are only at an experimentation stage and are conducted by rules (SKL 2011, p. 8). The duration of PB projects extended from one-year PB projects into five-year programs and were planned in advance in cooperation with local residents as was the case of Trelleborg (3 years) or Uppsala (5 years), which also allowed the allocation of larger sums for PB.

4.4   Citizens Participation

4.4.1   The Rules of Participation in Participatory Budgeting

The rules for participation are decided by the municipal councils. Sometimes, a wide group of citizens could participate in PB; sometimes a municipal council addressed PB to a special group of participants such as children and adolescents as was the case of Avesta, Haninge, Uddevalla, and Örebro. Another time, the PB projects concerned district or countryside development. In that case, all people who were either registered or owned a property in a municipality could participate by providing proposals for a PB project or by voting as was the case in the Municipalities of Upplands Väsby, Trelleborg, Uppsala, and Åre. Information about who could participate was found on the municipality's homepage when a local authority presented a PB proposal in a preliminary phase. Thus, the rules for citizen participation in PB varied due to the problem to be solved, the local needs, and the municipality's financial situation (Carlsson 2014, p. 49; SKL 2011). The first PB pilot projects conducted in Avesta, Haninge, Uddevalla, and Örebro, the local authorities addressed children as well as adolescents. Everyone could participate. The young people were usually underrepresented in existing citizen dialogues. Thus, the PB projects provided opportunities for them to influence local decision-making. Probably it was the conviction that the local authority's early dialogue and collaboration with children would have educational functions. The young people could gain knowledge about the municipality's budget work, understanding of the resources needed to make investments and take responsibility for their community and local decision-making.

Since 2015, the topics of participatory budgeting mostly concerned local development. Everyone, who had the interest and goodwill, was a resident in a specific area, or was an owner of a property, could participate in local decision-making. The municipalities that introduced the PB projects provided ample and timely information about every step of a process, which was in line with the Swedish model of PB. For example, the Municipality of Torsby while conducting its first PB in 2016–2017, addressed young people in grades 6–9. The pupils were asked to make suggestions on how the Tinghus Park (Tingshusparken) in the central part of Torsby urban area could be designed. The young people were informed about what their proposal would result in: (1) something that would remain for several years, (2) something that is suitable for all age groups, and (3) something that is accessible to all people (Torsby Kommun, 2018). In a similar spirit, other municipalities proceeded in a like manner, for example, the Municipality of Nässjöe. The aim of the Nässjöe PB project in 2016–2020 was to improve the physical environment. The participants were expected to: (1) make the area or location more attractive, (2) create a new meeting place or improve a meeting place that already existed in order to make it simply a place to meet in! (indoors as well as outdoors), (3) make the place safer and more comfortable, (4) strengthen the identity and future beliefs of those living in the area, (5) improve a new construction, for example, bathing bridge, playground equipment, benches, plantings in park, sculptures, and lighting.

4.4.2   Selection of PB Project and Citizen Participation in Voting

The winning PB projects were usually selected through voting independently if it concerned children, adolescents, or mature citizens. Sometimes, one person could vote on one proposal; sometimes one person could vote on three proposals. It was due to local needs. The sum of points scored by the proposals had decisive importance for which a given project won in the citizens' vote. Two exceptions to the rule were also apparent; in the Municipality of Göteborg, the civil servants selected the winning proposal, not the citizens. They proceeded in two stages: (1) by asking some questions about the degree to which a proposal fulfilled the rules of PB, and (2) by asking several questions about the nature of the proposal: whether it was innovative, providing conditions relevant to the topic of PB, and whether it was linked to other areas important, for example, social equality and justice within the municipality, and so on. The civil servants, being the jury, used matrices, tables, and color-coding to decide the winning proposal (see: Appendix; Göteborgs Stad 2020). In the Municipality of Åre, 2019–2020, the PB project dealing with the District of the Södra Årefjällen and Undersåker had the aim of appointing a resource person (a catalyst) who could drive the process of creating a new meeting place (all-activity house). Following that, the Rural Development Committee decided which project ought to be implemented (see: Appendix; Åre kommun 2020). It should be added that instructions for voting were in most cases clear. It was important which PB project received the first, second, and third prizes. In this order, the projects were implemented later on.

The number of participants in voting varied among the Swedish municipalities because the municipalities differed in size, voting rules, and methods to describe the PB projects on municipal homepages. The investigated municipalities seldom provided information about the percentage of voters in relation to the population within the area in which the PB was held. Hence those who wanted to answer the question—how many citizens did participate in voting?—had to count them themselves. In general, public participation in the PB projects seems to be rather low. Some exceptions concerned the projects addressed to young people, for example, in the Municipality of Uddevalla 2010. In the PB project: The odd choice, 10% of aged 13–19 and 87% and 76% of the pupils from two schools participated. In the PB projects dealing with the Square De Luxe: Park-Our-Path from the Municipality of Upplands Väsby everyone could vote, even those who did not live in the municipality. Finally, only 1337 citizens (2.8%) participated out of 46,786 (see: Appendix; Dialogguiden, 2017b; Uddevalla kommun, 2017). In the Municipality of Nässjö, the public officials did care about the participation of citizens in the voting. People could vote digitally, by e-mails, calls, by post and even by a mix of voting methods, but the number of voters remained unknown (see: Appendix; Nässjö kommun, 2020). According to the collected data, only 15 out of 33 PB projects conducted clear information about the number of voters participating in the PB project during the period of 2007–2020. Thus, transparency was disputable. Moreover, Information Communication Technology (ICT) became an integral part of the Swedish PB projects. ICT was widely used by local authorities to inform citizens about planned activities in a municipality and to receive feedback from residents via websites, e-mail, Facebook, Blogs, or Twitter.

4.5   Organization and Administration of Participatory Budgeting

The organization and administration of PB were usually presented on the municipal website in a special tab called Politics and Democracy. It was a Municipality Board that initiated a PB project. Public officials appointed a working group consisting of a project manager and some representatives from public administration responsible for technology and construction issues. Local officials also engaged the local media, radio, and TV, that is, those information channels that were available to disseminate information about PB among all citizens or target groups. Part of the advertising practices were posters hung in a city, shopping malls, pharmacies, community centers, youth clubs and schools, and so on. Such forms of advertisement always contained information about what issue the PB project was about and what criteria were applied to the submitted ideas.

Knowledge about how local authorities worked out such criteria for PB proved lacking, however, the Municipality of Avesta serves to illustrate how the first projects were organized. The PB pilot project was conducted in seven steps: (1) preparation that included technical IT support; (2) giving citizens a comprehensive opportunity to suggest what they want to be able to do in the areas proposed by the Municipality Board; (3) the Municipality Board received 127 proposals; (4) the 127 proposals were processed in the working group, with external consultancy support; (5) the proposals were divided into three "park" proposals: Feel Good Park; Sun & Bath Park; Sport Park, all 127 proposals then became part of one of three theme parks, except those which exceeded the budget, was impossible on safety grounds or were proposals where the municipality cannot operate (e.g., McDonald's and Burger King); (6) in some cases, the proposals were processed to be compared with the same type of proposal; (7) the proposers could find where their own proposal was finally placed (SKL, 2011). The appointed managers, in cooperation with their steering groups, were responsible for the process of conducting and implementation of the PB project. Such steering groups could have different names, for example, Citizens' Dialogue Steering Groups or Steering Committee and they had to create opportunities for the municipality inhabitants to influence their fellow citizens' life. Steering groups planned joint meetings between officials and citizens; they organized workshops or officials' meetings with residents in the open. During such meetings, officials and inhabitants discussed problems together, urgent matters deserving solutions in the municipality. A brief summary with conclusions were always presented on the municipality homepages or Facebook or Blog. Moreover, inhabitants were asked to make their own proposals how to solve a problem. In a relatively short time, the steering groups organized another meeting(s) open for officials and citizens to present the collected proposals from the citizens. The proposals were broadly discussed as well on purposely organized meetings, workshops, conferences, or digitally via the municipality homepage, Facebook, or Blog. Later on, the steering groups ensured that all proposals were published on the municipality homepages, Facebook, or Blog. The steering group controlled if the submitted proposals were in line with the criteria and budget of PB. Citizens or target groups were then encouraged to participate in voting.

Citizens could usually vote in the form of a survey on the Internet, but most municipalities did their best to make voting by e-mail, call, ordinary letters, or a mix of voting methods also possible. The methods of voting were selected conducive to the local context of area, population density or even creativity and engagement of the steering group, and so on. If people created numerous proposals, that is, over 100, as was the case in the Municipality of Haninge, then the number of proposals had to be limited. The steering group appointed a reference group consisting of 8 persons aged 16–78 who helped choose 12 proposals from 112. Those proposals were subsequently the subjects of citizens' voting (SKL, 2011).

The voting results were always published on the municipality's homepage, Facebook, or Blog. The winning proposal was approved by the Municipality Board and directed for implementation. Sometimes, the first three proposals were approved as was case in the Municipality of Uddevalla in 2010, which implemented: (1) the odd choice (200,000 SEK), (2) development of the school environment (250,000 SEK per school, two schools participated), and (3) safe walks organized by officials and politicians (175,000 SEK per district) (see Appendix; SKL, 2011, p. 35). Media contributed with the dissemination of this information among citizens.

4.6   Conclusions

The conducted PB projects give the impression that they are introduced under pressure from the EU, the Swedish central government, and the Swedish Association of Local Authorities and Regions. SALAR offered various incitements to motivate local authorities to experiment with PB projects, but only 12 out of 290 municipalities participated in such experiments. In fact, not one municipality continued with PB after the conducted pilot projects. In the municipalities of Avesta, Haninge, Uddevalla, Torsby, Nässjö, Upplands Väsby, and Uppsala, it was a one-two times event. PB probably causes negative emotions in local politicians, public officials, and professional groups which stunted its development. Independently, if we had to work with the first pilot projects or those in the second wave, PB in Sweden is still an immature institution. In order to understand what local politicians really think about PB, we need to conduct empirical studies. The SALAR report from 2011 emphasized that politicians and civil servants from the Haninge Municipality were skeptical about PB. They wondered, if "the citizen's budget really has any value" (SKL 2011, p. 34).

The research outcomes seem to be a paradox; the SALAR reports, the municipal websites, Facebook, and blogs from those municipalities conducting a PB project, confirmed that citizens were positive about such projects. They felt engaged and satisfied in helping to shape their own community. Local people appreciated the social integration by involving them in the decision-making process on the items to be prioritized in a municipal budget (e.g., in Avesta), even the participation of marginalized groups has increased but the Swedish local elected representatives, officials, and professional groups proved to be resistant to this knowledge.

The general conclusion is that the Swedish local authorities prefer a representative democracy with a citizen dialogue as sufficient support for decision-making on important local matters. Those in power at the local level do not want to share the real responsibility for the municipal budget, not even if it only concerns a fraction of it. It is surprising that the autonomy of the Swedish municipalities secured by the Local Government Act (1991: 900) and Constitution have contradictory effects on the central government's decisions and the signed international agreements by Sweden about the increase of citizen participation at the local level. The local politicians' passivity does not support the central government in fulfilling the given promises to the international organizations.

Having an organization promoting PB seems to be of the utmost importance because: (1) SALAR's systematic work to strengthen, and support addressed to the Swedish municipalities motivated them in their efforts to experiment with PB pilot projects, (2) the use of SALAR's financial incentives for municipalities has made some impact on even those municipalities that have no interest in trying to work with PB, and (3) SALAR's dissemination of information about the successful results of PB in other countries or municipalities has resulted in slow but growing interest in PB in Sweden.

Sweden has therefrom worked out its own PB model adapted to the Swedish context in which PB fulfilling an educational function for the young people is emphasized. It prepares them to take responsibility for their community in the future and to be more politically involved. Furthermore, PB may secure trust in local politics and can be perceived as a remedial measure to protect local politicians' legitimacy. Last but not least, PB support strengthens and not weakens representative democracy.

Such actors and perceptions have, however, to combat the firm tradition of Swedish representative democracy and the international reputation of Sweden in this regard in which it is already seen as one of the most democratic countries. Inherent in the national political system and cultural tradition is that it "should be as it currently is" and that local politicians are skeptics, reluctant, and have no interest in the direct involvement of citizens in decision-making. The culture is that citizen dialogue suffices for *deliberative democracy* and is sufficient in making good decisions.

In Sweden, local governance in which citizens are made (co-)responsible for decisions and the development of their community is not present. If the state does not develop its local participatory democracy, there will be stagnation, and when stagnation prevails, it will go in reverse and, as it goes backward, it will lose its leading position as a democratic country. Therefore, citizens' involvement in local decision-making seems to be of the utmost importance. Real governance includes cooperating citizens, politicians, and civil servants with the full understanding for the distribution of common municipal resources and the role that PB could play in local decision-making. It is a proven way to secure and build institutional trust and confidence in the merits of democracy.

Appendix: Municipalities That Introduced Participatory Budgeting in Sweden, 2000–2020 (An Alphabetic Order)

Name of municipality	Year	PB for project(s)	Populations by 2019	Number of participants and criteria for voting	Cost of project in SEK
Avesta	2010–2014	Avesta centrum—Lilla torget (Center of Avesta—Little square); Drömparken i Avesta (Dream Park of Avesta)	23,178	1033 Voters were available at all ages, but the emphasis was strong on those aged 10–19. The gender distribution was almost even (micro-local participation).	5,000,000 Local level funds. The maximum limit for investments was an investment budget of 10,000,000
Haninge	2007–2010	Eskilsparken (Eskil Park)	92,095	250 Young people were the part of local decision-making process, the goal was that young people should be seen as a natural part and not something that is done as secondary job.	400,000 160,000 Local level funds and other costs
	2014	Parkourbana (Park-Our-Path) in Jordbro		A reference group: 8 pers. 16–78 years old helped to choose 12 proposals of 112.	400,000
Göteborg	2017	District: Centrum—the safe Centrum	579,281	—	500,000
	2017–2018	District: Västra Hisingen—creating security through meetings between people who would otherwise not meet		1100 Everyone who is registered in Västra Hisingen, regardless of age.	500,000
	2019–2020	District: Östra Göteborg—meetings between people		—	400,000
	2019–2020	District Majorna-Linné (64,000 inhabitants)—Digidem Lab		—	450,000

Nässjö	2016–2020	The improvement of physical environment in the smaller planning areas: Flisby, Ormaryd, Solberga, Äng, Fredriksdal, Grimstorp, Stensjön, and Sandsjöbygde that: • Make the area or location more attractive • Is a new meeting place or improves a meeting place that already exists (can be indoors as well as outdoors—simply a place to meet!) • Make the place safer and more comfortable • Strengthens the identity and future beliefs of those living in the area • By physical action is meant improvement or new construction of a construction or site, for example, bathing bridge, playground equipment, benches, planting in park, sculptures, lighting, and so on.	31,538	Only for Flisby 360 It is unclear how many participated in voting in other planning areas. All the residents in the planning area, independently of age, can vote on the proposals they like best.	500,000
Stockholm	2016	District: Fagersjö (a forgotten neighborhood that has been like a colony in relation to Stockholm)	974,073	227	400,000
	2018	Vårgården as a meeting place	974,073	218 Everyone who lives and works in Vårberg, from middle school upward.	2,000,000
Torsby	2016–2017	Tingshusparken (Tingsbus Park)	11,616	189 All young people in grades 6, 7, 8, and 9 in Torsby Municipality.	500,000
	2018	Development of Oleby and Östmark	11,616	– All pupils attending grades 6–9 in Torsby Municipality.	500,000

(continued)

Name of municipality	Year	PB for project(s)	Populations by 2019	Number of participants and criteria for voting	Cost of project in SEK
Trelleborg	2019–2021	Planning of the Neighborhood Bath House (2 million SEK) Development of various stages of the Upper and Urban Parks Quarter (120 million SEK) Development of housing in Granlundaområdet/the Granlunda area (9 million SEK)	45,440	– All citizens, property owners, and traders in the southern rural area can vote—even children under the age of 18. Children who vote must be big enough to understand and want to be themselves and vote. It is up to each family to determine whether the child is mature or not.	131,000,000
Uddevalla	2010	Udda valet/The odd choice (200,000 SEK) Development of the school environment (250,000 SEK per school, two schools participated) Safe walks organized by officials and politicians (175,000 SEK per district)	56,703	10% of aged 13–19. 87% and 76% of the pupils from two schools that participated. The sum is not known.	625,000
Upplands Väsby	2013	The Square De Luxe (Torget project) Park-Our-Path (Parkourbana)	46,786	1337 When it comes to voting, everyone could vote, even those who did not live in the municipality. The voters could do this via the municipality's website, Facebook, or in the store in Väsby Centrum.	200,000

Uppsala	2018–2023	230,767	–	The aim is to increase local commitment and the opportunity for rural residents to influence their local environment and their rural development	The amount of budget each area receives depends on the number of inhabitants. Each area is allocated SEK 60 per inhabitant, but the maximum amount is SEK 900,000 for one area. The budget is adjusted for each year based on updated population figures. The figures for areas 2–5 are based on the population statistics for 2018.

Area 1

Countryside: Järlåsa, Vänge, South Hagunda

Residents and budget: 8803 inhabitants give SEK 528,180 (the figures for area 1 are based on the 2016 population statistics). Implemented in 2018

Area 2

Countryside: Björklinge, eastern and western Bälinge

Residents and budget: 14,406 inhabitants give SEK 864,360. Area 2 started in late 2019. See winning proposal in area 2

Area 3

Countryside: Gamla Uppsala, Storvreta, Vattholma, and Skyttorp. Residents and budget: 12,122 inhabitants give SEK 727,320. Submit proposals for projects and actions for area 3

Area 4

Neighborhoods: Vaksala area, Rasbobygden. Residents and budget: 8044 inhabitants give SEK 482,640

Area 5

Countryside: Denmark, Funbo, Almunge, and Knutby. Residents and budget: 8746 inhabitants give SEK 524,760

(continued)

(continued)

Name of municipality	Year	PB for project(s)	Populations by 2019	Number of participants and criteria for voting	Cost of project in SEK
Örebro	2006–2008	Traffic and environment	155,696	80 Pupils from three high school classes.	250,000
	2009–2010	Svartån	155 696	100 Pupils from four high school classes.	500,000
	2014–2015	Spontaneous sport site	155,696	150 Pupils from compulsory schools and young people from a Leisure Center.	800,000
Åre	June 17–July 1, 2019	District: Storlien/Västra bygden—Dredging and preparation of Handöl's Marina	11,727 Residents are spread over 7263 square kilometers.	104 people (311 votes) Those who either are written in or own a property in the western countryside (west of Staa Bridge to Storlien including Skalstugevägen). Each eligible person had 3 votes to cast on either one idea or several ideas.	300,000
	October 2019–December 2020	District: The Södra Årefjällen and Undersåker—Appoint a resource person/catalyst to drive the process of creating new meeting place/all-activity house.		Rural Development Committee decided which idea should be implemented.	300 000
	October 2019–December 2020	District: The West Storsjö Area—Improvement of the business climate by hiring a local rural developer for a needs inventory of the West Storsjö countryside.		60 people (180 votes), Residents either are written in or own a property in Västra Storsjö district (with settlements such as Mattmar, Kvissle, Arvesund, Hammarnäset, Hallen, Bydalen, and Månsåsen) voted for the ideas. Each eligible person had 3 votes to cast on either one idea or several ideas.	300,000

December 2019–January 2020	District: Åre and Duved—two projects wan: "Cultural Centre" and "Åre cultural arena" that share allocated money. Both projects will start 2020-12-15	—	300,000
Spring 2020	Improvement of the business climate and sustainable growth for cultural and creative industries in Åre municipality. PB for the whole municipality has been divided into 7 smaller part-projects. *PB for cultural and creative industries* The ideas that got the most votes and which thus can be shared on the citizen's budget are: idea 9 "Mountain festival with music, art, food and drink" (SEK 50,000), I. idea 11 "Craft & Art Festival" (SEK 50,000), idea 12 "Sauna festival" (SEK 47,500), idea 16 "Spectacle in Edsåsdalen" (SEK 27,500)	342 (Valid 316) A total of 342 people voted. Each person had three votes each, which could be put on one idea or distributed on several ideas. 26 of the votes were invalid because those who voted were not registered in the municipality of Åre or had voted too late. In total, there were 316 valid votes that distributed 948 votes on the ideas below. Implementation of the ideas should start no later than 2020-12-01	175,000
Spring 2020	Districts: Järpen and Mörsil—To look at Järpen and Mörsil with critical eyes.	—	300 000
March 2020	District: Kallbygden—"The Interest Association 2.0 of Kallbygden— Strengthening the Interest Association 2.0 with the remunerated persons"	35 people (105 votes) Those who either are written in or own a property in Kallbygden. Each person had 3 votes to vote on one idea or split on several ideas.	300,000

REFERENCES

Adolfsson, P., Solli, R., & Demediuk, P. (2012). *Medborgarbudget: erfarenheter från tre svenska pilotkommuner.*

Åre kommun. (2020). *En halv miljon idéer – Medborgarbudget.* https://are.se/kommunpolitik/medborgardialog

Carlsson, F. (2014). *Demokratisk innovation eller ett spel för gallerierna?: En demokratiteoretisk utvärdering av Participatory Budgeting i en svensk kommun. Masterprogrammet i statsvetenskap.* https://www.diva-portal.org/smash/record.jsf?pid=diva2%3A792418&dswid=1619560775837

Demediuk, P., Solli, R., & Adolfsson, P. (2012). People plan their park: Voice and choice through participatory budgeting. *International Journal of Interdisciplinary Social Sciences*, 6(5), 185–198. https://doi.org/10.18848/1833-1882/cgp/v06i05/52080

Dialogguiden. (2017a). *Medborgarbudget.* https://www.dialogguiden.se/article/show/1063

Dialogguiden. (2017b). *Medborgarbudget i Upplands-Väsby.* https://www.dialogguiden.se/article/show/458

Ekonomifakta. (2020). *Regional statistik.* https://www.ekonomifakta.se/Fakta/Regional-statistik/

Göteborgs Stad. (2020). *Medborgarbudget i Östra Göteborg.* https://goteborg.se/wps/portal/start/!ut/p/z1/04_Sj9CPykssy0xPLMnMz0vMAfIjo8ziAwy9Ai2cDB0N_N0t3Qw8Q7wD3Py8fdxNXU31w8EKTIzcDQy9TAy9_c1CTAwCnb0cLVxdPQwMXI30o4DSBjiAowFUPx4LCOgvyA0N-BQAizxAZ/dz/d5/L2dBISEvZ0FBIS9nQSEh/

Larsson, T., & Back, H. (2008). *Governing and Governance in Sweden.* Studentlitteratur AB. https://www.amazon.com/Governing-Governance-Sweden-Torbjorn-Larsson/dp/9144036825

Nässjö kommun. (2019). *En halvmiljon idéer – Medborgarbudget.* https://nassjo.se/nassjo-vaxer/utveckling-i-nassjo/en-halv-miljon-ideer.html

Nässjö kommun. (2020). *Om ½ miljon idéer.* https://nassjo.se/nassjo-vaxer/utveckling-i-nassjo/en-halv-miljon-ideer/om%2D%2D1-2-miljon-ideer.html

Petersson, O. (2010). *Den offentliga makten.* SNS Förlag. https://www.adlibris.com/se/bok/den-offentliga-makten-9789144125800

SCB. (2020). *Summary of Population Statistics 1960–2020.* https://www.scb.se/en/finding-statistics/statistics-by-subject-area/population/population-composition/population-statistics/pong/tables-and-graphs/yearly-statistics%2D%2Dthe-whole-country/summary-of-population-statistics/

Sintomer, Y., Herzberg, C., & Röcke, A. (2008). Participatory Budgeting in Europe: Potentials and Challenges. *International Journal of Urban and Regional Research*, 32(1), 164–178. https://doi.org/10.1111/j.1468-2427.2008.00777.x

SOU 2000:1. (2000). *Statens Offentliga Utredningar – En uthällig demokrati! : Politik för folkstyrelse på 2000-talet*. https://www.regeringen.se/49bb76/contentassets/69008696fa114a81837274bbf623793b/en-uthallig-demokrati%2D%2D-politik-for-folkstyrelse-pa-2000-talet

SOU 2001:48. (2001). *Statens Offentliga Utredningar – Att vara med på riktigt – demokratiutveckling i kommuner och landsting*. https://www.regeringen.se/rattsliga-dokument/statens-offentliga-utredningar/2001/01/sou-200148-/

SOU 2016:5. (2016). *Statens Offentliga Utredningar – Låt fler forma framtiden! Statens offentliga utredningar 2016:5*. https://www.riksdagen.se/sv/dokument-lagar/dokument/statens-offentliga-utredningar/lat-fler-forma-framtiden_H4B35

Stockholms stad. (2018). *Medborgarbudget – Stockholm växer*. https://vaxer.stockholm/omraden/fokus-skarholmen/dialog/medborgarbudget/

Sveriges Kommuner och Landsting (SKL). (2011). *Medborgarbudget – i Sverige, Europa och världen*. Sveriges Kommuner och Landsting.

Sveriges Kommuner och Landsting (SKL). (2019a). *Medborgarbudget – En världsomspännande modell för demokratisk inflytande*. https://webbutik.skr.se/bilder/artiklar/pdf/7585-779-4.pdf?issuusl=ignore

Sveriges Kommuner och Landsting (SKL). (2019b). *Medborgarbudget för demokratisk- och hållbar utveckling*. (Vol. 1, Issue 3). http://insyn.borlange.se/einsyn/registryentry/ShowDocument?registryEntryId=195694&documentId=210290

Sveriges Kommuner och Regioner (SKR). (2020a). *Fakta om kommuner och regioner*. https://skr.se/skr/tjanster/kommunerochregioner/faktakommunerochregioner.1022.html

Sveriges Kommuner och Regioner (SKR). (2020b). *Medborgarbudget*. https://skr.se/skr/demokratiledningstyrning/medborgardialogdelaktighet/medborgardialog/medborgarbudget.26603.html

Sveriges Riksdag. (1991). *Kommunallag (1991:900)*. https://www.riksdagen.se/sv/dokument-lagar/dokument/svensk-forfattningssamling/kommunallag-1991900_sfs-1991-900

Torsby Kommun. (2018). *Medborgarbudget*. https://torsby.se/%20kommunpolitik/dialogochsynpunkter/medborgarbudget.4.4dccf2b515940748fbf5c80b.html

Uddevalla kommun. (2017). *Medborgarbudget I Uddevalla*. https://dialogguiden.se/article/show/456

Uppsala kommun. (2020). *Medborgarbudget på landsbygden*. https://www.uppsala.se/kommun-och-politik/sa-arbetar-vi-med-olika-amnen/landsbygd/medborgarbudget-pa-landsbygden/

CHAPTER 5

Participatory Budgeting in Belarus

Yuri V. Krivorotko and Dmitriy V. Sokol

5.1   Introduction

The process of decentralisation to local communities and the participative approach is one of the most challenging ones of the last years in the post-soviet countries and Belarus as well. Thanks to decentralised cooperation, mutual cooperation between civil society and local governments occurs and it is possible to develop projects and activities that support local democracy and economic and social development. These projects also create strong links between communities and citizens, creating dialogue and trust.

One way of decentralised cooperation is in public participation in local budget processes or participatory budgeting (PB) where the citizens and active groups of population are setting up the local budget and include it in their projects. Thanks to PB, citizens have the right to discuss how part

Y. V. Krivorotko (✉)
BIP—University of Law and Social-Information Technologies,
Minsk, Republic of Belarus

D. V. Sokol
Belarus State University, Minsk, Republic of Belarus

© The Author(s), under exclusive license to Springer Nature
Switzerland AG 2022
M. S. De Vries et al. (eds.), *International Trends in Participatory Budgeting*, Governance and Public Management,
https://doi.org/10.1007/978-3-030-79930-4_5

89

of the public resources should be spent. PB is a tool for further civic education which leads to higher awareness of public issues and related policy-making.

Benefits from PB are found in 'pushing' the development of fiscal decentralisation in Belarus through the expansion of local democracy tools which is 'participatory budgeting'. It enhances openness, transparency and accountability in the local budgetary process.

The only model of participatory budgeting that could be discovered in Belarus is the so-called stakeholders PB. This model is open to third parties as partners of local communities and local authorities. The classical model of PB (as in Porto Alegre) or any form of it with direct or indirect participation in the local budgeting process is unacceptable in Belarus. So, the only working scheme of PB in Belarus is re-granting projects for local initiatives. Obviously, the key drivers for the development of such a model of PB are international organisations and programmes that propose granting money for local initiatives. PB in Belarus has a 15-year history. Over the past fifteen years and up to the present, many Belarusian public organisations (Educational institutions 'Office for European Expertise and Communication', New Eurasia Foundation and INGO 'ACT') have implemented projects within the territory of Belarus, in which civil initiatives aimed at solving problems at the local level were selected and funded on a competitive basis. Among them is the NGO "Lev Sapieha Foundation", which was liquidated by the decision of the Supreme Court of the Republic of Belarus under the pressure of Lukashenko's regime on August 20, 2021. It started in March 2006, when the ACSOBE (Acting Social and Cultural Rights in Belarus) project was first launched. This project was based on a re-granting model from the EU and its institutions and funds. In fact, it was PB's off-budgetary fund that was distributed on a competitive basis for the funding of a local community's development projects. Beginning in August 2010 and up to the present day, other re-granting models such as REACT (REinforcing Actions of Capacity Building for Civil Society), TANDEM (Cooperation for Development of Local Communities and Citizen Participation in Local Self-government) and SPREAD (Sustainable Partnership for REinforcement of Active Development in Belarus) began to be used (Organization of collaboration and project activity of NGO "Lev Sapieha Foundation" and ALDA, 2018). At the same time, the above participatory budgeting models were constantly updated. However, all these models combined one common idea, namely to find an optimal and effective scheme of interaction between citizens and local authorities for the benefit of the local community and its development.

5.2   PB Experience in Belarus

5.2.1   Characteristic of the PB Model in Belarus

The PB model in Belarus is based on an extra-budgetary fund, which is formed from funds of European organisations and institutions on conditions of co-financing from internal financial sources of local organisations. The extra-budgetary fund is used on a competitive basis to finance citizens' initiatives in local development and with their direct participation in budgeting.

PB in Belarus has been implemented since September 2006 in cooperation with the NGO "Lev Sapieha Foundation" and the European Association of Local Democracy—ALDA. Over the past fifteen years, experience in PB has increased through re-granting programmes: ACSOBE, REACT, SPREAD I–II and TANDEM I–V with support from the EU and other European institutions and foundations (Organization of collaboration and project activity of NGO "Lev Sapieha Foundation" and ALDA, 2018). The PB project results are shown in the following Table 5.1.

As the table shows, 110 out of 559 projects were selected on a competitive basis, and the total amount of EU funds raised to finance citizens' participation in local decision-making amounted to €558,000. The total amount under the mini-projects of funds amounted to €648,560. It means an extra 16.2% extra financing because of EU money. The final TANDEM-V project is the latest one under implementation and was due to be completed in December 2020. Programme applications for mini-projects by the PB model covered 128 municipalities at the basic level and the city of Minsk as the capital. Thus, for the entire period of the ongoing nine programmes, on average 4.3 project applications for each of the 129 municipalities were submitted.

These programmes were implemented through a PB method. Each programme identified winners who received EU funds for their mini-projects (along with co-financing). A separate extra-budgetary PB fund was used to accumulate these funds. This represented a kind of supplement to the main local budget. Therefore, additional public goods received through PB were not related to local budget expenditures. From these

Table 5.1   Project activity portfolio of PB by means of the re-granting models

Abbreviation of programmes	Full name of programme/project	Applications received	Applications selected	Funds (Euro)	Duration
ACSOBE	Acting Social and Cultural Rights in Belarus	22	12	36,000	September 2006–March 2008
REACT	Reinforcing Actions of Capacity Building for Civil Society	19	11	39,000	April 2009–August 2010
TANDEM-1	Cooperation for Citizen Participation and Community Development in Belarus	82	10	60,000	September 2011–April 2013
SPREAD-I	Sustainable Partnership for Reinforcement of Active Development in Belarus	15	10	9000	November 2012–June 2014
TANDEM-II	Cooperation for Citizen Participation and Community Development in Belarus	54	16	120,000	November 2013–April 2015
SPREAD-II	Sustainable Partnership for Reinforcement of Active Development in Belarus	44	19	54,000	July 2014–June 2017
TANDEM-III	Cooperation for Citizen Participation and Community Development in Belarus	24	9	70,000	April 2016–June 2017

(continued)

Table 5.1 (continued)

Abbreviation of programmes	Full name of programme/project	Applications received	Applications selected	Funds (Euro)	Duration
TANDEM-IV	Cooperation for Citizen Participation and Community Development in Belarus	160	11	85,000	October 2017– March 2019
TANDEM-V	Cooperation for Citizen Participation and Community Development in Belarus	132	12	85,000	May 2019 December 2020
Total	9 programmes (funded by EU)	559	110	558,000	September 2006– present

Source: Compiled by authors on the basis of NGO "Lev Sapieha Foundation" (Kobasa, 2020)

positions, local officials were very interested in the continuation of the PB method.

The analysis of a wide range of information collected during the implementation of all projects using PB showed that TANDEM programmes in Belarus have proved to be the most successful model for financing initiative projects of citizens. Visually, this picture can be seen by the example of TANDEM funding. To date, four TANDEM programmes have been successfully implemented, and a fifth is in the process of being completed. Applications for all TANDEM programmes exceed €1.5 million, as confirmed by the following Table 5.2.

The main content of TANDEM programmes is to find, support and implement initiatives of local citizens related to local development issues in cooperation with local authorities. TANDEM programmes have made many improvements to the PB model. First of all, mandatory co-financing was introduced, providing, along with grants allocated from EU funds, for the formation of PB by domestic financial sources of local enterprises and public organisations.

Table 5.2 Implementation of TANDEM's programme through PB

	Indicators	TANDEM-I	TANDEM-II	TANDEM-III	TANDEM-IV	TANDEM-V
Class A 'Partnership projects' (€10 000)	Total project cost, EUR	250,555	247,988	100,877	1,140,000	792,000
	Funding requested, EUR	182,127	194,030	83,262	946,000	609,000
	Co-funding	68,428	53,958	23,615	194,000	183,000
	Available funding, EUR	20,000	80,000	40,000	50,000	50,000
	Number of applications/ requests	33	21	8	97	63
	Number of projects	2	8	4	5	5
	On average per project	2074	2569	2952	2000	2900
Class B "Community initiatives" (€5 000)	Total project cost, EUR	317,332	225,438	96,560	390,000	423,000
	Funding requested, EUR	264,123	164,673	79,210	320,000	330,000
	Co-funding	53,209	60,765	17,310	70,000	93,000
	Available funding, EUR	40,000	40,000	30,000	35,000	35,000
	Number of applications/ requests	49	33	16	63	69
	Number of projects	8	8	6	6	7
	On average per project	1085	1841	1082	1111	1330
Total:	Applications/requests	82	54	24	160	132
	Projects	10	16	10	11	12
	Funding	567,887	473,426	203,437	1,530,000	1,215,000

Source: Authors, based on NGO "Lev Sapieha Foundation" data (Kobasa, 2020)

In TANDEM I–V programmes, 80.9% of the extra-budgetary fund of PB was formed by the EU funds and 19.1% by the local financial sources of organisations, which in turn are represented by financial sources of local enterprises and organisations and the civil society organisations in the share of 88.1% and 11.9%, correspondingly.

In addition, the project applications of TANDEM participants should provide for the creation (construction) of a socially significant object, such as a sports site, recreational zone, bike track, ecological trail and so on, or works on improvement of yards, parks, cultural and nature monuments and so on. At the same time, funds formed by the participation budget from EU funds, as a rule, should be used to purchase building materials and equipment and could not be used to pay for works and services that can be performed or provided for citizens free of charge.

From the very beginning, most applications were from Minsk. So, the first years of re-granting activities were mainly devoted to the education of local communities and to improve their ability to realise their initiatives through competition for grants.

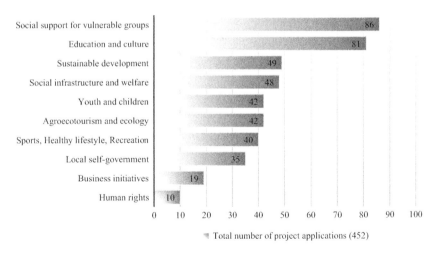

Fig. 5.1 Thematic directions of project applications in frame of competitions in TANDEM-I, TANDEM-II, TANDEM-III, TANDEM-IV and TANDEM-V. (Source: Compiled by authors on the basis of NGO "Lev Sapieha Foundation" data (Kobasa, 2020))

The TANDEM programmes aimed to involve NGOs and citizens' initiative groups in socially relevant activities at the local level in order to strengthen their influence in local development issues, adjust confidential interaction with local authorities and effectively share best practices among partner organisations. All the thematic applications of TANDEM projects are presented in Fig. 5.1.

The thematic areas of use of the extra-budgetary participation fund were solely based on the initiatives of local residents and active groups within the population. At the same time, PB was not in conflict with municipal policies, the interests of local officials or local budget projects. All presented PB projects complemented the lack of existing public goods of a particular municipality, and local authorities provided them with every support. The geography of TANDEM projects for participatory budgeting is very diverse and covers almost all regions of Belarus. The leaders in applications submitted and selected for funding are in the regions of Hrodna voblast: 89 applications, of which 12 were selected for funding, and Vitsyebsk voblast: 85, of which 10 applications were approved for funding.

Thus, the established model of Belarus PB, based on the formation of an extra-budgetary fund by sources from EU funds and their own funds of local organisations, has become a firm part of the practice of a participatory approach in decentralised governance at the local level and the solution of local development problems.

5.2.2   PB Organisation and Rules Implementation

PB contains three mandatory conditions to be met under the submitting applications for funding from an extra-budgetary fund:

- Mandatory participation of citizens in decision-making and problem-solving at the local level. Citizens should be active participants in the project implementation at the stages where necessary and possible.
- The project application must contain the creation or construction of a socially significant object (sports ground, recreational zone, bike path, ecological trail, etc.) or improvement of yards, parks, monuments of culture and nature and so on.
- EU funds submitted for financing shall be used to purchase building materials and equipment and may not be used to pay for works and services that may be performed or provided for citizens free of charge.

In the selection applicant process, along with civil society organisations, local authorities were represented. They acted as applicants or co-applicants for projects that civilian organisations implemented through the PB. Civil society organisations were represented by public associations, institutions, as well as by citizens' initiative groups, acting with applicants together with local authorities and representing them or civil society organisations as legal entities. Local authorities were most often represented by departments of ideological work, culture and youth affairs, sports and tourism, ecology, environmental, representative bodies of municipal (rural) Councils of Deputies, as well as of village chiefs (elders), collegial bodies of territorial public self-government.

Thus, the local authorities' interest was embodied in the fact that the projects implemented through PB were in line with the policies of the rayon municipalities in ensuring the current quality of life of its residents. From these positions, local officials were very interested in the continuation of PB on the basis of re-grant schemes funded by the EU and its institutions and funds together with their own financial sources' local organisations. The share of local officials exceeds a quarter of all applications (Table 5.3).

The number of applications from NGOs is 73% and from representatives of local authorities—27%. The lower activity of local authorities can be explained by the 'non-core' nature of this type of activity for them, their employment in their official duties, as well as their lacking knowledge and skills in the preparation of competitive applications, which affect the quality of their input.

All projects were implemented by means of PB in cooperation with the NGO "Lev Sapieha Foundation" and the European Association of Local

Table 5.3 Participation of local authorities and civil society organisations in Tandem-IV and Tandem-V programmes

Projects TANDEM-IV and TANDEM-V

Applicant's status	Number of applicants	Share of applicants
Civil society organisations	252	73.0%
Local (rayon) executive power	132	15.4%
Local (rural) executive power	68	11.6%
Total:	452	100%

Source: Compiled by authors on the basis of NGO "Lev Sapieha Foundation" data (Kobasa, 2020)

Democracy (ALDA). In tender commission for determining the winner among the submitted applications for funding from the additional budget, the experts—representatives from ALDA and the NGO "Lev Sapieha Foundation" and other Belarusian and foreign partner organisations—were included as well. After careful examination, all project applications were selected by the tender commission for nomination in several stages. In each case, the selection process was carried out on an impartial and competitive basis. The tender commission was guided by published requirements about the conditions for competition and the pre-agreed system of winner selection. The basis was a scoring scale used by three independent experts. Each expert evaluated all incoming projects using this assessment. The results of the experts for each submitted project were combined and subsequently averaged. As a result, the projects that received maximum points in competition were nominated. However, there were situations where two or more projects got the same score. In this case, a system of criteria came into force in the second stage. For example, in case of social projects tied with small business projects the former were preferred, and when projects in rural areas tied with submitted projects in cities, the former were judged to be preferable.

In the selection process of the best project applications, the tender committee members simultaneously sought to ensure the maximum possible diversity of project activities, taking into account the capabilities of applicants from the organisation, regional specificity or settlement, as well as the interests of those groups.

After the completion of project competitions to determine the winners and allocate funding, individual work with each of them was carried out. The aim of this work was to provide successful and effective implementation of the project in accordance with the conditions and requirements of national and international sponsors. The work consisted of providing advice and organisational support by ALDA specialists and the NGO "Lev Sapieha Foundation" through the signing of contracts between each winner and sponsor.

5.2.3   PB Performance Process

The process of organising and implementing of PB was jointly administered by the ALDA and NGO "Lev Sapieha Foundation" and comprised six main stages as follows:

- NGO "Lev Sapieha Foundation" receiving a grant from the EU (ALDA) for funding mini-projects in local development
- Announcement of the contest among municipalities and locals
- Consultations among the NGO experts
- Receiving project applications from active citizen groups
- Competition (tender) provided by NGO "Lev Sapieha Foundation" and the ALDA group
- Winner definition and providing funding

All TANDEM programmes were implemented within 16–20 months. They consisted of the following activities:

- Preparation of tender documentation, the announcement of the contest, dissemination of information about the contest, provision of advice to the participants of the contest and summing up the results of the contest.
- At this stage, oral and written consultations for bidders were provided. This made it possible to significantly reduce the number of applications that did not comply with the competition conditions and requirements. Advice was provided by experts from Lev Sapieha Foundation and ALDA's representatives. Common evaluation criteria, which guided all experts involved in project evaluation, were developed. As a result, the first or preparatory stage took approximately four months.
- Contract signing with the winners, the opening of accounts and credit of funds and registration of mini-projects.
- At this stage, by means of the bilateral consultations (coordinator of the project and applicant), the application of the winning organisation was clarified and detailed, and the legal agreement was subsequently formalised. The contract specified the terms of the mini-project implementation, a sum of funds (including co-financing fund), a detailed budget, a step-by-step of the plan of action for the of the mini-project implementation, the rights and obligations of the parties and other significant provisions. The contract parties were ALDA and the winning organisation. This phase was the most complex and time consuming, aimed at providing each party with a clear understanding of the goals and objectives of the mini-project and a realistic plan for achieving and addressing them. The main difficulty of the stage was that the TANDEM programme was funded through

foreign grant assistance, and according to the Belarusian legislation it required bureaucratic registration in the Department of Humanitarian Activities of the Presidential Office for Affairs. Taking this procedure into account, it took up to 5 months, and the total terms of this stage were delayed by up to 6–7 months.

- The third stage consisted of educational activities (opening conference, a seminar for the preparation of financial and analytical reports, a study of foreign experience and the development of domestic and international relations).
- The fourth stage consisted of civic initiatives. Within the framework of one completed cycle of the TANDEM programme, typically 10–12 civic initiatives are included. The tender documents indicate the topic of a mini-project, the requirements to applicant organisations, the terms of application acceptance, the maximum amount of financing and a framework version of the budget. According to the terms of reference, the projects are divided into Lot A and Lot B. Within Lot A (up to €10,000), joint partnership initiatives of civil society organisations and local authorities are financed. Lot B (up to €5000) funds comprise initiatives proposed by one applicant: either a civil society organisation or local authority. The implementation stage of the initiatives took approximately 8–10 months. Throughout the initiative process of the TANDEM programme, the coordinators monitored the process on-site and provided advice on emerging issues and agreed on informed proposals and changes to the working plan, as needed.
- The final stage consisted of financial and analytical reports' preparation and the holding of a final conference. In the process of initiative implementation, the organisations are obliged to provide interim and final (financial and analytical) reports. As a rule, interim reports are provided in the middle of the 4th stage, and final reports are provided 15 days before the completion of the mini-project. At the end of the TANDEM programme, a final conference was held, during which the participating organisations presented their results, discussed the overall results of PB and analysed achievements and shortcomings.

5.2.4   PB Results

Twenty in-depth interviews in Belarus with representatives of State administration bodies (8 persons), self-government bodies (5 persons) and civil society organisations (7 persons) from different localities (from rural municipalities to Minsk) were conducted. This was done in order to assess the prerequisites for the PB introduction to all municipalities in Belarus. The researchers were interested in the attitude of respondents towards PB and to assess the readiness for its possible implementation, the regulatory context for the PB implementation, the vision on key principles for PB functioning in Belarus, as well as the responsibilities and functions of interested parties.

According to respondents, PB brings the following advantages:

- Promoting constructive interaction between citizens and local authorities (local problems become more visible and understandable).

Representatives from local authorities told, for instance, that, *"It is quite possible that we do not always see where things need to be done. We see where it is broken, and people may no longer need it where it is broken"* and *"More and more requests are coming from citizens for the development of urban space, for the development of architecture and some regional initiatives. The state does not have time to respond to all these requests. And I think that public budgets will help solve these issues."*

- Stimulating civic activism.

Respondents told that, *"This is a good tool for a person to try offering their idea, to be useful, to be heard"* and *"This has a social effect, because people are becoming more active, they put forward some kind of initiative groups, they offer their projects"*.

- Support for bureaucratic decisions by local residents.

Involved participants told us, *"So, residents get the opportunity to participate in solving problems relating to themselves, as well as their immediate environment"* and *"The public's confidence in the authorities is increasing, i.e., it looks like the authorities consult with the population, how best to use budget funds, and after that they are already working together on the implementation of these projects"*.

- More efficient spending of budget funds to solve problems significant for citizens.

To give some more quotes: *"This is a way to solve many issues on the ground with the participation of people themselves. Nowadays, issues are usually resolved, but without the participation of citizens themselves. This sometimes leads to a lack of active participation by citizens themselves, creates dependency, and sometimes, perhaps, even not fully done what is necessary. If it involves people themselves, it is more targeted."* And *"The population knows the local needs. When they are directly involved in the* budget process, *i.e., they submit some initiatives, and then monitoring the implementation of this process, the efficiency of using budget funds increases."*

The representatives of local government and self-government bodies also expressed the hope that PB introduction will guarantee to secure some additional funding for solving urgent problems of local communities. As they said: *"This money should go to the development of the region, localities, where we do not have enough funds. Therefore, we can include this budget and actively turn it to the needs of the population, which is located on the periphery of the district—this is important."* And *"We are looking for ways to satisfy people, including finding additional funding. Since we, on the one hand, seem to be considered rich region, but, on the other hand, in fact, they give us less subsidies."*

The respondents from civil society organisations noted such possible positive effects of PB introduction as rapprochement with local authorities to strengthen cooperation, support and assistance from them in the implementation of projects, as well as promotion of this form of citizen participation among local communities.

> *"The participation budget, in principle, implies a public process, which also makes it possible for as many people and all interested parties to know about your initiative as possible, for example, through the media, etc."*

When describing local problems that could be solved with the help of PB, the respondents were also in tune and named infrastructure problems and landscaping. This is understandable. First, these problems affect all residents and are most noticeable. Secondly, given the subsidised nature of local budgets, the social sphere relegates solution of infrastructure issues due to lack of funds to the background.

> *"Just an example: we have several such streets that play a very important role for neighbourhoods, but they still can't be completed. Relatively speaking, there you need to lay 200 metres of asphalt to the main street, and they have not been laid for years. Finally, entire neighbourhoods are cut off from others. This does not require large finances; it could be spent on it and solve transport problems."*

All respondents agreed with the idea of introducing the PB institution in Belarus. Representatives of local government bodies also expressed the hope to introduce PB which would guarantee the consolidation of additional funding to resolve pressing problems of the local community.

The results of the local development initiative mini-projects using PB were subject to many roundtable talks in which also representatives and executive authorities of the regions participated. For example, during the roundtable talks in Vitebsk, representatives of executive committees, councils of deputies and members of the NGO "Lev Sapieha Foundation" discussed experiences to promote and implement local civil initiatives through PB and firmly decided to continue it everywhere (Chashniki Regional Executive Committee, 2019).

5.3   FINDINGS IN INNOVATIONS AND LESSONS LEARNED

A visible innovation caused by this kind of PB was the emergence of a new in-depth form of communication between residents and official local authorities. Such communication created a participatory approach to local governance and showed the possibility of cooperation between residents and local authorities at the decentralised level.

The innovative features of PB were primarily evident in the new approach to achieving fiscal decentralisation in local governance. It is known that since the 1990s the newly democratic states have had problems to start up a power transfer to the local governments and that such transfers did not always pass flexibly. In the post-soviet countries, some steps to diminish the centralised decision-making in favour of decision-making procedures at the local level were taken. However, they did not bring about the desired results in fiscal decentralisation because of a rigid vertical and central power and lack of decentralised cooperation between citizen groups and local government. The examples in PB show that the approach to implement fiscal decentralisation through PB and decentralised cooperation between residents and local authorities could push fiscal decentralisation processes in Belarus from below.

PB has proved to be an anti-corruption tool. The use of PB funds was carried out by the residents themselves and under their control on a targeted basis, which prevented the emergence of corruption cases.

Finally, innovations are seen in the skills and knowledge acquired by the citizens in the field of public finance, budgeting and financial control.

Research studies carried out by experts of the NGO "Lev Sapieha Foundation" on PB during the TANDEM project implementation have produced a number of important lessons. Below, they are summarised

Table 5.4   SWOT analysis of participatory budgeting in Belarus

Strong (+):	Weakness (-):
• Neutralisation of corruption • Providing the most exact definition of inhabitants' needs for public services • Development and deepening of the decentralised cooperation • Use of public resources (extra-budgetary funds) by a targeted principle • Development of skills and knowledge of population in the field of public finance, budgeting and financial control	• Weakness of civil society • Lack of active groups of the population • Lack of the legislative base and framework for public budgeting • The weakness of financial sources base of PB for large local projects implementation
Opportunities (↑):	**Threats (↓):**
• The way to reach fiscal decentralisation • Achievement of a profound partnership between locals and local authorities • An instrument of civil society development	• Economic crisis and recession in the country • Possibilities of manipulations with projects of active groups from the side of local authority officers • Lack of political will of the authorities in PB development

Source: Compiled by the authors

through a SWOT analysis, presenting the strong and weak sides, opportunities and threats (see Table 5.4).

PB weaknesses and threats are of greatest concern in the SWOT analysis. The first point concerns the weakness of civil society, that is the inability in breaking old constructions in public administration and putting forward innovations in fiscal decentralisation and democratisation into governance as a whole. The lack of active groups (actors) is also considered one of the weak links in the civil society chain. This weakness is more pronounced in rural areas than in urban areas. At the same time, the citizen groups' activity can be subject to restrictions and even suppression by the authorities that could bring the effects of hopelessness and indifference in PB development.

The lack of PB legislative regulation is one of the more complicated issues in furthering the development of such processes in the country. The absence of the PB concept in the Budget Code and in the Local Self-government's Law slows down the spread of PB processes in Belarus. It is possible that in this situation PB process could be considered by officials as illegal if it is not in their interest.

In view of the absence of the PB legislative base, there could appear quasi-PB and manipulated cases created by the local officials. For example, the creation of online platforms by local authorities for collecting citizens' projects on the improvement of public goods and servicing. It looks very often like the local authority PB model. However, in this case, citizens are not really participating due to the separating from the budgeting and financial control processes.

The weakness of many municipalities in their own revenue base may be the real obstacle to PB. Almost quarter of the poor municipalities receive over 65% of the central budget transfers (see Fig. 5.2). It reduces the space for PB realisation due to difficulties in allocating even 1–2% of the local budget independently.

The economic crisis is most serious obstacle among the strategic threats to PB development in Belarus. Difficulties with financial sources in local financial management have appeared. Nowadays, it is becoming clear that

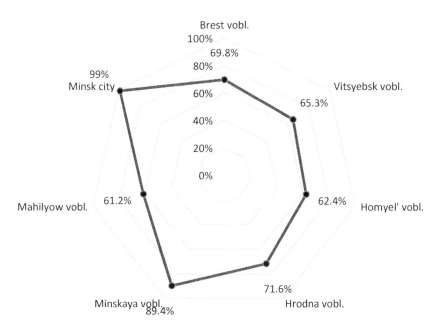

Fig. 5.2 Level of own revenues in regional local budgets in 2019. (Source: Authors, based on the data of Ministry of Finance of the Republic of Belarus)

the global COVID-19 pandemic has negatively affected economic growth and deteriorated revenue structure of local budgets.

Finally, the lack of political will is a drag factor in PB development. At this time, the officials are still not ready to say 'Yes', to open the way for PB in budgetary decision-making processes. The PB development process without the appropriate public administration support is sometimes perceived to be a threat and results in discrediting the PB idea among local residents and to induce an atmosphere of hopelessness and indifference.

Nevertheless, the SWOT analysis confirms the opportunities and strong sides of PB in the local budgetary process in Belarus.

5.4   Thoughts for the Future

The experiences with PB within the re-granting programmes/projects in Belarus testify to the opportunities to transfer part of the allocation within budgets to citizen initiatives on the base of the participation principle. There are, however, some conditions to be fulfilled.

1. The presence of active citizen groups capable of taking the lead in the project proposals and implementation and to have this included in the local budget.

The importance thereof is that without such a presence it is impossible to have meaningful participatory budgeting in local budgets or to transfer the responsibility for budget control and monitoring the budget spending. An increase in initiative groups and active citizens promotes the potential increase in the share of the budget which can be allocated by citizens through participatory budgeting. Experiences in PB in other countries show that, even if the initial sum of PB is small, initiators can attract interest from both citizens and business (Klimovský & Grynchuk, 2017).

However, it is necessary to also note certain obstacles in the development of civil activity in budgeting. First of all, civil society is not so well developed and in general citizens are hesitant and sometimes even unwilling to participate in public affairs. Experiences within the Central and Eastern Europe countries demonstrate that this model implies a high degree of political activity of the population and a readiness by politicians to cede considerable powers in the adoption of public decisions. Notwithstanding this impediment, even with a weak civil society, involvement of citizens in consultations regarding local finances and policy implementation of pilot participatory projects on drawing up the local budget could be a feasible model (Klimovský & Grynchuk, 2017).

It is also necessary to bear in mind that citizens' participation in drawing up the local budget can be substituted by quasi-forms of PB. For example, the citizens' autonomy in drawing up the local budget can be substituted by special public platforms created by the official authorities for collecting proposals and requests of citizens. In that case the officials have to promise to include these proposals and requests in expenditure assignments of the local budget.

2. Capacities of local budgets to execute a mission of PB.

This factor may be regarded in a great extent by the competence of the Ministry of Finance which acts as the regulator and controller of local budgets. Local budgeting through the participatory budgeting principle is not mentioned in the Budgetary Code of the Republic of Belarus yet. Therefore, to consider recommendations about the size and shares of the budget of participation in the general local budget has to be approved by this regulator.

This applies especially to the funding municipalities receive from the national level. To choose for PB projects in local budgeting, this is most likely to be approved; if it concerns money the municipality collected itself and independently, that is in those municipalities with a maximum of self-reliance in collecting its own revenues. In other words, PB is most likely in those local budgets which have a maximum share of own revenues in the total local budget revenues and a minimum amount of central government transfers. The explanation is that the fact that an increase of a share of transfers from the central budget to a locality potentially inhibits possibilities proposals to be financed, chosen by citizens and initiative groups. It must be kept in mind that the allocation of transfers for equalisation of fiscal capacity most often has a strict special purpose character and therefore cannot be allocated differently out of initiatives of citizens. Thus, with increasing dependence on central budget transfers, the possibilities of PB diminish.

The extent to which localities in Belarus depend on the transfer of revenues from central government is seen in Fig. 5.2.

The range of autonomy in generating own revenues in regional local budgets is between 61.2% and 99.0%. On average, it is 71.6% in Belarus. Research has also shown that within regions there are self-sufficient rayon budgets with a high share of own revenues (own taxes and non-tax payments) and which can create more opportunities for participation in an experiment of PB. Many municipalities have a high range of own revenues in total local budgets. There are 15 municipalities with more than 83% of their own revenues in their budgets, plus 11 with their own revenues that exceed 67%. This could be considered as quite sufficient for allowing a larger share of the budget to become subject to participatory budgeting. However, even when municipalities are self-reliant regarding their local budgets to a high degree and when active citizen groups are present, the future of participatory budgeting projects primarily depends on the political will of the central authorities and the desire of local government authorities to include this in the local budgetary process. Notwithstanding the suggestion that given the autonomy of many a municipality to generate is own revenues, PB could be more widespread, the data provided do not allow for such concrete recommendations. This is because of the following reason:

3. Political will of the central power and desire of local authorities to introduce PB in practice is a necessity.

Political will, courage, absolute understanding of innovation needs and belief in its success are necessary for the implementation of PB. Examples of many countries in Central and Eastern Europe show how the lack of the political will accompanied with the general interest of citizens results in disappointment and the premature ending of participatory budgeting projects. Totally different examples have shown how the existence of political will, even a small initial budget sum for PB, could attract and connect interested citizens, business and authorities. It could convince local authorities to deal with this issue more seriously and to increase the share in the local budget process for PB.

It is also necessary to get political support for this innovation from the central and local authorities of the country and beyond its borders: EU Commission, Council of Europe, international organisations and funds, neighbouring countries and so on. The advancement of the process of PB also implies the professional development of active citizen groups in the sphere of the public and local financial management.

In implementation of PB in Belarus, the threats can be the following:

- Resistance of officials ('incompleteness' of the measures put in Laws, Decrees of the President, Resolutions of Council of Ministers and bureaucratic procedures).
- Discrediting of the PB's idea among citizens through the distortion of its purposes and tasks.
- Mistakes and miscalculations at a stage of adoption of PB projects.
- Conflicts of interests both horizontally (between public bodies) and vertically (between the public administration and local governments) in the decentralised cooperation process and the financing of the participatory budgeting.
- Fear of change and, as a result, lack of support for PB by the civil society.
- Staff deficiency for PB innovations.

5.5   Conclusions

Citizens' participation in budgeting is extremely important for providing democratic, transparent and responsible decision-making in public finances. Public policy in view of a good governance philosophy has to be focused on granting opportunities for and managing abilities of citizens to influence budgeting processes. Participatory budgeting is a very good example of it. The wide development of participatory budgeting in Belarus could be the first step in strengthening of the decentralised cooperation between local authorities and citizens and in developing fiscal decentralisation. However, it will require political will and consent of the central government. At the same time, central government's behaviour regarding the introduction of participatory budgeting may be obstructive and conservative.

Participatory budgeting is a good tool for civil society development and direct local democracy in Belarus. The motivation of citizens in participatory budgeting discovered in opportunities to improve the quality of their lives through implementation their projects and financial management of it.

The interests of local authorities are the additional possibilities in funding local development and the ability to correspond the needs of local communities for public services in better way. However, the further development of participatory budgeting requires a shift to more complex forms of public budgeting, based on direct participating of citizens in the local budgeting and allocation of a certain share of local budget for their projects.

Participatory budgeting as innovation in the local financial management turns up also in Belarus as in other Central and Eastern European countries. It started from the simplest forms of participatory budgeting and continues to delegate it to more difficult models for the creation of local budgets. The PB approach develops mutual interest and interaction of citizens representing civil society and local authorities. Through this alliance, the projects performed by citizens' initiatives have succeeded with means of allocated grandees of the EU and their direct budgeting by citizens.

In Belarus, PB projects developed by means of re-granting funding from the EU funds. It allowed accumulating experience and skills in project budgeting and in public finance among active groups of citizens. This stakeholders PB experience could serve as spin-off for more advanced public participation in local budgeting. At the same time, this method of PB created an 'embryo' of the decentralised cooperation of local authorities and local citizens.

The key drivers of public budgeting development and implementation of participatory budgeting in Belarus are as follows: (a) local initiatives—active citizen groups that are capable to undertake the project implementation and budgeting; (b) abilities of local budgets in Belarus to realise the PB mission, and (c) political will and desire of the central and local authorities to introduce PB into the local budgetary process.

The last key factor is the most complicated for Belarus as it is accompanied by a perception of financial decentralisation needs in view of public finance. This points to a number of hidden threats, such as resistance of officials; discrediting participatory budgeting's idea among citizens through the distortion of its purposes and tasks, mistakes and miscalculations in adoption of participatory budgeting projects, conflicts of interests both inside (between public bodies) and outside (between public administration, local governments and local communities) during the decentralised cooperation and participatory budgeting, fear of changes and resulting lack of participatory budgeting support by civil society and staff deficiency for innovations of participatory budgeting.

Assessment of local budgets' capacities in implementing participatory budgeting mission has shown that in Belarus there are 15 municipalities with more than 83% own revenues in their budgets, plus 11 with own revenues that exceed 67%. This is sufficient for starting pilot projects of participatory budgeting in frame of local budgets.

Civil society and local authorities should initiate and promote both existing and new forms and methods of participatory budgeting in Belarus. It is crucial to introduce participatory budgeting into the 'institutional shell', to create a legislative framework for it and put it into the Budget Code. The international stakeholders will play a big role in development of those processes. The Belarusian governmental bodies, local communities and municipalities, NGOs and active citizen groups are in need of full technical assistance and support from EU, international financial donors and international reputable NGOs.

REFERENCES

Chashniki Regional Executive Committee. (2019). *Five projects for the realization of local civil initiations have received grants.* http://chashniki.vitebsk-region. gov.by/ru/region-news-ru/view/pjat-proektov-po-realizatsii-mestnyx-grazhdanskix-initsiativ-iz-vitebskoj-oblasti-poluchili-granty-16809/

Klimovský, D., & Grynchuk, N. (2017). *Participatory budgeting.* NISPAcee. https://doi.org/10.4018/ijpada.2015040103

Kobasa, M. (2020). *Citizen Participation in the Process of Decision Making on Local Level in Belarus: Current State, Experience and Perspectives.* http://sapieha. org/2020/06/citizen-participation-in-the-process-of-decision-making-on-local-level-in-belarus-current-state-experience-and-perspectives/

Organization of collaboration and project activity of NGO "Lev Sapieha Foundation" and ALDA. (2018). Bulletin of self-government № 1 (28), 2–9. Retrieved April 14, 2019, from http://sapieha.org/wp-content/uploads/201 8/10/%D0%91%D1%8E%D0%BB%D0%BB%D0%B5%D1%82%D0%B5%D0 %BD%D1%8C-%E2%84%9628%D0%B0%D0%BF%D1%80%D0%B5%D0%BB %D1%8C-2018.pdf. (In Russian)

CHAPTER 6

Participatory Budgeting in Croatia: A Mixed Bag of Good, Bad, and Indifferent

Jasmina Džinić

6.1 Introduction

Participatory budgeting (PB) appeared in Croatia several years ago when very few proactive towns in cooperation with NGOs decided to experiment with this new form of democracy. Therefore, the idea to include citizens in the preparation of local public budgets has come from "the bottom", having in mind both civil society and local self-government. In Croatia, the central government had no direct influence on local self-government in this respect. However, legal regulation on the obligation of all public bodies to provide citizens with public information and to carry out public consultations fostered the opening of local government to citizens. Some mayors might have recognised PB as an innovative approach to improve communication and trust with citizens. Although very slowly and still insufficiently, Croatian towns and municipalities have been opening to the public.

J. Džinić (✉)
Faculty of Law, University of Zagreb, Zagreb, Croatia
e-mail: jdzinic@pravo.hr

© The Author(s), under exclusive license to Springer Nature
Switzerland AG 2022
M. S. De Vries et al. (eds.), *International Trends in Participatory Budgeting*, Governance and Public Management,
https://doi.org/10.1007/978-3-030-79930-4_6

However, it should be noted that not any kind of citizens' participation could be marked as PB. When criteria for PB indicated by Sintomer et al. (2008, p. 168) are taken into consideration, it can be noted that most towns in Croatia with some form of direct involvement of citizens in the preparation of the local budget have not implemented "real" PB. The emphasis is on transparency, but the door of opportunity to spread and discuss ideas, and even to make decisions on local finances is still only ajar for citizens. Accordingly, existing practices of involving citizens in the processes related to local public finances in Croatia could be grouped as follows (Džinić, 2021):

1. "Real" Participatory Budgeting concerns processes fulfilling (almost) all above-mentioned criteria;
2. Participatory Budgeting Trials are PB processes that have lasted for a year or two (as long as the project introducing PB in selected towns), but have not continued;
3. Learning through Play and Digitisation relates to online games aimed to introduce citizens to budgetary processes and provide them with the opportunity to manage local finances by proposing the projects to be financed, and austerity measures to be taken;
4. Traditional Approaches with the Touch of Modernisation usually using classical, legally prescribed forms of citizens' engagement in deciding on local public affairs;
5. Informal Participation that lacks formally defined elements and processes of PB and other forms of citizens' participation, and relates to collecting citizens' opinions and proposals "on-site", in direct communication with individuals or groups of citizens.

In the following part of the chapter, the emphasis is on towns having "Real" PB, but other participatory processes having some elements of PB will be also described and analysed. Factors that could determine (non) existing PB practices in Croatia will be discussed. The study is based on desk research and information obtained through the survey on experiences in PB and similar forms of participation in Croatian towns.

6.2   Introduction of Participatory Budgeting

In Croatia, the first formal projects of PB commenced in 2014, although some practices with characteristics of PB have been existing since the beginning of 2000. Despite the crucial role of the town council in the acceptance of the final budget (including the amounts decided in the PB process), the councils in general have not had a significant role in the introduction of PB projects. There was no council hearing on that subject, and in Pazin the aldermen have been just informed of the intention to start with the PB project.

In 2014, the town of Pazin in cooperation with several NGOs launched a pilot PB project called "Pazi(n), proračun!" (Watch out the budget!). The aim of the project was to involve the citizens in the planning of the budget for the year 2015 (Džinić et al., 2016), and more generally, to strengthen the capacity of various stakeholders (especially citizens) in decision-making in order to improve quality of public policies and good local governance. As of its introduction, PB has been implementing each year, and so far, seven cycles have been passed.

The town of Pula introduced e-consultations on local finances and public hearings at the sub-municipal level in 2012, and in the end of 2014, together with towns Mali Lošinj and Karlovac, was included in the two-year project "Participatory budgeting: citizens monitor local budget". The project was initiated and coordinated by several NGOs, and financed by the EU. The main aim of the project was to provide the citizens with the opportunity to informatively and actively participate in the preparation of local budgets and to control its implementation. However, after the finalisation of the project, Karlovac and Mali Lošinj have not continued with PB in the form provided by the project.

The PB project in the town of Trogir started in 2018 with the campaign "I tebe se pita!" ("You are asked, too!"). It is an annual project related to the local budget, and so far, three cycles have been held. The incentives to introduce PB were the need for better communication between local government and citizens, and the willingness to help citizens get more active. The campaign was aimed to involve citizens in making decisions on public money spending, to encourage them on setting priorities of small utility actions in neighbourhoods, and to establish trust relationships. The proposal of the project on PB was prepared by the mayor and top civil servants and included in the budget proposal for 2018.

Rijeka has developed several models of PB and other forms of citizens' participation in budgetary processes. They had existed earlier than projects on PB started in other towns, but were not labelled as PB. The Local Partnership programme was launched in 2004 with the following aims: (1) to stimulate citizens, their associations, councils of sub-municipal entities to participate in the accomplishment of local community needs, and to resolve problems existing in the community; (2) to speed up the realisation of utility projects for the groups of citizens, citizens' associations, and sub-municipal entities willing to contribute and actively participate in the realisation of projects; (3) to develop partnership and common responsibility of the City and citizens in the realisation of projects, and to provide citizens with direct impact on the local budget allocation; (4) to achieve wider social and economic effects by pooling sources from public and private sectors, and the local community contribution; (5) to stimulate value of volunteering in the community and contributing with the aim to accomplish the common good. Small utility actions are the activities aimed to increase the quality of life by improving utility standards, and standardisation of sub-municipal entities' equipment. In the current form, this PB model was also introduced in 2004. As of 2011, City of Rijeka offers an online Educational budgetary game—Proračun(ajme) which provides citizens with the opportunity to "manage" local budget by changing planned projects and financial amounts. Besides educational purpose, the intention is to improve transparency and communication of local self-government with citizens. Also, citizens of Rijeka are invited to submit their proposals on the local budget electronically or via surface mail, using the template provided.

Educational games have also been introduced in Sisak, Labin, and Bjelovar. Application My town budget was introduced by Sisak in 2016 and by Labin in 2019. This way citizens have insight into the budget proposal and can submit their own suggestions and comments. The most numerous proposals are then added to the budget proposal by the mayor. Unlike Sisak and Labin, Bjelovar offers a game based on fictive town and fictive amounts of the town budget. The aim is to introduce citizens to the budget structure, and the enactment of the local budget, but the budgetary process is simplified and lacks basic elements of any kind of citizens' participation.

Dubrovnik commenced with the PB process in 2018 and within the project divided into two phases: preparation (2018 and 2019) and implementation (2020). The general aim of the project is the democratisation of public resources management, development of active citizenship, and contribution to the quality of life. Specific goals are the development of cooperation between town administration and sub-municipal entities, development of PB model, and education on the possibilities of contributing to local community development.

There are several other towns providing possibilities for the citizens to participate in the preparation of the local budget in the form of public hearings, e-consultations, calls for the submission of proposals, and so on. However, those possibilities often lack wider discussion, feedback, public information on submitted proposals, the direct participation of citizens, and other basic elements of PB.

6.3   CHARACTERISTICS OF PARTICIPATORY BUDGETING

Characteristics of particular elements of PB or "areas of difference" (Cabannes, 2004, p. 28) form the basis for distinction among various models of PB. This part of the Chapter is devoted to the description and analysis of PB elements grouped as follows: (1) administration and subject of PB and (2) participation in PB.

6.3.1   Administration and Subject of Participatory Budgeting

The PB process is administered by the city/town administration, often with the support of sub-municipal entities in the form of technical assistance and logistics. Employees of local organisations directly providing public services (local transportation, utility services, etc.) are also included in the process. During the implementation of the PB projects initiated by NGOs, the latter were also providing assistance to town administration. Representatives of civil society and media form the committee for evaluation of proposals submitted within the Rijeka local partnership programme. In Pazin, public hearings are chaired by a person who is not a town civil servant. In Dubrovnik, the idea of future PB is to include citizens in the preparation of projects with the assistance of specially trained coordinators. The whole PB project is coordinated by the Dubrovnik Development Agency and the city administration.

Special procedure for PB is not always prescribed (e.g., in Pula and Pazin). However, in Trogir, the team from the town administration responsible for PB has passed the action plan of implementation of the PB.

The complexity of administration depends on the model of PB. When the PB is about small utility actions, evaluation of submitted proposals is more complex and elaborated than in the cases of Rijeka local partnership programme, general consultations lacking concrete financial amounts or educational games. For instance, the analysis of proposals of small utility actions in Rijeka last more than six months and comprises more than 15 activities before the councils of sub-municipal entities form the list of priorities. Based on the lists of priorities, the local administration prepares the Allocation plan for utility priorities and submits it to the City council for final approval. However, in Trogir, the evaluation of proposals conducted by the team of civil servants appointed by the mayor lasts four weeks before the final list of proposals is presented for public discussion. After the collection of proposals, the latter are grouped according to sub-municipal entities, and the costs of each proposal are estimated. The analysis of more than a hundred proposals on small utility actions submitted in Pazin in 2014 lasted for a month (Džinić et al., 2016). The difference between Rijeka on the one hand, and Trogir and Pazin, on the other, might emerge from the size of those local units, the amount of money allocated for small utility projects, and consequently on the complexity of projects.

Further issues in the PB processes are related to the level of participation provided for PB as well as policy areas and percentage of total budget citizens are invited to discuss.

In several towns, PB and other forms of citizens' participation in deciding on local finances are carried out on the level of sub-municipal entities as a "form of direct citizens' participation in deciding on local affairs of direct and everyday impact on citizens' life and functioning" (Art. 57 of the Act on LRSG). However, it should be emphasised that some towns organise public hearings for discussion and deciding on projects within rather well-defined PB process (Pazin, Trogir, as it is planned in Dubrovnik), while in others decisions are made by elected bodies of sub-municipal entity (councils) (Rijeka in relation to small utility actions). It is not clear if the latter hold public hearings for the citizens since no detailed information is provided in that respect. Few towns organise online or offline consultations and/or discussions on the level of the whole town (e.g., Sisak, Labin) or have a combination of the two (Pazin, Rijeka).

When PB is organised on the sub-municipal level, citizens are usually invited to propose, discuss, and/or decide on small utility actions (e.g., repairs of local roads and construction of a playground). Even in the cases when they can propose projects from other sectors such as in the town of Trogir, most proposals relate to utility actions. In Pazin, decision-making authority is limited to small utility actions, but they can also comment or propose activities in other local affairs.

When participation is organised on the town level, citizens can propose and discuss projects in any area of town's responsibility. In 2014, Pazin organised public hearings within the sectors of social security and health, economics and tourism, culture and tourism, education and sport, and one additional hearing on special citizens' proposals (Džinić et al., 2016). Also, in 2016, citizens of Pazin were invited to vote for priority among four proposed large projects. The project with the biggest number of ballots was included in the budget.

Amounts allocated for PB (excluding educational games) extend between 0.02% of the total budget (approx. € 26,700.00) for the Rijeka local partnership programme to 1.19% of the total budget (approx. € 180,000.00) in Trogir, and 1.39% of the total budget (approx. € 106,000.00) in Pazin. However, the percentage of Rijeka budget intended for small utility actions in 2020 amounts to 0.9% (approx. € 1,583,066.00). On average, each sub-municipality entity in Rijeka obtains approx. € 46,560.00, but concrete amounts depend on population, surface area, utility rate, and condition of existing infrastructure. Population and existing infrastructure are also criteria for allocation of amounts of the total budget for PB to sub-municipal entities in Pazin. In order to make possible planning larger and more expensive projects, just a half of sub-municipal entities in Pazin participate in PB every year (since 2018). In Dubrovnik, only 0.009% (approx. € 9000.00) of the local budget is allocated for PB so far, but this is due to the partial implementation of the PB project. In 2019 six schools and in 2020 seven schools participated, and the students of each had the opportunity to decide on projects worth approx. € 1300.00. The analysis of the percentages of total local budgets and the amounts of money intended for PB shows that the amount of budget for PB is smaller when citizens are allowed to decide on local projects and activities. On the other hand, when they are just invited to submit proposals or play educational games, they "can dispose of" a larger percentage of the budget or the amount of money is not defined. Furthermore, despite smaller percentages of the total budget intended for PB, in larger cities (Rijeka) the total amount of money for that purpose is in some cases higher than in other towns due to the high amount of total budget.

Nevertheless, the amount of money intended for PB in Pazin has been increasing—since the beginning of the project, it has increased 2.7 times. In very few examples, participants are invited to give their contribution to selected projects. In Mali Lošinj, citizens have been invited to decide on the location for the street workout they proposed in the PB process and to participate in the cleaning of selected locations (Džinić, 2018). In the Rijeka local partnership programme, one of the requirements for participation is that 10% of the project value comes from the contribution of the local community (in the form of volunteering, donations, etc.). In those cases, PB is not confined to discussion and decision-making, but also includes other forms of citizen co-production.

6.3.2   Participation in Participatory Budgeting

In most cases, participants are citizens as such. In addition, proposals for small utility actions in Rijeka can be submitted by the councils of sub-municipal entities, representatives of co-owners of residential-business buildings, and citizens' associations. Councils of sub-municipal entities, citizens' associations, and groups of citizens are allowed to propose projects within the Rijeka local partnership programme. Educational games in Rijeka, Sisak, and Labin are publicly available, and anyone (not just citizens of selected towns) can play the games. The Dubrovnik model of PB is only partly implemented since so far it has been confined to PB in elementary schools. The plan is that PB in Dubrovnik includes broader citizenry, but the proper form of the selection has to be still defined.

Towns participating in special projects of PB started with promotions of the projects through leaflets, radio shows, public presentations, special websites, social networks, personal contacts in sub-municipal entities, and so on. Also, in some cases education is provided in the preparatory process as a part of the presentation of the PB projects, by publishing guidelines for participants (Trogir), informing citizens and representatives of sub-municipal entities (Pazin), and in the form of workshops for the wider community after special education of PB coordinators (Dubrovnik). In parallel, participants are invited to submit their proposals and to participate in discussions. During the years in which PB was introduced, the time left for submission of proposals was rather long (more than a month as of invitation). It had to be even extended in the case of Pazin since citizens were not willing to participate. Nevertheless, since PB takes place in cycles, after gaining some experience, participants have enough time (a whole year) to think about and prepare proposals for another PB cycle.

In the PB processes, several ICT instruments have been used. Participants are often invited to submit their proposals by email, but in very few towns (Pazin, Trogir, and Rijeka; and Karlovac, Pula, and Mali Lošinj) proposals serve(d) as a basis for further public discussions within the PB process. In many other towns, citizens are invited to submit their proposals and comments on the local budget, but the latter are followed neither with discussion nor with the (publicly available) feedback. In some analysed cases, participants are provided with the templates for the sub-mission of their project proposals and comments on the local budget (Trogir and Rijeka—small utility actions, Rijeka local partnership pro-gramme, e-consultations in Rijeka). In order to provide citizens with the opportunity to discuss proposed small utility actions electronically, Pazin has introduced an online moderated forum. Educational games are pro-vided exclusively online. Most indicated forms of "participation" are lim-ited to mere consultation, that is, collecting citizens' and other participants' proposals. A step further is planned to be taken by Dubrovnik in the form of an online platform for PB, and e-voting. Citizens and other participants can also submit their proposals personally or by surface mail.

Public hearings on small utility actions are organised on the level of sub-municipal entities, usually once in each entity. An exception is made by Pazin where two public hearings are held—first when the citizens sub-mit their proposals, and the second when they vote for the priorities of small utility actions. In addition, after the first reading of the budget pro-posal, a final public hearing on the overall content of the budget (includ-ing proposals of small utility actions the citizens have voted for) is held on the town level. The schedule of public hearings is announced at least a week earlier (Trogir). The meetings start with the presentation of techni-cal issues (estimated expenses, photos of the location, and other informa-tion for each proposal) by local civil servants administering the PB. Public hearings are held also in order to discuss general issues in selected sectors in the town of Pazin. The latter also provides an online forum as an addi-tional channel for discussion in the PB process. However, a discussion is not provided in the case of Rijeka PB on small utility actions. When the city administration gives feedback on technical aspects of proposed proj-ects, councils of sub-municipal entities select and prioritise projects to be financed and implemented. Nevertheless, this approach can be considered as indirect citizen participation in the PB process. Furthermore, public hearings are neither provided within the Rijeka local partnership programme where the committee passes the decision on the acceptance of proposed projects without any prior discussion among participants. Also, educational games on the local budget do not include discussion.

When a discussion on small utility actions is provided for, participants have an opportunity to deliberate, and not just to express their opinion. This especially comes to the fore when public hearings include voting on priorities of small utility actions (Pazin, Trogir). There were cases when citizens from one sub-municipal entity have quitted their proposals in favour of another sub-municipal entity after deliberation and exchange of arguments (Pazin). Although a final decision on the acceptance of the budget proposal (including the part relating to PB) is passed by the local council, decisions on the priorities of small utility actions in Pazin, Rijeka, and Trogir made by the participants in the PB are included in the budget for the following year. Therefore, besides expressing their opinions on local activities, citizens participate in decision-making on the part of the local budget. Voting is conducted by using ballot papers (Pazin) or by hand-raising (Trogir, in Pazin if all participants agree). Co-deciding is also provided in the Dubrovnik plan of the PB, but in the electronic form. In other models of PB in Croatia (Rijeka local partnership programme, educational games, and discussion on large utility projects in Pazin), the exclusive aim of the PB is to obtain an opinion and advice from the participants, that is, their proposals of the projects in the local community.

In general, the participation of citizens in fiscal policy and budgetary processes in Croatia is rather low (Ott & Bronić, 2015). The number of participants in the PB just confirms this statistic. It ranges from zero (when no proposals have been submitted) to 10% of the town population. The biggest score has been achieved in the town of Mali Lošinj with the increase in the number of participants in the second year of the PB project (from 7% to 10%) (Džinić, 2018). However, Mali Lošinj has not continued with PB. The number of participants in the public hearings has increased also in Trogir from 2.47% to 3.75% of the population eligible to vote. In the well-experienced town of Pazin, approx. 2.26% to 3% of inhabitants have participated in public hearings on small utility actions until 2017. In 2018 the number of participants slightly decreased which might have been the consequence of the new model of PB (half of the sub-municipal entities included), but increased again in 2019. Since educational games are the least demanding in the sense of the effort required, the citizens are the most willing to participate in this kind of process. For instance, Rijeka online game registers 7.000 visits a year out of which 1.500 games were finished (Džinić, 2018).

6.4 OUTCOMES OF PARTICIPATORY BUDGETING

In all cases, final decisions on the projects proposed, discussed, and selected as priorities during the PB process are passed by the local (city/town) council within the decision on the local budget. Nevertheless, when a certain amount of money is intended for the PB (small utility actions and Rijeka programme of local partnership), and the costs of selected projects do not exceed that amount, proposals selected in the PB are mostly accepted by the councils. However, the council in the town of Karlovac has rejected all proposals submitted by the PB project leaders (Mužar, 2017), and in the town of Pula few proposals (those already planned by the budget) have been accepted (Matić, 2017). In other towns, proposals and opinions on larger projects, whether collected on public hearings (Pazin) or without any discussion (including online games) are also taken into consideration during the preparation of the budget. In the town of Sisak, the feedback of the online game is provided in a way that citizens can see the amounts of money that had been proposed per each item, and the ones that were later accepted by the council.

The part of local budgets concerning communal economy and investments is most affected by the PB since the greatest number of participants' proposals relates to utility actions. However, in some cases, the actions and projects selected during the PB process would be implemented in the local budget notwithstanding the PB process. Therefore, it is hard to measure the direct impact of PB on the final contents of the budget. Besides, PB is limited to traditional local activities. An innovative approach to PB is implemented through the online games, but on the other hand, the latter are limited to informing and consultations with weak feedback by the local government, and lack of strong citizen engagement. The innovativeness of the town of Pazin has been recognised by other towns and the URBACT programme of the European territorial cooperation that awarded the town of Pazin for its PB project in 2017.

A formal survey on the satisfaction about the PB process has been conducted only in Dubrovnik where 90% of students who had participated in the PB in elementary schools expressed their interest to participate in the PB again. 65% of the students marked the PB project as excellent. In other towns, positive feedback has been provided only during public hearings.

Nevertheless, the increase in the number of participants and the amount of money intended for PB shows some positive effects of PB on citizen participation and mutual trust between citizens and local government. The improvements in this respect are still very modest, but it seems that continuous development of existing PB processes could result in higher participation and even partnership of local government and citizens. Towns that have not implemented PB yet have expressed their interest, so positive effects of PB on policy diffusion can be expected, taking into consideration other factors that might impede the process.

In the survey, the respondents have been asked to indicate the lessons learned during the PB. In the town of Pazin the lessons have been divided into three categories (the period of preparation, the period of discussions and co-deciding, and the period after the public hearings), and explained in detail (e.g., it is important to take sufficient time for preparation, to determine the exact amount of money for each sub-municipal entity, to ensure good guidance of public hearings, to fulfil all accepted proposals in order to keep the citizens' trust in future PB processes, etc.).

6.5   DISCUSSION

When compared to international trends in the development of PB (Nelson Dias, 2014; Sintomer et al., 2010), Croatia is lagging behind, both in the number of cities applying PB and in the elaboration of existing practices of PB. Taking into consideration the typology of PB developed by Sintomer et al. (2008, 2010), the analysis of the above-mentioned PB practices shows that Pazin, Trogir, and Rijeka (small utility actions) have been implementing a combination of the "Porto Alegre adapted for Europe" and the "Proximity participation". Rijeka local partnership programme can be indicated as the model of "Participation of organised interests", while educational games and other forms of informing citizens on local finances represent the model of "Consultation on public finances" aimed, first of all, to make local finances transparent. There are no other types of PB recognised in other countries. In Croatia, most of the towns have not been led by international developments in the field. Analysis of PB in Pazin and its cooperation with foreign scholars shows that it is the only town that has taken into consideration internationally recognised advantages of PB. When PB is not dealt with just by town administration and when NGOs and other institutions (such as Dubrovnik Development Agency) are included, it can be expected that international experiences will be taken into account. Otherwise, the capacities are limited due to other obligations of town staff.

Towns with more elaborated PB models (Pazin, Rijeka, Trogir, and Dubrovnik) set the aims of PB projects and formed the processes accordingly. Thus, the instruments ensuring more specific goals like involving citizens in decision-making, standardisation of the equipment on sub-municipal level, or stimulation of volunteering have been introduced. However, when coming to more general aims such as the improvement of trust, good governance, and quality of life, PB itself might contribute to the achievement thereof, but there are other factors that interfere and determine the quality of PB processes.

The characteristics of described processes in Croatia might be determined by several factors. PB is not an obligation prescribed by law but depends on the goodwill of local government. In the environment of a legalistic culture where things are done only when required by law, and where administrative capacities are rather weak, it can be expected that voluntary mechanisms of citizen participation will not be implemented to a wider extent (Džinić, 2016). Besides, despite legally required transparency of local finances and the improvement in that respect, Croatian local units are not sufficiently transparent yet (Ott et al., 2020). The least transparent are municipalities as a type of local units established in more rural areas, but room for improvements exists also in towns, cities, counties (units of regional self-government), and central state institutions. Despite decentralisation reforms launched in 2000, Croatia is still a highly centralised country. The main factors impeding genuine decentralisation are fragmented territorial structure, uneven level of economic development, and huge variations in the capacity of local governments, all resulting in an overall lack of local capacities. There are 556 local governments with approximately 7 inhabitants on average per local unit. Besides, the range between the smallest and the largest municipality is 1:50, and the range between the smallest and the largest city (excluding the City of Zagreb) is 1:118 (Koprić, 2013). Territorial fragmentation affects the fiscal capacity of local governments and in the case of Croatia confirms the linkage between the size of local units and their role in the provision of local public services (Koprić, 2012). Most local authorities are not capable of performing constitutionally guaranteed local competencies. Small local governments do not necessarily mean higher citizens' participation in political processes. In Croatia, citizens do not trust local authorities and think that their opinion will be ignored (Švaljek et al., 2019). Sometimes they are even afraid to express their opinion or are just not well-informed. Therefore, they are not highly engaged in public affairs. It seems mistrust is mutual since existing PB processes are often limited to pure consultation with the unwillingness of local governments to provide citizens with decision-making authorities. In the field of civic engagement, an institutional framework for co-production was set up in some policy fields by a reformist government during the 2000s (Howlett et al., 2017). However, as an analysis of co-production in disability policy shows that "in a clientelist context, such as Croatia, co-production may generate adverse effects when misused by policy-makers to expand their discretionary powers through patronage practices" (Sorrentino et al., 2018, p. 288). Also, other circumstances such as unresolved property relationships, local civil servants' resistance, the weak position of sub-municipal entities, and so on might have affected the state of PB in Croatia (Džinić, 2018).

Therefore, the reasons for the rare implementation of PB, insufficiently elaborated processes, narrow authorities provided to citizens, and their low response should be looked for in above-mentioned environmental factors. Accordingly, strengthening of local capacities, transparency and openness impose as basic preconditions for the diffusion of PB and successful implementation.

6.6   CONCLUSION

In Croatia, PB is not well developed, either as a widespread practice among towns and municipalities or as a form of participatory democracy with well-elaborated elements required for a process to be called PB. There are nine towns that used to have (Karlovac and Mali Lošinj), have (Pazin, Trogir, Rijeka, Pula, Labin, and Sisak), or are in the preparatory phase to introduce (Dubrovnik) some kind of PB. They represent only 1.62% of local units in Croatia (128 towns and cities, and 428 municipalities). There are other towns providing some forms of citizen participation in local budgets, but they lack most of the crucial elements of PB. Even in the group of the nine towns mentioned, not all of them have well-elaborated PB. They lack either deliberation, citizens' authority to decision-making or control, and accountability for the projects selected in the PB process. A part of PB projects was quitted after a very short period of implementation. Non-elaborated "PB projects" imply that it is more about another political gimmick, and not a real intention to empower citizens and improve local public policies.

The most serious approach to PB has been taken in Pazin, Rijeka, Trogir, and Dubrovnik. In most models provided by those towns, citizens can discuss and make decisions. However, sometimes it is hard to determine the real impact of citizens' decisions on the content of local budgets because some of the selected projects would be included regardless of citizens' opinion. Positive results are present in relation to learning on own experience followed by improvements of the PB process itself. Making local finances transparent and providing citizens with the opportunity to participate in the creation of local budgets has educational effects for citizens, too. In Pazin, there is a slight increase in the number of citizens participating and in the amounts of money allocated to PB projects which might be the consequence of strengthening the mutual trust between local government and citizens.

However, there is still room for improvement since the part of the budget allocated for PB is rather low, especially where citizens have decision-making power. Besides, they are not willing to participate in public hearings, but participate the most in processes without authority to decide on local finances (online games). The example of Pazin confirms that the evaluation of existing processes, learning, and improvements based on experience is of utmost importance for gaining positive outcomes from the PB processes. Learning from the experience of others and following international developments in the field are also important.

Nevertheless, broader factors impeding diffusion of PB and positive effects of its implementation have their roots in high territorial fragmentation, weak decentralisation, and capacities of local governments, insufficient transparency, and underdeveloped culture of citizens' participation in public affairs. Until real reforms in this respect are not implemented, it is hard to expect broader diffusion of PB. It is more probable that PB projects will be confined to a smaller number of more developed towns resulting in further disparities among Croatian citizens living in different local communities.

References

Act on LRSG. (n.d.). Act on local and regional self-government. *Croatian Official Gazette*, no. 33/01, 60/01, 129/05, 109/07, 125/08, 36/09, 36/09, 150/11, 144/12, 19/13, 137/15, 123/17, 98/19.

Cabannes, Y. (2004). Participatory budgeting: A significant contribution to participatory democracy. *Environment and Urbanization, 16*(1), 27–46. https://doi.org/10.1177/095624780401600104

Džinić, J. (2016). Komparativna iskustva upravljanja kvalitetom u javnoj upravi. In I. Koprić, J. Džinić, & R. Manojlović (Eds.), *Upravljanje kvalitetom i učinkovitošću u javnoj upravi* (pp. 129–157). Institut za javnu upravu. https://www.bib.irb.hr/800523

Džinić, J. (2018). Participatory budgeting in Croatia: A way to improve quality of local governance? In J. Nemec, V. Potier, & M. S. de Vries (Eds.), *Alternative service delivery* (pp. 73–81). IASIA/IIAS.

Džinić, J. (2021). Participativno budžetiranje u službi razvoja dobrog lokalnog upravljanja. *New regulation of referendum in the Republic of Croatia and other forms of direct citizen participation in decision-making—What position of citizens in the democratic system we need?*

Džinić, J., Svidroňová, M. M., & Markowska-Bzducha, E. (2016). Participatory budgeting: A comparative study of Croatia, Poland and Slovakia. *NISPAcee Journal of Public Administration and Policy, 9*(1), 31–56. https://ideas.repec.org/a/vrs/njopap/v9y2016i1p31-56n2.html

Howlett, M., Kekez, A., & Poocharoen, O.-O. (2017). Understanding co-production as a policy tool: Integrating new public governance and comparative policy theory. *Journal of Comparative Policy Analysis: Research and Practice, 19*(5), 487–501. https://doi.org/10.1080/13876988.2017.1287445

Koprić, I. (2012). Lokalna i regionalna samouprava u Hrvatskoj: k policentričnoj zemlji. In J. Barbić (Ed.), *Hrvatski pravni sustav*. HAZU. https://www.bib.irb.hr/671607

Koprić, I. (2013). Dvadeset godina lokalne i područne (regionalne) samouprave u Hrvatskoj: Razvoj, stanje i perspektive. In V. Đulabić (Ed.), *Lokalna samouprava i lokalni izbori* (pp. 3–63). Institute for Public Administration. https://www.bib.irb.hr/725485

Matić, G. (2017). Pula. In *E-participativno budžetiranje: iskustva iz Karlovca, Malog Lošinja i Pule.*

Mužar, I. (2017). Karlovac. In *E-participativno Budžetiranje: Iskustva iz Karlovca, Malog Lošinja i Pule.*

Nelson Dias. (2014). *Hope for democracy—25 years of participatory budgeting worldwide*. Loco Association.

Ott, K., & Bronić, M. (2015). Sudjelovanje građana u fiskalnoj politici i proračunskim procesima. *Newsletter of the Croatian Institute of Public Finances, 96*, 1–6.

Ott, K., Bronić, M., Petrušić, M., Stanić, B., & Prijaković, S. (2020). Proračunska transparentnost županija, gradova i općina: studeni 2019.—travanj 2020. *Newsletter of the Croatian Institute of Public Finances, 119*, 1–13.

Sintomer, Y., Herzberg, C., & Allegretti, G. (2010). *Learning from the South: Participatory budgeting worldwide—An invitation to global cooperation*. Global Civic Engagement.

Sintomer, Y., Herzberg, C., & Röcke, A. (2008). Participatory budgeting in Europe: Potentials and challenges. *International Journal of Urban and Regional Research*, *32*(1), 164–178. https://doi.org/10.1111/j.1468-2427.2008.00777.x

Sorrentino, M., Sicilia, M., & Howlett, M. (2018). Understanding co-production as a new public governance tool. *Policy and Society, 37*(3), 277–293. https://doi.org/10.1080/14494035.2018.1521676

Švaljek, S., Bakarić, I. R., & Sumpor, M. (2019). Citizens and the city: The case for participatory budgeting in the city of Zagreb. *Public Sector Economics, 43*(1), 21–48. https://doi.org/10.3326/PSE.43.1.4

CHAPTER 7

Project-Oriented Participatory Budgeting in the Czech Republic

Lucie Sedmihradská, Soňa Kukučková, and Eduard Bakoš

7.1 Introduction

Participatory budgeting (PB) is a democratic innovation that literally stormed into Czech local government in the last six years: From the very first enlightening articles in 2012 to a real chance to take part for almost 20% of the Czech population. The purpose of this chapter is to map and evaluate the development of PB in the Czech Republic. It assesses the

L. Sedmihradská (✉)
Faculty of Finance and Accounting, Prague University of Economics and Business, Prague, Czech Republic
e-mail: sedmih@vse.cz

S. Kukučková
Faculty of Business and Administration, Mendel University in Brno, Brno, Czech Republic
e-mail: sona.kukuckova@mendelu.cz

E. Bakoš
Faculty of Economics and Administration, Masaryk University Brno, Brno, Czech Republic
e-mail: eduard.bakos@econ.muni.cz

131

process, analysing various quantitative indicators such as the number of municipalities and inhabitants involved, the amount of money allocated, and the number of projects proposed and realised. Special attention is paid to utilised voting rules and public participation.

This study is based on an extensive database of municipal PB between 2014 and 2019 in the Czech Republic, a literature and media review, participation in several thematic workshops and conferences aimed at practitioners, and personal experience of one of the authors as an elected municipal official in charge of PB in her municipality. Our database was compiled manually using publicly available information on the websites of the individual municipalities. It contains 133 PB cases in 59 municipalities. Data on the number of inhabitants and voter turnout came from Czech Statistical Office (CSO) and data on municipal expenditure came from Monitor (an open data portal of the Ministry of Finance).

While at first sight the numbers show a clear increase, a deeper analysis reveals many issues that may significantly slow down this process. There are only a handful of municipalities with really performing PB processes at the moment and a growing number of downgrading municipalities between 2018 and 2019. Many municipalities observe a decline in the number of submitted proposals and in order to reduce implementation problems the rules get stricter every new round. The likely impact of the COVID-19 pandemic and subsequent deep economic slowdown is unfortunately strongly negative.

7.2   PARTICIPATORY BUDGETING IN THE CZECH REPUBLIC

Participatory budgeting (PB) is a decision-making process through which citizens deliberate and negotiate over the distribution of public resources (Wampler, 2007). It is an element of direct democracy that enters the budgeting process. There is no unique model of PB and we can observe numerous experiments worldwide based on different patterns in relation to specific contexts (Stewart et al., 2014). In the Czech Republic the so-called project-oriented participatory budgeting (Sintomer et al., 2008) prevails when suitable projects are selected for implementation according to predetermined rules within a given amount of funds. Besides this project-oriented participatory budgeting, some cases of the consultation on the public finance model can be found. In that model, citizens do not vote for proposals and local governments freely and arbitrarily integrate some proposals in the public policy (Sintomer et al., 2008). This type of participatory budgeting with certain variations is used in some municipalities (e.g. Litoměřice, Ústí nad Labem).

PB in the Czech municipalities generally has the following phases with little variation among the individual municipalities: (1) announcement of a call for projects including total predetermined amount (usually already approved in the budget), (2) collection of project proposals, (3) feasibility or technical analysis realised by the municipal office and exclusion of unfeasible projects, (4) voting on feasible projects and (5) implementation of successful projects.

Thus, PB is kind of outside of the standard budgetary process. The municipal council first approves the amount dedicated for PB in the annual budget and then a separate process of PB takes place. While the promoters of PB deem the involvement of the broader public in the budgetary process to be one of the key benefits (Fölscher, 2007), this is not really happening. That cannot be blamed on current Czech legislation. The legislation does leave enough space for public participation in the budgetary process as it poses significant information disclosure requirements and allows active citizens' participation in finance committee meetings and municipal council meetings. Unfortunately, these occasions are rarely utilised (Sedmihradská, 2016).

The history of participatory budgeting in the Czech Republic is relatively short. The first initiatives were seen in the non-profit organisation Alternativa Zdola. It established the first website related to participatory budgeting in the Czech Republic in 2012 (Exner, 2018). The first municipal participatory budgeting project was implemented in the city district Praha 7 in 2014. In the same year, the Czech Pirate Party started to distribute its own funds to projects proposed by party members using PB practices (Czech Pirate Party, 2020).

The year 2015 was a turning point: First AGORA Central Europe (Agora Central Europe, 2015), a non-governmental organisation, piloted participatory budgeting in two Prague districts (Praha 10 and Praha Zbraslav). Second, initiative Democracy 2.1 (D21) launched a voting platform using a novel voting method as proposed by Karel Janeček. Under this voting method, voters utilise multiple positive votes and usually also negative vote(s) (Janeček, 2016). In addition to these initiatives, a pilot project of the city of Litoměřice took place within the concept of the Healthy Cities, which applied the principles of the Local Agenda 21. It used the "Healthy Cities Forum" for voting on proposed projects. All the above concepts contributed to the development of participatory budgeting in the Czech Republic.

The four non-governmental organisations mentioned above played a key role in the spread of PB in the Czech Republic. They were able to bring the novel concept not only into the public debate but predominantly on the political agenda and to provide services which made the implementation quick and cheap (and uniform). While the first case of PB in the city district Praha 7 took place before the municipal elections in 2014, all the other cases started after that election. Whereas the buzzword in the 2010 election was "transparency", it transformed to "public participation" in 2014, and as budget explorers are a fulfilment of the transparency commitment (Sedmihradská, 2019), PB is that of public participation.

The number of municipalities experimenting with PB grew steadily over the last five years and in 2019 it was implemented in 48 towns and municipalities (Table 7.1). Compared to the total number of municipalities (over 6200) it is still not a high number. Nevertheless, participatory budgeting is used especially by relatively large cities (e.g. Prague districts, Brno, Ostrava districts), so the share of the total population involved is fairly high: In 2019 almost one-fifth of the country's population had the possibility to participate in such initiatives and to decide on the amount of almost CZK 150 million (i.e. €5.6 million). From a single project

Table 7.1 PB in Czech municipalities during 2014–2019

Year	Number of municipalities	Inhabitants of municipalities with PB	Amount allocated (€)[a]	Number of approved projects
2014	1	42,381	36,298	1
2016	11	549,780	1,087,796	58
2017	32	1,364,405	2,950,932	189
2018	41	1,742,496	4,936,614	232
2019	48	1,869,836	5,615,043	246

Source: Authors

Note: The year of the PB was set based on the date of the voting for PB projects. In some municipalities, preparation of the process started the year before; thus the year in the name of the PB process used by municipalities could differ from the year used in this chapter

[a]A single exchange rate announced by the Ministry of Finance each year for tax purposes was chosen for the conversion of Czech crowns into euro

implemented by one municipality, the number of projects increased to 246 in 48 different municipalities across the whole country.

Despite this encouraging growth, it is worth mentioning that the percentage of the total municipal budget allocated through PB is very low, ranging from 0.02% to 1.94%, with a median of 0.38%. There is no clear relationship between the size of the municipality and the share of PB expenditure, although big cities tend to allocate a pretty low share of expenditure (Fig. 7.1).

7.3 Participation and Voting

PB is seen as a tool for public participation and therefore the rules for participation are often more open than general election rules, with its strictly required minimum age of 18 years and permanent residence in the municipality.

In the Czech case, we can analyse participation rules first for those who vote and second for those who propose a project.

The selection criteria to become eligible to vote in the PB process are linked to age, the address of residence, and the relationship to a

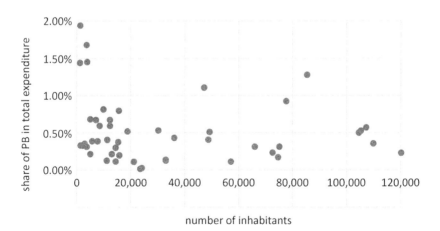

Fig. 7.1 Share of PB expenditure in total expenditure and the size of the municipality (Source: Authors). Note: Data for the most recent case of PB in the given municipality (2018 or 2019), Brno with 380,000 inhabitants and share of PB in total expenditure 0.23% is not shown for sake of the figure clarity)

municipality. In many municipalities (46% of cases), the age can be lower than 18 as the PB is considered a tool to enhance civic participation among younger citizens. Other frequently used criteria for voting are a permanent address in the municipality (62% of cases) and even an address in a specific district to vote for a project located in that district of a municipality (e.g. Český Krumlov). Nonetheless, citizens without permanent residence can often participate, if they can prove a proper relationship to a municipality, for instance, by owning real estate (Starý Plzenec, Golčův Jeníkov), if they study, work or spend free time in the municipality (e.g. Příbram, Praha 14). Some municipalities did not specify age limits (35% of cases) or have a permanent address in their rules (4 cases). In one municipality (Ostrava—Mariánské hory a Hulváky) there was no limitation at all on who could vote for online voting.

The criteria for those who can propose projects usually mirror those for voting. The age can be lower than 18 years in 73% of all cases, which confirms that the PB was indeed used to encourage young citizens to participate. Mostly, when a proposer is younger, a guarantor/legal representative over 18 years is needed. Sometimes, even more, guarantors are required (e.g. five persons in Husinec Řež). Similarly, to the voting criteria, in some cases a permanent address is required (e.g. Slaný, Praha 20), or just a relationship to the municipality is needed (e.g. Praha 11, Dobříš). A proposal can be submitted by an individual (or a group of individuals) or a legal entity (company, institution, NGO). A legal entity's proposal is accepted when the entity has a registered office or place of operation within the municipality (e.g. Krnov, Praha 20). In most of the municipalities, only individuals can be proposers (e.g. Brno).

In many municipalities, the proposer submitting a project needs to get some form of support from other citizens beforehand. It can be proven with a physical collection of citizens' signatures on the list or a certain number of "likes" on the municipality's webpage (e.g. in Brno a project must collect 300 likes to be supported). The desired number of signatures on the list varies from none (Mníšek pod Brdy) to 50 citizens (Litoměřice in 2017). Sometimes, too many required supporters resulted in fewer submitted proposals and the municipalities watered down the condition. Another potential problem discouraging young people to participate is that a proposal made by 15-year-olds must be supported by a higher number of older citizens (e.g. Mnichovice and Orlová).

Similarly, the obligation to participate in public hearings/meetings to be accepted for voting and to present the project can be problematic for some proposers (Příbram or Dobříš in 2018). When there is a pilot project of PB, the meetings are rather informational to promote and explain participatory budgeting. About 65% of the municipalities hold public meetings before the voting to present the pre-selected projects eligible to be voted upon. The municipalities without them are mostly small municipalities where the projects are presented on their websites only.

In bigger municipalities, there is usually a PB coordinator who assists the proposers to adapt their projects to comply with the rules. Proposers are present in 23% of PB cases. In some cases, the coordinator has the right to approve the projects (e.g. Ostrava Poruba). In case more districts are involved in one PB process (e.g. Brno) the coordinator can help to negotiate with and to inform the district officials at the town level. When the municipality belongs to the Healthy Cities, there is often a commission of the Healthy Cities that must confirm the selected PB projects to be eligible for voting (e.g. Nový Jičín). A meeting of PB coordinators in Ostrava in March 2019 showed that their role, especially personal engagement, is a key factor in the development of PB in particular municipalities. Very often the PB coordinators are part of the mayors' offices, which is important from the point of political support of the whole process.

Almost always a pre-selection is performed by the municipality office or by their technical evaluators before voting. This pre-selection made by officials could be called project filtering (Smith, 2009) or cherry-picking (Font et al., 2018) when a non-random selection of proposals is made by the authorities based on their feasibility evaluation. We measure the project filtering based on the rate of the number of selected projects for voting on the number of originally proposed projects. We checked the fate of 2785 original PB proposals presented on the websites in the period 2016–2019 and on average 71% of the cases were approved for voting (Fig. 7.2). However, there are other proposals that could be excluded from our data set when a municipality officer did not recommend the projects even to be proposed.

This step is crucial for the success of the whole process. In the early rounds, attention was predominantly paid to the encouragement of citizens to submit proposals and generally to participate. However, subsequent implementation revealed too many administrative and technical obstacles (e.g. need of projects, permits, public procurement, shared responsibilities in case of statutory cities) that prolonged the implementation process. While these obstacles are real in the Czech public

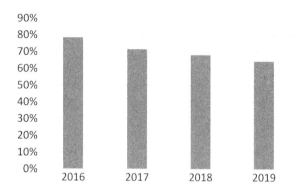

Fig. 7.2 % of proposals approved for voting in 2016–2019. (Source: Authors)

administration and imply nothing about the engagement, competence, or efficiency of the particular municipal office or officials, it is hard if not impossible to explain it to the proposers of the successful projects. The delay between submission of a project and its implementation can be very long and cause unnecessary distrust in the municipality or its officials.

During the process, municipalities encounter additional issues that originally nobody considered. Klihavcová (2019) found that municipalities do not have any rules regarding future operational costs or costs higher than the original budget. Some municipalities stated that operational costs must be reasonable, and majority of municipalities pay some expenditure over the allocated PB amount from the general budget.

After public voting, the winning projects are approved by the municipal council and in the case of a town with more districts (e.g. Brno), ratification of the winning project by the concerned district is needed. Again, we can find different selection practices among municipalities: while some select those according to the support seen in the number of casted votes regardless of whether a part of the budget stays unused, other municipalities try to utilise as much from the allocated PB budget as possible even when smaller projects with fewer votes surpass costlier projects with more votes. In this case, it is deemed important to publish the reasons for rejection and to inform the proposers. According to Font et al. (2018), the excluded proposers have difficulty accepting the fact that their proposals get less financing than the accepted ones. Similarly, Allegretti (2014) emphasises the need for detailed information on the reasons that resulted in the refusal of some proposals and the acceptance of others. The possibility to get feedback from participants including the proposers during the evaluation meeting was identified in 20% of Czech PB cases.

7.4   ORGANISATION AND RULES FOR PB VOTING

The spread of participatory budgeting is often presented as the result of more frequent use of ICT tools. Most of the PB voting is realised only online (57%) or in combination with physical voting (30%). Some municipalities offer possibilities to use the computers inside the municipal office because the preference for online voting could be considered as discrimination against older citizens lacking ICT facilities. Only 9% of the analysed municipalities required physical voting exclusively (e.g. Sadská, Hlučín).

In 64% of cases, the municipalities use services of external companies/NGOs, which provide websites for projects presentation, voting systems, or which organise the whole process. Agora and Participace 21 (former D21) prevail with an 86-percentage share on all external companies used by municipalities for services linked to PB. Typical for them is that they promote the voting system using the D21 method proposed by Karel Janeček and offer all services mentioned above. Other companies involved are IT companies providing IT solutions (e.g. Neogenia, NIC CZ). Smaller municipalities rarely outsource these services. Sometimes they only use their original websites. The online voting system often enables the display of projects in random order which could prevent the preference of projects on top of the list (e.g. Praha 10).

The verification of the identity of those eligible for voting is limited in many cases. Usually, the municipalities using the systems of external companies/NGOs check the duplicity of the votes using IP address, registered email address, or SMS code on the phone number. The permanent address or the age is rarely controlled, not even when these are criteria for the eligibility to vote. The city of Brno is an exception. Here, a voter is verified in the registry and both conditions must be fulfilled. The 'voter' must give their date of birth and ID number—this data is checked in the registry of citizens and a unique encrypted token is generated. This token enables voting and is cancelled after the voting is completed.

In 71% of the cases, the D21 method was used to choose the winning projects. In this case, voters have several votes to cast. A voter may give only one vote to any project. To use a minus vote, it is necessary to cast at least two plus ones. The number of pluses and minuses can change according to the specific electoral context (www.participation21.com). This method is presented as a better way to express the preferences with more information based on more votes which could motivate the voter to participate (Janeček, 2016). Through negative votes, controversial projects could be identified or even excluded from winning options. Similarly, the opposition of residents to a proposed project in their local area expressed by the acronym Not in My Back Yard (NIMBY) could be demonstrated by negative votes.

The model used is based on a modified majority rule which is based on the assumption of an informed voter motivated by the possibility to cast more than one vote. A risk is posed by the possibility of strategic voting and the complexity of the rules as perceived by voters. Voting proposers and their supporters could abuse the possibility to cast negative votes— using these just to beat their rivals. When there are few voters, this might substantially change the result. Some municipalities have changed the D21 method and now use positive votes only (Havířov, Brno). In Brno, the negative votes are used, but for evaluation purposes these are relevant only in the case of an equality of positive votes. This rule has been applied since 2019, as there was a critique on the use of negative votes from PB participants (both proposers and voters). In 8% of the cases, positive votes were determinative without the application of the method D21. Different rules are used in Healthy Cities. Usually, there is a public hearing called a forum, where participants can vote on projects after the presentation thereof (e.g. Nový Jičín and Znojmo).

There is frequent criticism that PB does not represent the interests of the majority when only few citizens participate. During the implementation stage, the problem described as asymmetry of information may occur. Lack of communication from the municipality could cause that only a few potential participants have information about the realisation of PB implying their higher possibility to enforce their proposals. This advantage could be misused by an informed minority, such as by friends of the organisers or by some incumbent group of interests. Therefore, a higher participation rate is desirable to confirm the legitimacy of the process. From the opposite view, it has been observed that communities are less likely to participate once their demands are met (Baiocchi & Ganuza, 2014; Bhatnagar et al., 2003; Zepic et al., 2017).

In 2019, the PB voter turnout varied from 1.22% to 18.88%. The rate was calculated as the share of the number of PB voters in relation to the number of all potential voters in the list for the Czech municipal election in 2018. More than 50% of the analysed cases showed a PB voter turnout lower than 5%. Approximately 20% of cases have a PB voter turnout higher than 10%. Three municipalities with the highest PB voter turnout are smaller ones with 3000–4000 inhabitants (Mnichovice, Golčův Jeníkov, Praha Kolovraty). The probable reason is the size of the projects. While in a small town a project of CZK 1 mil (i.e. €40,000) has a town-wide impact, a project of the same amount is a small local project in a city. None of the municipalities used PB for bigger projects.

7.5   CLASSIFICATION OF PBs IN 2019

While the number of Czech municipalities experimenting or utilising PB is growing, it is worth exploring this development more in-depth. The literature on PB offers at least two typologies allowing such an in-depth analysis: Alves & Allegretti (2012) differentiate between ongoing (upgrading or downgrading) and abandoned PB processes and based on Statusbericht des Portals Buergerhaushalt.org (e.g. Ermert et al., 2015; Ruesch & Ermert, 2014) the evolution can be divided into four phases: pre-form, introduction, continuation, and sliding.

According to Alves and Allegretti (2012) we can distinguish between an ongoing (upgrading or downgrading) and abandoned PB process. The upgrading PB means that at least one of the following three conditions is met: the growth in the number of proposals, the number of votes, or the amount of allocated funds. Duration of the PB for at least two years is required to enable comparison of the last two years. This classification reflects the fate of PB and its actual state (Fig. 7.3).

We compared the parameters of 59 PB processes between two years— the years 2017 and 2018 to obtain the result for 2018 and the years 2018 and 2019 for 2019.

The total number of abandoned PBs in the period 2014–2018 is 10 (Fig. 7.4). While this total is relatively low, the increase in 2018 is significant. The predictive capacity of this classification is surprisingly good: 60% of the downgrading PBs identified in 2018 did not continue in 2019. The growing number of downgrading PB can be a possible alert to signal the bad fate of PB. Abandoned PBs were identified from 133 cases between 2014 and 2018.

The second classification was designed according to the methodology used in Statusbericht des Portals Buergerhaushalt.org (e.g. Ermert et al., 2015; Ruesch & Ermert, 2014). We selected four categories from the

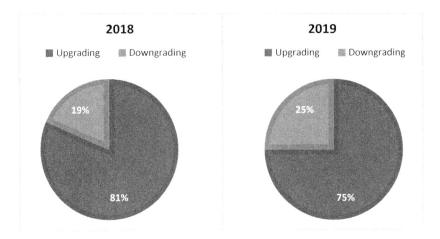

Fig. 7.3 Ongoing PBs: the share of upgrading and downgrading PBs in 2018 and 2019. (Source: Authors)

Fig. 7.4 Abandoned PBs (2014–2018). (Source: Authors)

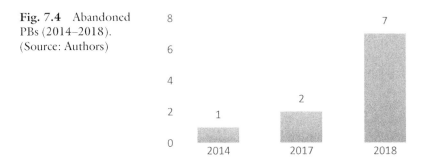

original seven that relate to PB implementation reflecting duration and character of PB process suitable for Czech cases:

- Pre-form: PB is not fully implemented, such as proposal through online forms or emails without interactive discussion possibilities,
- Introduction: PB realised for the first or the second time,
- Continuation: PB realised for the third time or more times,
- Siding: the last PB was realised two years ago and at the moment there is no perspective to start again.

We analysed 58 municipalities with PB in the period 2016–2019 and classified them based on the situation in the year 2019. This year, slightly more PBs were introduced than considered as a continuation, two PBs were in pre-form and 11 PBs were siding (Fig. 7.5).

Using these classifications sheds new light on the evaluation of the PB development in the Czech Republic as we see a high or growing number of abandoned or sliding cases and a limited number of upgrading or continuing cases. This is alarming as the COVID-19 pandemic and subsequent economic decline may have a strong negative impact on municipal management in particular, and on the novel and unstable projects such as PB in general.

7.6   DISCUSSION AND CONCLUSION

The study of the effects of PB on society has a relatively long tradition in different countries. Unlike Porto Alegre, the PB in the Czech Republic is project oriented. It is used for the implementation of specific and usually not very costly projects. Thus, it can be said that it mostly serves as an

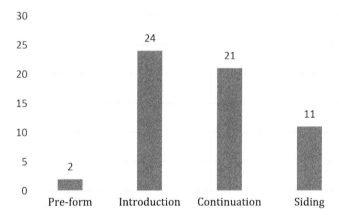

Fig. 7.5   Classification of Czech PBs reflecting their duration and character in 2019. (Source: Authors. Note: Pre-form PB not fully implemented, for example proposal through online forms or emails without interactive discussion possibilities; Introduction: PB realised for the first or the second time; Continuation: PB realised for the third time or more times; Siding: the last PB was realised 2 years ago, at the moment there is no perspective to start again)

"extension" or "supplement" to existing events or investments financed by the municipality. In this sense, the nature and extent of participatory budgeting in the country are influenced by slightly different factors compared to Brazil, where the prevalent emphasis was on social investment, solving social issues, and infrastructure building (Bhatnagar et al., 2003; Goldfrank, 2007; Goldsmith, 1999; Jacobi, 1999; Wampler, 2012).

On the other hand, when participatory budgeting penetrated Europe, a change was witnessed compared to its original intention and method of implementation. In Germany, for example, participatory budgeting is associated with the aim for greater efficiency (Fölscher, 2007; Herzberg et al., 2014; Sintomer et al., 2010, 2012). In the Czech Republic, project orientation means the selection of suitable projects for implementation, especially in the sense of improving the quality of life for citizens. This is quite like developments in Canada and the US (Hagelskamp et al., 2016) where project orientation in PBs prevails. For this reason, the factors influencing the participatory budgeting process are the following: the amount of the participatory budget, the defined rules for participatory budgeting including participation criteria for proposers and voters, the voting method, the project selection procedure, and the realisation of approved projects, which are the focus of this chapter.

So far, there are only a few studies on the effects of PB in Central and Eastern Europe. PB is often considered as a pioneering instrument to enhance good governance. Based on the results of a study by Kukučková and Bakoš (2019) it is not possible to confirm its impact on higher voter turnout in municipal elections conclusively without deeper qualitative analysis in every single municipality. Džinić (2018) postulates that the significance of the participation of the local population in managing public finances through PB depends on the degree of fiscal decentralisation and whether the amount of the budget reserved for PB projects represents a substantial share of public finance. Therefore, it is questionable whether the PB expenses are high enough to motivate the Czech citizens to participate (Kukučková & Bakoš, 2019). This is in line with Zepic et al. (2017) who describe a relatively small PB budget as one of the possible reasons why inhabitants decline to participate in the PB process. However, according to Gondášová and Svidroňová (2016), when citizens play a crucial role in the realisation of projects and in the co-creation of PB processes, their civic involvement increases. From this perspective, the Czech model of PB is quite close to co-creation as the realisation is done by the municipality itself.

Our research shows that PB spread among Czech municipalities in a short time. While the general pattern is quite similar across the municipalities, there is a huge experimentation regarding details on who can participate, how to vote, and especially how to utilise ICT for the various phases of the PB process and for communication in general. Many municipalities have promoted networking of active citizens and civil society organisations and many creative or original proposals got a chance to be realised. From the voting systems point of view, the experimentation with the D21 voting can be of both research and practical interest.

The PB process is usually framed either as public budgeting or as citizens' participation and the evaluation focuses on the impacts thereof. Unfortunately, such impacts are not very impressive in the case of Czech municipalities. PB takes place outside of the standard budget process and only small resources are allocated through this process. Participation in PB is lower than participation in the general election and the representativeness of PB remains questionable.

Nonetheless and despite the varying professional background of the authors of this chapter, from a perspective of municipal communication and marketing, we are impressed by the impact of PB thereon, that is both the acknowledgement of their relevance and the practical implementation using professionals in that field, experimenting with social media and others. Definitely, this impact is worthy of continuation and of continued investigation.

Participatory budgeting in the Czech Republic emerged in times of economic growth. The impending economic slowdown and likely long-term time of resource scarcity will show whether PB was a profligate new fashion or an efficient tool of resource allocation.

REFERENCES

Agora Central Europe. (2015). *Výroční zpráva 2015.* http://agorace.cz/wp-content/uploads/2019/05/Vyrocni_zprava_2015.pdf

Allegretti, G. (2014). Paying attention to the participants' perceptions in order to trigger a virtuous circle. In N. Dias (Ed.), *Hope for democracy: 25 years of participatory budgeting worldwide* (pp. 495). In Loco Association. https://www.buergerhaushalt.org/sites/default/files/downloads/Studie_Hope_for_democracy_-_25_years_of_participatory_budgeting_worldwide.pdf

Alves, M. L., & Allegretti, G. (2012). (In) stability, a key element to understand participatory budgeting: Discussing Portuguese cases | Estudo Geral. *Journal of Public Deliberation, 8*(2), 1–19. https://estudogeral.sib.uc.pt/handle/10316/41025

Baiocchi, G., & Ganuza, E. (2014). Participatory budgeting as if emancipation mattered. *Politics & Society, 42*(1), 29–50. https://doi.org/10.1177/0032329213512978

Bhatnagar, D., Rathore, A., Moreno Torres, M., & Kanungo, P. (2003). Participatory budgeting in Brazil. In *Worldbank Working Paper No. 51418. Empowerment case studies.* World Bank. http://documents.worldbank.org/curated/en/2003/01/11297674/participatory-budgeting-brazil

Czech Pirate Party. (2020). *Participativní rozpočet.* https://wiki.pirati.cz/fo/rozpocty/participativni/start

Džinić, J. (2018). Participatory budgeting in Croatia: A way to improve quality of local governance? In J. Nemec, V. Potier, & M. S. de Vries (Eds.), *Alternative service delivery* (pp. 73–81). IASIA/IIAS.

Ermert, J., Pützer, H., Ruesch, M., & Zebralog GmbH & Co KG. (2015). *8. Statusbericht des Portals Buergerhaushalt.org Juni 2015.* Bundeszentrale für politische Bildung. http://www.buergerhaushalt.org/sites/default/files/downloads/Statusbericht_2015_Stand_24052015_aktualisierteVersion.pdf

Exner, V. (2018, April 16). *Participativní rozpočet—něco končí, něco začíná.* Alternativa Zdola. http://alternativazdola.cz/vaclav-exner-participativni-rozpocet-neco-konci-neco-zacina/

Fölscher, A. (2007). Participatory budgeting in Central and Eastern Europe. In *Participatory budgeting, public sector governance and accountability series* (pp. 127–156). World Bank.

Font, J., Smith, G., Galais, C., & Alarcon, P. (2018). Cherry-picking participation: Explaining the fate of proposals from participatory processes. *European Journal of Political Research, 57*(3), 615–636. https://doi.org/10.1111/1475-6765.12248

Goldfrank, B. (2007). Lessons from Latin American experience in participatory budgeting. *Participatory Budgeting, 143*(March), 91–126.

Goldsmith, W. W. (1999). *Participatory budgeting in Porto Alegre, Brazil.* Planners Network. http://www.plannersnetwork.org/2000/03/participatory-budgeting-in-porto-alegre-brazil/

Gondášová, L., & Svidroňová, M. M. (2016). Participatory budgeting as an innovation in local public services delivery: The Slovak case. In D. Špalková & L. Matějová (Eds.), *Current trends in public sector research: Proceedings of the 20th international conference* (pp. 248–256). Masarykova univerzita.

Hagelskamp, C., Rinehart, C., Silliman, R., & Schleifer, D. (2016). Public spending, by the people: Participatory budgeting in the United States and Canada in 2014–2015. *Public Agenda.* https://www.publicagenda.org/reports/public-spending-by-the-people-participatory-budgeting-in-the-united-states-and-canada-in-2014-15/

Herzberg, C., Sintomer, Y., Allegretti, G., Röecke, A., & Alves, M. (2014). *Bürgerhaushalte weltweit. Aktualisierte Studie. Dialog Global. Heft 25.* Engagement Global gGmbH.

Jacobi, P. (1999). *Challenging traditional participation in Brazil—the goals of participatory budgeting.* Woodrow Wilson International Center for Scholars.

Janeček, K. (2016). *Democracy 2.1.* https://uploads.ssl.webflow.com/5a61da42 ae3f8f00019b46bd/5a893542d9716c0001a4a80d_d21.pdf

Klihavcová, M. (2019). *Participativní rozpočty v obcích.*

Kukučková, S., & Bakoš, E. (2019). Does participatory budgeting bolster voter turnout in elections? The case of the Czech Republic. *NISPAcee Journal of Public Administration and Policy, 12*(2), 109–129. https://ideas.repec.org/a/vrs/njopap/v12y2019i2p109-129n5.html

Ruesch, M., & Ermert, J. (2014). *7. Statusbericht des Portals Buergerhaushalt.org. Juni 2014.* Bundeszentrale für Politische Bildung.

Sedmihradská, L. (2016). *Rozpočtový proces obcí.* Wolters Kluwer. https://obchod.wolterskluwer.cz/cz/rozpoctovy-proces-obci.p2862.html

Sedmihradská, L. (2019). Budget transparency innovation in the Czech local government. *Central European Journal of Public Policy, 13*(1), 23–32. https://ideas.repec.org/a/vrs/cejopp/v13y2019i1p23-32n2.html

Sintomer, Y., Herzberg, C., & Allegretti, G. (2010). *Learning from the South: Participatory budgeting worldwide—an invitation to global cooperation.* Global Civic Engagement.

Sintomer, Y., Herzberg, C., & Röcke, A. (2008). Participatory budgeting in Europe: Potentials and challenges. *International Journal of Urban and Regional Research, 32*(1), 164–178. https://doi.org/10.1111/j.1468-2427.2008.00777.x

Sintomer, Y., Herzberg, C., Röcke, A., & Allegretti, G. (2012). Transnational models of citizen participation: The case of participatory budgeting. *Journal of Deliberative Democracy, 8*(2), 9. https://doi.org/10.16997/jdd.141

Smith, G. (2009). Democratic innovations: Designing institutions for citizen participation. In *Democratic innovations: Designing institutions for citizen participation.* Cambridge University Press. https://doi.org/10.1017/CBO9780511609848

Stewart, L. M., Miller, S. A., Hildreth, R. W., & Wright-Phillips, M. v. (2014). Participatory budgeting in the United States: A preliminary analysis of Chicago's 49th ward experiment. *New Political Science, 36*(2), 193–218. https://doi.org/10.1080/07393148.2014.894695

Wampler, B. (2007). A guide to participatory budgeting. In A. Shah (Ed.), *Participatory budgeting* (pp. 21–54). World Bank Publications.

Wampler, B. (2012). Participatory budgeting: Core principles and key impacts. *Journal of Deliberative Democracy, 8*(2), 1–13. https://doi.org/10.16997/jdd.138

Zepic, R., Dapp, M., & Krcmar, H. (2017). E-partizipation und keiner macht mit E-participation without participants. *HMD Praxis Der Wirtschaftsinformatik, 54*(4), 488–501. https://doi.org/10.1365/s40702-017-0328-z

CHAPTER 8

The Beginning of a Beautiful Friendship? Participatory Budgeting in Hungary

Péter Klotz

8.1 Introduction

The theory and practice of participatory budgeting can be traced back some three decades. Although different models and practices of participatory budgeting have developed over the years in relation to the theory of good governance, one of its main goals is to involve citizens in the decision-making process on the use of public funds and thereby strengthen trust in public bodies. Consequently, participatory budgeting can be defined as "*a mechanism or process through which people make decisions on the destination of all or a portion of the public resources available, or are otherwise associated with the* decision-making *process*" (Cabannes, 2019, p. 1).

Tanaka (2007) summarises the self-reinforcing benefits of public engagement as overall improvements consistent with good government and stresses especially that engaged citizens feel empowered because they

P. Klotz (✉)
University of Public Service, Budapest, Hungary
e-mail: klotz.peter@uni-nke.hu

© The Author(s), under exclusive license to Springer Nature Switzerland AG 2022
M. S. De Vries et al. (eds.), *International Trends in Participatory Budgeting*, Governance and Public Management,
https://doi.org/10.1007/978-3-030-79930-4_8

149

have more input into the establishment of priorities and feel that they have a stake in outcomes; that citizens feel that government works for them and as a result, they place greater trust in government and public officials; that the interests of under-represented and vulnerable groups (including the poor, women, and children) can be better protected, and there is greater equity in the allocation of public resources; that the government can exhibit greater transparency, making it more accountable to citizens; that the government can be more open, allowing expanded access to information and that the opportunities for waste, fraud, and abuse decrease as accountability improves and public awareness and scrutiny increases.

Participatory budgeting also creates a climate for the development and pursuit of good fiscal policy, because citizens' access to information and participation in the public debate leads to a more accurate understanding of public finances, particularly basic questions like where the money comes from and where it goes; because voters confront fiscal realities and acknowledge the need to make trade-offs; because citizens become aware of issues related to intra- and inter-generational equity and can cultivate a stronger sense of stewardship and because public thinking becomes more realistic, providing expanded opportunities for negotiation, compromise, and consensus.

Among these aspects, in the case of Hungary, as this chapter will show, the transparency of budgetary resources and the active involvement of citizens in decision-making processes are of particular importance.

8.2   Trends of Participatory Budgeting in Hungary

The practice of participatory budgeting in Hungary can be traced back only a few years. The primary reason for this is political and stems from the different perceptions of the role of the governing party and the opposition parties on self-government and the involvement of citizens in public decisions. Following the 2006 elections, the vast majority of county and local governments came under the control of the current governing party and, although good practices on participatory budgeting were available, their practical implementation did not begin.

Following the change of government in 2010, a new law was adopted on local governments. The Act CLXXXIX of 2011 on the local governments of Hungary significantly reduced the tasks and powers of local governments, increased state control over them (especially by restricting borrowing), and at the same time consolidated their economic operations by taking over their debts.

In 2011, Hungary adopted a new regulation on public finances with the aim of modernising the rules of budget planning and management. However, the law coming into force does not contain provisions on whether the solutions developed by the literature and practice on participatory budgeting can be applied when planning the budget of the state, county governments, or local governments.

In the past decade, political and professional debates on the budget are not primarily about the forms and ways of creating a participatory budget, but about the use of budgetary resources and the enforcement of the principles of budget transparency. In the 2019 Open Budget Survey (OBS), Hungary scored 45 out of 100 in the area of budget transparency, while the OECD member countries averaged 68 points (International Budget Partnership, 2019, p. 2). The OBS also assesses the formal opportunities offered to the public for meaningful partitioning in the various stages of the budget process. It examines the practices of the central government's executive, the legislature, and the supreme audit institution using 18 equally weighted indicators. In the Public Participation sub-index, Hungary scored only 4 points, while the OECD average is 23 points (International Budget Partnership, 2019, p. 6). In order to strengthen public participation in the budget process, the report recommended among others to "*expand mechanisms during budget formulation that engage any civil society organisation or member of the public who wishes to participate*" (International Budget Partnership, 2019, p. 6).

According to the international literature, the use of a participatory budget is mostly a practice among local governments (Cabannes, 2020; Goldfrank, 2007; Sintomer et al., 2008). However, based on the above, it is not surprising that few of Hungary's 3155 municipalities have practical experience in applying participatory budgeting. This approach changed in the 2019 municipal election campaign, during which the active involvement of voters in municipal decision-making became an important message for opposition parties. This vision of a new, transparent, participatory self-government, which considers voters as partners and is open to their activities and expressed needs, has been well received in many places, most notably in county capitals and districts of the capital. As a result, for the first time in Hungary, local decision-makers were elected en masse with such a programme (Merényi, 2020, p. 5).

This electoral success was also accompanied by the possibility of the election of one deputy mayor and rapporteurs responsible for public participation. The following is the practice of planning and implementing a participatory budgeting. It is important to note that in Hungary we cannot talk about participatory budgeting, neither in terms of the central budget nor in terms of county self-governments, so the presentation of cases is limited to the presentation of local self-governments, including local governments in Budapest.

This study follows the presentation and comparison of participatory budgeting in the most experienced local governments, Kispest (District XIX of Budapest), Budafok-Tétény (District XXII of Budapest), and Budapest City. Kispest is the District XIX of Budapest with a garden city character in the south-eastern part of the capital, with a population of about 60,000. Budafok-Tétény is Budapest's dynamically developing District XXII in the south-western part of the capital with a population of about 55,000, while Budapest has 23 districts, with a population of 1.75 million (excluding the population of the agglomeration). The districts of Budapest have their self-government, and within the district there are quarters. Both the city and the districts are local governments, not subordinated to one another, each having specific duties and powers, specified by law. Both are eligible to exercise the basic rights of local governments.

8.3   Participatory Budgeting in Practice

8.3.1   The Effects of International Trends

The impact of international examples can be seen in the design of participatory budgets, sometimes explicitly. The adaptation of these international good practices facilitated the spread of participatory budgeting in Hungary. Among the practical manuals, the work of Miklós M. Merényi can be highlighted, which was published with the support of the Friedrich Ebert Stiftung (Merényi, 2020).

In Kispest, the beginnings of participatory budgeting go back to 2016, when the elected mayor announced it in his mayoral programme as 'Community Budget 2017'. This initiative was not only the first in Kispest, but it was a pioneer in the whole of Hungary. There is no specific information on the model in which participatory budgeting was introduced in the district, but it was presumably also inspired by international good practices.

In Budafok-Tétény, the district's participatory budgeting was launched immediately after the municipal elections, in October 2019, to strengthen participation in important joint decisions. The planning process is supported by a dedicated website, which also presents good practice in Boston for participatory budgeting. As can be seen from the examples presented, the municipal elections held in the autumn of 2019 were crucial for the application of participatory budgeting. As a result, the parties that came to power began to implement a new model of self-government based on transparent operation, which sees voters as partners. It was a spectacular and symbolic step for the first time that the General Assembly of Budapest elected a Deputy Mayor for Smart City and Participation. When the mayor took office, he also appointed a chief adviser responsible for participation, the founder of a website receiving public interest announcements.

The city presented good international examples of the participants' budget (Bologna, New York, Cascais, Madrid) together with their specifics on the website created for this purpose. Due to the cultural similarities, Budapest chose the Paris participatory budgeting as a model for its own participatory budgeting. It was of significant help that the software used to support the process was made available to anyone free of charge by the Paris municipality. Concerning international trends and good practices, it can be stated that international good practices not only had an inspiring effect on the participatory budgeting initiatives in Hungary but in the case of Budapest, the practical implementation of the participatory budgeting was significantly advanced by adopting the voting software.

8.3.2 The Framework of Participatory Budgeting

In the planning and implementation of participatory budgets, it is crucial which percentage of the budget is made by decision-makers 'free to use' for citizens, and the extent to which citizens are mobilised during preparation and decision-making.

In Kispest, within the framework of the first participatory budgeting in 2017, the local government provided HUF 4 million (approximately €13,000) per city quarter for the winning projects, a total of HUF 16 million (approximately €52,000).

The successful community budget programme has continued in recent years. The budget planned for the projects increased significantly to a total of HUF 42 million (€131,000), while the willingness of citizens to participate is also significant: the community budget for 2019 received 2142 votes (Gajda, 2019, p. 1). While in the initial period the amount allocated for the implementation of participatory budgeting was a fraction of the budget, even the significantly increased budget for 2019 is only 0.3 per cent of the annual budget of the municipality.

In Budafok-Tétény, in the first year, HUF 100 million (approximately €312,500), a total of HUF 300 million (approximately €937,500), was available for the implementation of the plans for the three quarters of the district. That is about 1.5 per cent of the annual budget. Encouraged by the success of the first year, the municipality of Budafok-Tétény continued the project for planning participatory budgeting in 2020. In the course of this, not only the residents of the district can decide on the use of another HUF 100 million (approximately €312,500) per quarter, but also on the fate of the remaining HUF 48 million (approximately €150,000) from the previous year's participatory budgeting. Thus, the total sum to decide is amounting to more than €1 million.

Proposals related to participatory budgeting are subject to registration, and participation in the process is only available to the residents of the district. In the first year, a total of 2500 people registered on the website and 360 project proposals were received (Karsay, 2020). In the first year, the residents of the district cast a total of 10,400 votes on the developed project proposals. According to the rules, everyone had five votes. Three votes could be cast for the projects of the quarter where they live, and they were free to have two more votes, so they could vote for the project of their own quarter or the project of another quarter. After the vote is over, the ideas are realised from the project with the most votes down to the project with the fewest votes until the available budget is exhausted. In 2020, 2080 people took part in the voting based on the votes cast.

In the city, the development of the organisational structure presented above greatly facilitated the implementation of the ideas for the creation of participatory budgeting. The city has allocated HUF 1 billion (approximately €2.8 million) to the 2020 budget. This amount is about 0.25 per cent of the city's planned expenditures for 2020. Participatory budgeting started on 1 October 2020 and first requested the submission of ideas for implementation in the city in the following categories:

- Whole Budapest: ideas for the whole City (but at least 3 districts). In this category, it will be possible to implement 2 major ideas, each with a maximum budget of HUF 250 million (approximately €700,000).

- Green Budapest: ideas to promote the development of green spaces in the capital and adaptation to climate change. In this category, the cost of a project may not exceed HUF 50 million (approximately €140,000), there is no lower limit. The total amount is HUF 250 million (approximately €700,000).
- Caring Budapest: proposals promoting social solidarity or community development. The upper limit of a project is HUF 50 million (approximately €140,000), there is no lower limit, and the total amount allocated to the category is HUF 250 million (approximately €700,000) (Budapest Részvételi Költségvetés, 2020b).

A total of 687 ideas were received during the three months open for proposals. Of these, 261 are in the Whole Budapest category, 282 in the Green Budapest category, and 144 in the Caring Budapest category. Based on the data on the website, most of the proposals, a total of 42, are listed in District III and the fewest proposals, only one, came from Kispest (District XIX) (Budapest Részvételi Költségvetés, 2020a).

Regarding the financial background of participatory budgeting, it can be stated that they concern only a small part of the municipal budgets and do not exceed 1.5 per cent of the budget. One possible reason for this is that local governments have few budgetary resources for development. This is largely due to EU funding, which is managed in most cases by the government. The government has a state secretary responsible for the development of Budapest and the metropolitan agglomeration since 2018, and since February 2020 the Budapest Development Centre has been managing the city and its agglomeration transport investments.

As for the participation of the population in decision-making, it can be said that it is difficult to formulate trends based on the last few years, but the initial results are encouraging based on the submitted proposals, the proportion of registered users, and the number of votes cast. The successful operation is also indicated by the fact that the affected local governments plan to continue participatory budgeting and further increase the available resources.

8.3.3 The Process of Participatory Budgeting

Of particular importance for the implementation of the participatory budget is the procedure by which citizens can decide on the use of available resources. From this point of view, the process can be divided into two major stages, proposing and voting.

In Kispest, citizens were able to submit their development proposals to the local government. There is no formalised framework for this, so the local government also has access to proposals that are minor repairs and do not require substantial development resources.

These proposals have been examined and evaluated by municipal officials for feasibility. Based on the evaluation, the following categories were established:

- the proposal is automatically planned by the local government among its tasks for the following year;
- the proposal was considered unfeasible by the local government office for some reason (legal, technical, material, etc.);
- is not a municipal competence, but is forwarded to the competent organisation; and
- proposal to be put to the vote.

As can be seen, the automation built into the planning of the community budget makes it possible for the municipality to become aware of minor development needs (such as tree maintenance, sidewalk renovation, the removal of abandoned cars) that make citizens' everyday lives simpler and more comfortable. This significantly strengthens the relationship of trust between the population and the municipality and encourages social participation in public affairs. Typically, about 60 per cent of the proposals received from citizens fell into the category of minor repairs that could be resolved within their competence (Gajda, 2017).

In the first year of the programme, more than 180 proposals were received, from which citizens could choose which of the four quarters the municipality would implement next year. The invitation to vote and the ballot paper were published as an appendix to the local newspaper and were also available online (Gajda, 2017, p. 1). Community developments are also supported by an interactive urban development map available on the city's website, on which developments under the community budget are indicated by coloured diagrams.

In Budafok-Tétény, citizens must register on the website created before submitting their proposals. Proposals shared on the website should include the title of the idea, the exact location of the implementation, a short description, and, if possible, a photo of the site or other information that will increase the popularity of the project to be implemented. For the submitted ideas, the municipality prepares a feasibility plan, which also includes the project budget. The proposals, which do not fall within the competence of the municipality, are forwarded to the competent authority, and a detailed justification is given for the impracticable ideas.

On the website of the participatory budget, the local government regularly reports on the status of the projects, so that those interested can monitor the implementation of the projects. The process of the participatory budget was supported by the local government with a communication campaign; a high-quality video was made about the implementation and the winning proposals (Budafok-Tétény Önkormányzata, 2020).

As for the city, it should be emphasised that in preparation for participatory budgeting, the capital held several events during 2020, although the implementation of the planned events was significantly hampered by the coronavirus epidemic. These include the public information forum associated with board games, the joint brainstorming with the leaders of each district, or the online reception hours announced for planners to submit ideas. The ideas could be submitted on a separate website for the given three categories (Whole Budapest, Green Budapest, and Caring Budapest), followed by a legal, financial, and formal analysis of the ideas. The peculiarity of this process is that the examined ideas are submitted to a council of Budapest residents, who finalise the list of eligible ideas. It is planned that the ideas can be voted on for a month between March 1 and 31, 2021.

An important experience in the management of participatory budgeting is that the smaller local governments try to solve the minor repairs in their own competence, so participatory budgeting also provides a good opportunity to map and solve people's everyday problems and shortcomings. The city has neither the capacity nor the competence to solve such minor repairs, so it expects well-developed, larger budget development concepts, for which it also provides technical support with its own resources. Among the tools supporting the implementation of the process are the creation of one's own website and the communication support of the process in the local newspaper, on social portals, or by creating a video report. The website can also be highlighted in terms of ensuring the sustainability of the process as well as the monitoring of the implementation of the results.

8.4   RESULTS

Although only a few years have passed since the beginning of the application of participatory budgeting in Hungary, favourable results can already be reported. These results can be examined in terms of specific projects implemented based on citizens' decisions, as well as structurally in terms of the extent to which views on local government, civic participation, and the management of public funds have been shaped.

Analysing the concrete results, we can see that in Kispest, in the first year, in 2017, the local government renovated a 120-metre-long sidewalk, surrounded a playground with a fence, placed five new drinking fountains, and renovated a tennis court (Gajda, 2017, p. 1).

In Budafok-Tétény, only five projects selected with the support of the population can be reported so far. These include the modernisation of a playground, the construction of a track for runners and street workout track, the creation of the Danube garden cinema and community space playing classic Hungarian films, the creation of a family park, and a programme for catching, chipping, and the return of stray dogs.

The city is gathering ideas for implementation, but many of them, such as the network of public gardens, the revision of the public transport tariff system, or the renovation of public toilets, already seem to be forward-looking initiatives (Budapest Részvételi Költségvetés, 2020a).

In addition to these results, the presented initiatives also point to the weaknesses of the implementation of participatory budgets in Hungary. Although the community budget programme in Kispest has been operating successfully for many years, its disadvantage is that it restricts civic participation primarily to proposals and voting, and devotes less space to the elaboration and discussion of proposals. Its budget is limited (only 0.3 per cent of the municipality's annual budget) and it does not have a separate website, which makes it difficult to monitor the year-over-year process and related measures.

Summarising the experiences of the Budafok-Tétény participatory budget, we can state that the order of usable resources exceeds 1.5 per cent of the annual budget of the local government, which is an outstanding amount in Hungary. The implementation of the project and the elaboration of the project proposals are much more complex than in the case of Kispest. The communication and the monitoring of the implementation are facilitated with a dedicated website, which also presents international good practices. The design of the voting process allowed residents to weigh their votes and also ensured that there was wider social support for the planned projects. It can be considered a practical and fair solution that several projects can be implemented in a quarter, up to the available budget. This can also be seen from the fact that the most popular project, the budget for catching and chipping stray dogs, was only HUF 1 million (€3125), barely 1 per cent of the available budget.

Analysing participatory budgeting in the city, we can state that the city provided an order of magnitude more resources for the participatory budgeting project than the districts presented. However, if we look at the share of this amount within the budget, we find that it represents only 0.25 per cent of the total budget expenditures, significantly lagging behind international good practices and district indicators.

It can be seen that the city placed great emphasis on the preparation of participatory budgeting tasks by studying and implementing international examples, as well as by providing information and ideas for citizens. The establishment of a participatory organisational structure and the appointment of a Deputy Mayor for a Smart City and Participation were of great help in this. At the same time, careful preparation also brought about a slowdown in the project, which could only start one year after the municipal elections.

Examining the attitude-shaping effect of participatory budgeting in Hungary, we can say that the legal-regulatory environment does not support the application of participatory budgets. This area appears as a white spot in the regulation, so there are no laws, guidelines, or information on its implementation. Consequently, there are no guarantees or mandatory elements for the application of participatory budgeting. In recent years, the transparency of budgetary processes in Hungary has significantly deteriorated and public participation in matters concerning the use of budgetary resources is low in international comparison (International Budget Partnership, 2019), and we do not encounter any efforts to offset this at the government or county level. The application of participatory budgeting is thus typical in Budapest City and the districts of Budapest under opposition control.

8.5   CONCLUSION

We can agree with Krenjova and Raudla (2013) that the New-Weberian State argues for the supplementation of representative democracy by devices for consultation and that participation is very important for CEE countries. Participatory budgeting charges citizens with new resonances of 'co-producers' of public services and in general 'co-deciders' in political decisions which in turn fits with the 'post-post-NMP' rhetoric (Pollitt & Bouckaert, 2004; Herzberg, 2011).

Undoubtedly, as Fölscher (2007) argues, local governments in the Central and Eastern European region have had to struggle to overcome the inherited weaknesses of local-level decision-making structures. At the same time, it can be seen in Hungary that the application of participatory budgeting is not primarily influenced by post-communist civic or local government attitudes, but by governmental and opposition narratives about the role and tasks of local governments. While the ruling party, and the local governments under its control, seek to centralise power and narrow the roles and powers of local governments, opposition-led local governments are taking significant steps to make local government budgets transparent and to involve citizens in decision-making.

This trend is well reflected in the treatment of the COVID-19 pandemic. The pandemic has increased the burden on municipalities that have daily contact with citizens, while closures and the economic downturn have also eroded their revenues. Based on the government's decision, parking became free during the pandemic, so local governments lost a significant part of their own revenue. In the case of downtown of local governments in Budapest, this could be 5–10 per cent of their revenues (Bucsky, 2020). According to the calculations of the Települési Önkormányzatok Országos Szövetsége (National Association of Local Governments), this means a deficit of about HUF 150 billion (about €417 million) for local governments, and about 70 per cent of this will be missing from the budgets of larger cities (TÖOSZ, 2020). It is estimated that with this decision, cities will lose more than one-eighth of their revenues and the city about 18 per cent (Bucsky, 2020).

This situation affects not only the performance of local government tasks but also the planning and implementation of participatory budgeting, which was intended to recover after the 2019 local government elections. Due to the loss of revenues connected to the COVID-19 pandemic, Kispest suspended the implementation of the projects voted for 2020 already in September 2020 (Gajda, 2020). At the same time, it is an encouraging sign that the participatory budgeting planning processes have not been stopped by any local government, and work is still underway to seek the opinion of citizens and involve them in decisions, laying the foundations for a new local government operating model.

REFERENCES

Act CLXXXIX on the local governments of Hungary. (2011). https://net.jogtar.
hu/jogszabaly?docid=a1100189.tv

Bucsky, P. (2020, December 22). *Teljesen kiszolgáltatottá teszi az ellenzéki városo-
kat Orbán Viktor bejelentése.* https://g7.hu/kozelet/20201222/
teljesen-kiszolgaltatotta-teszi-az-ellenzeki-varosokat-orban-viktor-bejelentese/

Budafok-Tétény Önkormányzata. (2020, May 5). *Közösségi fejlesztések, közös döntés
alapján.* https://budafokteteny.hu/hir/kozossegi-fejlesztesek-kozos-dontes-
alapjan

Budapest Részvételi Költségvetés. (2020a). *Beküldött ötletek.* https://otlet.buda-
pest.hu/pb/jsp/site/Portal.jsp?page=search-solr&conf=proposals_
list&query=&fq=&fq=

Budapest Részvételi Költségvetés. (2020b). *Indul Budapest részvételi költségve-
tése—budapestiek ötletei alapján költ el 1 milliárd forintot a Fővárosi
Önkormányzat.* https://otlet.budapest.hu/pb/jsp/site/Portal.jsp?document_
-id=1&portlet_id=159

Cabannes, Y. (2019). The contribution of participatory budgeting to the achievement of the Sustainable Development Goals: Lessons for policy in
Commonwealth countries. *Commonwealth Journal of Local Governance,
21*(21), 6707. https://doi.org/10.5130/cjlg.v0i21.6707

Cabannes, Y. (2020). *Another city is possible with participatory budgeting.* University
of Chicago Press. https://books.google.cz/books/about/Another_City_Is_
Possible_with_Participat.html?id=EmDOtgEACAAJ&source=kp_book_
description&redir_esc=y

Fölscher, A. (2007). Participatory budgeting in Central and Eastern Europe. In
A. Shah (Ed.), *Participatory budgeting* (Public Sector Governance and
Accountability Series) (pp. 127–156). World Bank.

Gajda, P. (2017). *Kispesti Közösségi Költségvetés 2017.* https://uj.kispest.hu/
felhivasok/5789-kispesti-kozossegi-koltsegvetes-20171025

Gajda, P. (2019). Beszámoló a Kispesti Közösségi Költségvetés 2019 Programról,
javaslatok a 2020-as közösségi költségvetésre. *Kispest, 25*(9). https://uj.kispest.
hu/images/kepek/kiadvany/2019/kispest_ujsag2019/kispest_ujsag_
201911.pdf

Gajda, P. (2020). *Beszámoló a Kispesti Közösségi Költségvetés 2020 Programról,
javaslatok a 2021-es közösségi költségvetésre.* https://uj.kispest.hu/felhivasok/
9649-beszamolo-a-kispesti-kozossegi-koltsegvetes-2020programrol-
javaslatok-a-2021-as-kozossegi-koltsegvetesre

Goldfrank, B. (2007). Lessons from Latin American experience in participatory
budgeting. *Participatory Budgeting, 143*(Mar.), 91–126.

Herzberg, C. (2011). Democratic innovation or symbolic participation? A case
study of participatory budgeting in Germany. 6th ECPR General Conference,

Panel 25, "Democratic Innovations in Europe: A Comparative Perspective", 25–27 August 2011, Reykjavik, Iceland. https://ecpr.eu/Events/Event/PaperDetails/8236

International Budget Partnership. (2019). *Open Budget Survey—Hungary.* https://www.internationalbudget.org/sites/default/files/country-surveys-pdfs/2019/open-budget-survey-hungary-2019-en.pdf

Karsay, F. (2020). *Budafok-Tétény/Közösségre kapcsolva.* https://kozossegrekapcsolva22.hu/kuldetesunk/

Krenjova, J., & Raudla, R. (2013). Participatory budgeting at the local level: Challenges and opportunities for new democracies. *Halduskultuur, 14*(1), 18–46. http://halduskultuur.eu/journal/index.php/HKAC/artile/view/78

Merényi, M. (2020). *A részvételi költségvetés esélyei a magyar önkormányzatokban.* K-Monitor. https://www.fes-budapest.org/fileadmin/user_upload/dokumente/pdf-dateien/A_reszveteli_koltsegvetes_eselyei_20200210.pdf

Pollitt, C., & Bouckaert, G. (2004). *Public management reform: A comparative analysis* (2nd ed.). Oxford University Press. https://books.google.cz/books/about/Public_Management_Reform.html?id=rei8DGQQoooC&redir_esc=y

Sintomer, Y., Herzberg, C., & Röcke, A. (2008). Participatory budgeting in Europe: Potentials and challenges. *International Journal of Urban and Regional Research, 32*(1), 164–178. https://doi.org/10.1111/j.1468-2427.2008.00777.x

Tanaka, S. (2007). Engaging the public in national budgeting: A non-governmental perspective. *OECD Journal on Budgeting, 7*(2), 139–177. https://doi.org/10.1787/budget-v7-art12-en

Települési Önkormányzatok Országos Szövetsége (TÖOSZ). (2020, December 21). *150 milliárdos kiesést okoz az iparűzési adó megfelezése.* http://töosz.hu/news/656/73/150-milliardos-kiesest-okoz-az-iparuzesi-ado-megfelezese/

CHAPTER 9

Participatory Budgeting in Poland

Artur Roland Kozłowski and Arnold Bernaciak

9.1 Introduction

The systemic and economic transformation in 1989 in Poland did not result in a permanent, deep social change that would lead to developing the idea of a civil society based on Western patterns. Social activities were focused on everyday affairs, such as work, business or the struggle with reality. Higher social needs were of secondary importance. Despite some temporary upheavals, the involvement of the Poles in social life after three decades since abandoning the previous system, often erroneously referred to as a communist system, has to be assessed as low (Kozłowski, 2019; Suteu, 2019). Some scholars emphasise the fact that this kind of change is the most difficult one and takes the longest time: first of all, it requires a change in human awareness and character, namely focusing on

A. R. Kozłowski (✉)
Law and Security Science Institute, WSB University in Gdańsk, Gdańsk, Poland
e-mail: akozlowski@wsb.gda.pl

A. Bernaciak
Institute of Economics and Finance, WSB University in Poznań, Poznań, Poland
e-mail: arnold.bernaciak@wsb.poznan.pl

cooperation, participation and involvement and not on negation, distance and criticism; it also requires respect for the law and new institutions and civil culture. Some scholars, self-government activists and observers of the Polish social life have accepted the idea of participatory budgeting (PB) with interest and hope, seeing it as a form which can directly affect citizens' involvement in social life.

The first participatory budget (PB) in Poland was implemented in Sopot in 2011. Located in the centre of the Tri-city metropolis (Gdańsk, Sopot, Gdynia), this small city (33,000 inhabitants) is characterised by a high level of citizen affluence, when seen from the economic conditions in Poland, and a high level of their cultural, social and professional activities. The progressive uniqueness of the urban fabric of Sopot comes as a factor which fosters searching for innovative solutions in numerous fields of life. However, it would not have found its expression in the implementation of participatory budgeting in the city if the proper conditions of the local policy had not been provided (Kempa & Kozłowski, 2020, p. 67). For the first time since the introduction of local self-government in Poland, the city found itself in a political impasse: the mayor and the majority of the City Council took opposite positions. Both local political forces were looking for new ideas to win support and to tip the balance in their own favour during the next elections. Hence, the implementation of participatory budgeting resulted from the process of political rivalry; however, it was also intended to include the local community into the co-management of the city.

The project in Sopot ended in success and it became an impulse for other cities in Poland to follow this model. At the central level, the government decided to regulate this area of territorial self-government unit management by issuing relevant legislative acts (Journal of Laws 2018 item 130, n.d.). Since 1 January 2019, participatory budget has been a statutory obligation for municipalities with county rights.

9.2   Participatory Budgeting Models and Experience

The source of political conditions for implementing PB does not necessarily determine its future role in a particular country. However, the history of the first project implemented in Porto Alegre should be remembered, as it underwent gradual erosion because of some fundamental differences which divided the local political parties (Rodgers, 2010, p. 25). Similarly, a fundamental polarisation can be observed at all the levels of the Polish political scene. This fact negatively affects administrative and legislative support for PB, especially since 2015, when the right-wing parties took control of the country under the leadership of PIS (Law and Justice). Despite some similarities, some clearly distinguished differences can be observed in the PB origin.

In numerous places around the world where PB has been implemented it has been aimed at meeting the need to improve democracy, to reduce corruption and clientelism and to improve living conditions for the most deprived. The role of civil emancipation has been emphasised and the hope to open a path to a wider social change has been expressed (Célérier & Cuenca Botey, 2015, pp. 759–760). The traces of social pedagogy and constructive influence of PB or rather of some hope for such influence can be found in numerous research studies in terms of civil perception (Bryer, 2011, 2014), pedagogy of reasoning (Rose, 1991), and strengthening of social solidarity at the local level (Lederman, 2015, p. 259). Considering the Polish conditions, it can be found in reference to education of citizens, with the indication of the authority of democratisation function (Naumiuk & Bron Jr., 2017, p. 42). The common feature of this stream is the hope to strengthen democracy through the adaptation of PB for the administration practice at the local level.

During the implementation of PB to the international practice, the key intentions include: bringing governing parties and society closer to each other; empowerment of citizens based on the right to manage their own (public) funds; transparency of the criteria and process of selecting projects for further implementation; and providing technocrats and citizens with joint supervision over project implementation (Bocatto & Perez-De-Toledo, 2019, p. 145). Although the PB implementation models in the world differ, PB implementation is presented in a similar way as it has the character of a cyclical process which includes the following stages: diagnosis, deliberation, collective decision-making, execution and monitoring. The differentiating factors are the levels of process of democratisation which are expressed by, among others, equal access to information and funds, the type and scope of social participation in the process, objectivity of project assessment and transparency.

Regardless of the procedural issues, a noticeable difference in the attitudes presented by the particular countries and, respectively, by units of territorial self-government towards PB, can be observed in the aims for which the funds have been allocated (Pinnington et al., 2009, p. 459). In this respect, the hierarchy of needs can be presented starting from the most basic ones which are related to infrastructure, such as road paving, constructing sewage systems, constructing health care centres, sports facilities and ending with meeting social-cultural needs. Between the above-mentioned areas and outside them, there are sublime fields which are characteristic of the societies whose basic needs have already been met. The fulfilment of such needs brings a new value to the civil relations.

9.3   THE SCOPE AND FORMS OF PB IMPLEMENTATION IN POLAND

In Poland, statistical data on participatory budgeting are not collected anywhere in any systemic way. All the information on the number and amounts of participatory budgets implemented at the territorial self-government units in Poland is taken from the partial scientific research and documentation provided by the particular self-governments. In this respect, a report provided by the Supreme Audit Office on the functioning of participatory budgeting in Poland comes as valuable material to study. The report presents the results of the audits carried out for participatory budgeting in Polish cities in the years 2016–2018 (Najwyższa Izba Kontroli, 2019, p. 10). The most recent list of units which implement participatory budgeting can be found in the report published by the Urban Policy Observatory at the Institute of Urban and Regional Development. It provides the data referring exclusively to cities in 2017 (urban and urban-rural municipalities).

As already mentioned, the first process of participatory budgeting was implemented in Poland in 2011 in Sopot, when the decisions about the budget for 2012 were made. In cooperation with the City Council, the mayor set up the participatory budget at the amount of PLN 7 million (€1,560,300), which was 2% of the city budget expenditures planned for 2012. There were over 500 projects submitted. The preliminary verification of the projects was done by the Participatory Budget Committee which was appointed by the Sopot City Council. There were eventually 22 suburban projects and 49 local projects (in 4 districts) submitted for voting; 2448 (7%) inhabitants participated in the voting. The voters were asked to select 5 projects from the suburban list and 5 from the local list.

There were 36 projects selected for the implementation.[1] In the subsequent years, it was possible to observe some dynamic growth in the number of territorial self-government units which implemented participatory budgeting. In 2012, voting for participatory budgeting for the subsequent year was conducted by the authorities of 12 other cities. In 2013, there were 68 cities. The most recent list of cities where participatory budgeting has been implemented is presented by the authors of the Report on the Polish Cities and Public Participation. The data refer to the participatory budgets in 2017 (the processes of collecting applications and voting carried out in 2016). At that time, 322 cities were implementing participatory budgets—64 of them for the first time. It was almost 35% of all the Polish cities (urban and urban-rural municipalities) (Fig. 9.1) (Pistelok & Martela, 2019).

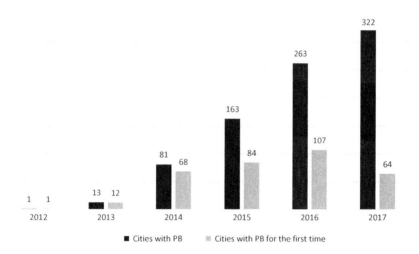

Fig. 9.1   Polish cities which implemented participatory budgeting in the years 2012–2017. (Source: Authors, based on Pistelok and Martela (2019))

---

[1] Resolution no. XV/178/2012 of the Sopot City Council of 3 January 2012 on adopting the report on the work undertaken by the Participatory Budgeting Committee; E. Stokłuska, A Description of an Example of Participatory Budgeting in Sopot. The Unit for Social Innovation and Research—Shipyard, pp. 7–9 https://partycypacjaobywatelska.pl/wp-ontent/uploads/2015/09/praktyka_budzet_obywatelski_sopot.pdf (dostęp:10.11.2020); Report on the implementation of the city budget in Sopot in 2012 https://bip.sopot.pl/a,15743,budzet-sopotu-2012.html (access: 12.11.2020).

At first, participatory budgeting was mainly implemented in large and medium-sized cities. In the subsequent years, participatory budgeting was also implemented by some smaller units. After several years of implementing participatory budgeting in cities, this instrument was also introduced to rural areas. As the research studies presented by Leśniewska-Napierała indicate, the first editions of participatory budgeting in rural and urban-rural areas took place in 2015. In 2017, the processes of participatory budgeting were implemented in 96 territorial self-government units (4.4%) located in rural areas (Leśniewska-Napierała, 2019, p. 81). Drawing on the experience gained by cities, other units of territorial self-government started to implement the processes of participatory budgeting too: county self-governments (at the local level) and provincial self-governments (at the regional level).

The analysis of participatory budgeting implemented in the years 2016–2018 provided by the Supreme Audit Office for 22 selected cities indicates that the local self-governments allocated from 0.2% to 1.5% of their expenditure to participatory budgeting. The highest share was recorded in Sopot, where in 2017 it was 1.5% and 1.4% in 2018. The lowest share among the analysed cities was recorded in Kraków: in each analysed year it was 0.2% (NIK, 2019, 37). In absolute terms, during the analysed period of time, the highest amount allocated to the projects implemented within the framework of participatory budgeting was recorded in 2018 in Warsaw, which was over PLN 61 million (€13.5 million). During the analysed period of time, PLN 40 million (€8.9 million) was allocated to participatory budgeting each year in Łódź; in Wrocław it was PLN 25 million (€5.6 million) and in Katowice it was PLN 20 million (€4.5 million) (Twojbudzet, 2020).

Pistelok and Martela present the average amounts of participatory budgets in Polish cities per capita. The highest average amount can be observed in large cities with over 100,000 inhabitants, including the provincial capital cities (€7.58 per capita). The lowest amount was recorded in Supraśl with about 15,000 inhabitants, where €35.91 per capita was allocated to the participatory budget (Table 9.1) (Pistelok & Martela, 2019, p. 82).

The analysis provided by the Supreme Audit Office also indicates a high differentiation in the interest displayed by the inhabitants. In 2017, the highest voter turnout was recorded in Kalisz (73%) and in 2016 in Pleszewo (71%). In 2016, the lowest voter turnout of 3% was recorded in Piotrków Trybunalski and in 2017 in Aleksandrów Łódzki (Najwyższa Izba Kontroli, 2019, p. 44).

Table 9.1   The amounts per capita allocated to participatory budgeting in Polish cities in 2017

City category	Average amount	Maximum amount	Minimum amount
Total	4.60	35.91	0.45
Provincial capital cities	7.58	16.28	3.12
Large cities (>100,000 inhabitants)	6.91	16.28	3.12
Medium-sized cities (50–100,000 inhabitants)	4.91	13.83	0.67
Medium-sized cities (20–50,000 inhabitants)	4.68	24.31	0.45
Small cities (20,000 inhabitants)	4.01	35.91	0.67

Source: Authors, based on Pistelok and Martela (2019)

While analysing the implementation of PB in Poland, it is difficult to broadly discuss a cooperation network between public administration and citizens. As scientists suggest, it is difficult because of the law or the sense of primacy (not of partnership) presented by territorial/local self-government units (Filipiak, 2017). PB is often treated as a kind of social security valve and an instrument to eliminate the negative moods of voters (Filipiak & Dylewski, 2018, p. 15). The implementation of PB in Poland has got two current aims: (1) involving local communities in co-management of the city through joint decisions about how to spend some part of public funds (it is reflected in the voter turnout) and (2) promoting the authority which originally comes from political rivalry. The extreme form of the latter aim can be a travesty of a particular project, turning PB into an instrument used for political fighting.

In most territorial self-government units in Poland, the implementation of PB is based on the decision-making process which is provided by the local executive bodies or their appointed representatives. The implemented procedures are not of a permanent character but they are renewed within the framework of activities undertaken to work on the subsequent annual budget of a territorial self-government unit. Furthermore, the conditions and instruments applied by various territorial self-government units to implement PB procedures can be also highly significant. Some possible intentional exclusions of citizens from the decision-making process have been emphasised (Filipiak & Dylewski, 2018, p. 16).

During the implementation of participatory budgeting processes, the authorities of territorial self-government units have to face numerous obstacles, difficulties and ambiguities. Błaszak indicates 4 types of dilemmas related to participation budgeting in Poland: legal, economic, organisational and social (Błaszak, 2019, pp. 203–220). Legal dilemmas pertain to the following:

- the possibility for the authorities to make changes to the projects selected through the voting; the law states that these can only be minor changes, however, it is not clear what should be understood as minor;
- disparities among territorial self-government units in terms of the obligatory character of participatory budgeting implementation; this obligation refers only to one group of such units, namely to cities with county rights;
- lack of any legal basis for inhabitants to decide how funds will be spent; the only competent bodies in this field are executive and regulatory organs of self-government units;
- lack of legal procedures for submission and selection of projects.
- indicated by Błaszak, economic dilemmas pertain to the following:
  – high differentiation in the amounts of participation budgets in particular self-government units;
  – lack of clear definition of tasks which can be financed (own, obligatory, optional, project-related, process-related).

Numerous organisational dilemmas pertain to the ways of project submission, organisation of voting, economic efficiency of the process and decision about who has the right to vote. Social dilemmas pertain to the lack of well-developed, efficient systems of communication between local authorities and inhabitants and also to the open attitude and involvement of inhabitants in public affairs. Among the most important problems of Polish participatory budgeting processes, Nykiel enumerates the following (Nykiel, 2020):

- no reporting on the implementation of participatory budgeting;
- no national standards for the implementation and reporting on participatory budgeting;
- no social control over the implementation of participatory budgeting;
- weak communication between administration offices and inhabitants;

- domination of strong lobbies;
- making decisions based on the current political needs.

The weaknesses of the participatory budgeting processes in Polish self-government units have also been identified by the Supreme Audit Office and they include, among others (Najwyższa Izba Kontroli, 2019, pp. 10–18):

- necessity of collecting inhabitants' signatures on the project submission forms;
- obligation of providing voters' PESEL personal identification numbers during the voting;
- introduction of age limits for people who wish to participate in consultations on participatory budgeting;
- reliability of verifying project submission forms.

The regulations of participatory budgets often require project submission forms to be supported by a particular number of inhabitants' signatures on them. However, not all the inhabitants who have good ideas and who wish to submit their projects also want to become involved in the process of collecting signatures. As a result, inhabitants resign from submitting their projects and applying for funds for their projects. It should be noted that supporting project submission forms by signing them comes as an unnecessary limitation because the verification of project submission forms and their social substantiation takes place at the voting stage and by the inhabitants' choice. The necessity to provide PESEL personal identification numbers limits the number of inhabitants who can vote only to the group of citizens who have been provided with such numbers. Foreigners or Polish citizens' children born abroad are excluded from this group.

The age limit for voters is introduced by most territorial self-government units. The age limits are differentiated in the national scale—it is usually 13, 16 or 18 years of age. The age limit comes as a restriction to the statutory entitlements in the light of which the participation in consultation should be accessible to all inhabitants.

There should be one more remark added to those mentioned above as it is presented in the report provided by the Supreme Audit Office. It has been indicated that the criteria applied to assess projects in most cities take account of the conformity with the community's own tasks or the possibility to implement tasks during the budget year. In some territorial self-government units, projects have been assessed in terms of their social significance, their importance for the local and supra-local communities, their advantages for the city and possibilities of external co-funding. There has also been a criterion of the reputation of the city or non-damaging the good name and dignity of people, institutions and respect for the places in the submitted investment projects (Najwyższa Izba Kontroli, 2019, p. 10). The widespread lack of procedures to appeal against decisions about not putting particular projects to the vote has also been defined as an error.

The Supreme Audit Office has also indicated another drawback, namely verification of project submission forms. Project submission forms for participatory budgeting should meet some specific requirements which are defined in the regulations. The organisers of the participatory budgeting process should make sure that the requirements are met. However, it is still possible to observe the lack of reliability and consistency in this respect and, as a result, some project submission forms which do not meet the requirements are still put to the vote.

The important aspects of PB implementation also include territorial allocation of funds within local self-government units themselves. The legislator provided self-governments with a lot of freedom in this respect too. Hence, it is possible to observe open solutions, including general urban projects and such allocation of funds in which one part of the amount is dedicated to general projects and another part is dedicated to the areas defined by the executive body within a particular territorial self-government unit. It should be emphasised that some cases of corrections made to the previous divisions have been observed. However, it is also necessary to note that a commune can be divided only into some specific auxiliary units. Other divisions are impossible (organised in a different way than auxiliary units, e.g., residential areas, streets). It is also impossible to divide the defined auxiliary units into smaller units.

The prohibition to divide districts into units which are smaller than auxiliary units is also controversial. The experience in the field of participatory budgeting in Sopot and other municipalities indicates that allocation of funds to smaller units is beneficial and it integrates smaller urban communities. The analysis of urban districts indicates that city centres, residential areas and single-family housing estates which can belong to one bigger unit are, in fact, highly differentiated in terms of the number of inhabitants and problems which are faced there (Kempa & Kozłowski, 2020, pp. 71–72). Furthermore, in this situation, the projects intended for the auxiliary units (districts) that are more densely populated will win—more inhabitants mean more votes.

Initially, only the traditional methods of voting were implemented. However, because of the low voter turnout, an additional formula of electronic voting was adopted, following which the voter turnout was improved for a while (Filipiak & Dylewski, 2018, p. 19). The scientists indicate that had the above-mentioned decision not been made, the traditional voting method would have buried the validity of PB functioning in numerous places. The audit carried out by the Supreme Audit Office indicates that in the years 2016–2018 the voter turnout reached the levels of 16–19% of people with the right to vote (Najwyższa Izba Kontroli, 2019, p. 14), which is certainly less than the voter turnout during the elections; however, it is not a rate that could discredit the implementation of PB in these places. Unfortunately, there are also large cities where the voter turnout is very low; worthy of mention are Warsaw (5.11% in 2018) and Kraków (4.52% in 2018). Among the reasons explaining the very low voter turnout in the capital city, there is its more cosmopolitan character and inhabitants' orientation towards national affairs rather than local ones. At the same time, it is indicated that there is some positive correlation between the voter turnout and the PB scale, as confirmed by the data provided from Łódź, Gdańsk, Poznań and respectively low allocation and voter turnout in Kraków (Miasto 2077, 2019, pp. 4–6).

A controversial factor during the assessment of the PB implementation in Poland is constituted by the regulations limiting freedom of municipalities in the substantive evaluation of submitted projects. Self-government councillors and officials analyse projects in terms of implementing tasks assigned to territorial self-government units. Hence, they willingly adjust the procedures to the implementation of aims they have been given rather than allow inhabitants to freely decide about the funds allocated to participatory budgeting. In literature or in councillors and officials' statements, it is often possible to find an argument that the obligation of implementing each project which has been passed through the formal assessment can supposedly lead to some investments that may hardly ever contribute to the development of the city (e.g. they are incompliant with the development strategy of the city). Trying to avoid such a situation, some municipalities may decide to follow the complicated application procedures, for example, by imposing additional requirements on substantive and financial justification of the submitted projects. This, in turn, can be discouraging for applicants (inhabitants) to fully engage in participatory budgeting

(Kempa & Kozłowski, 2020, pp. 71–72). Appointed by the Supreme Audit Office, the experts do not notice the above-mentioned problem. They say that *an important issue is to relate participatory budgets to the spatial and investment policy of the particular municipalities. It is also important that inhabitants learn the financial policy of their municipality, observing various limitations to the municipal funds. Participatory budgeting is an instrument applied to stimulate inhabitants to take part in a discussion about their needs and wishes in their nearest environment* (Najwyższa Izba Kontroli, 2019, p. 16).

The fact that various practices can be observed during the implementation of PB is proved by the disappointment in the lack or detachment of participatory projects from the strategies followed by the particular cities, expressed by, among others, the authors who analyse implementation of projects at the local level. They emphasise the fact that only a small number of projects refer to all inhabitants of a particular city and they are fully in line with the objectives of the city development strategy. The submitted projects reflect unmet needs expressed by some particular groups of inhabitants. Among the winning undertakings in Rybnik, the projects related to sport and recreation dominate. Hence, there is a lack in co-funding dedicated to school facilities because many of these projects refer to the modernisation of school playing fields. We can also observe some needs which refer to the construction and modernisation of playgrounds, outdoor gyms, revitalisation of green areas and repairs of roads and pavements (Żabka & Łapińska, 2014, p. 60).

Infrastructural projects are most frequently submitted also in other parts of Poland. The audit carried out by the Supreme Audit Office indicates that 25% of PB expenditure refers to transport and communication, 23% to municipal management and protection of natural environment, 21% to physical culture and 15% to education (NIK, 2019, 16). Although adequate, this systemisation does not fully reflect the essence of the submitted projects, mainly because of its high aggregation. In this respect, it is interesting to analyse some research studies at the level of the particular cities or counties, for example, Poznań which is a highly developed city in terms of economy and the adjacent municipalities (Smalec et al., 2018, p. 53). In 2017, the projects intended to meet the needs referring to the number of playgrounds, integration places, municipal infrastructure (roads, pavements, street lighting, sewage systems), more and more popular bicycle lanes, dominated. The next position was taken by the projects which referred to educational and cultural infrastructure. They were followed by individual projects oriented towards urban green areas or zoo infrastructure—the last one quite unusual on the list. It is indicated that PB only partially reflects the needs and interests expressed by inhabitants (Naumiuk & Bron Jr., 2017, p. 42) and it will probably not be changed before most of the infrastructural needs are met and/or the level of citizens' social activity is raised at the same time. It is also emphasised that the general number of submitted projects is relatively low. However, despite the decreasing voter turnout observed in many places, attractive and needed projects can still draw a lot of public attention.

The criticism of PB in Poland is usually focused on the uniform way of implementing PB and the trite acceptance of the procedures. In their analysis of 15 Polish cities in 2017, Kłucińska and Sześciło indicate that participatory budgets do not differ enough to significantly (and positively) affect the implementation of the whole process and the activation of passive members of the community. The field providing an opportunity for municipalities to shape their independent, original approach towards PB, which could result in a variety of local practices, remains unused. As a result, the development of the whole PB process can be blocked in the future (Kłucińska & Sześciło, 2017, p. 116). Considering the low level of participation, the PB model dominating in Poland does not foster developing a new type of relationship between inhabitants and local authorities based on deliberation and agreement to the lines of action undertaken by the municipality. The PB procedures in the particular territorial self-government units which ignore or limit room for consultations, debates and opinion exchange are also criticised. Moreover, the transparency of norms applied to evaluate PB is also questioned (Kłucińska & Sześciło, 2017). The factors which hinder the development of PB in Poland include relatively small funds allocated to projects. Considering the weak promotion of projects and the way they are proceeded (to make them meet the needs of a municipality rather than express inhabitants' aspirations), socially inactive inhabitants are even more convinced that their civil alienation is the right choice. The politicisation of PB in the way similar to political campaigns additionally discourages inhabitants and it does not positively contribute to the co-management culture.

9.4   The Method Applied by Polish Territorial Self-Government Units to Design Participatory Budgeting Processes

Considering the current formal and legal conditions in Poland, the process of participatory budgeting involves mainly two groups of entities: the authorities of territorial self-government and inhabitants of particular territorial self-government units. Other entities of social life, such as central authorities or social organisations, participate in this process to a very limited extent (Table 9.2).

The central authorities have provided participatory budgeting with the legal statutory rank.[2] A relevant legal act defines the legal formula of participatory budgeting, indicating that it is a form of public consultations. Participatory budgeting can be implemented at each level

Table 9.2   Entities involved in the implementation of participatory budgeting in Poland

Entity	Scope of involvement
Central authorities	Statutory definition of a framework for the principles of participatory budgeting
Self-government authorities (regulatory bodies of a municipality, country, province)	Definition by a resolution of formal requirements for the submitted projects, the number of signatures provided by inhabitants who support the project (not more than 0.1% of inhabitants in the area covered by participatory budgeting), the principles for evaluation of the submitted projects, voting standards
Inhabitants	Submission of projects, lobbying among inhabitants, participation in voting
Organisations and associations	Support and promotion of the selected projects, lobbying among inhabitants
Groups of inhabitants	Support and promotion of the selected projects, submission of projects, lobbying among inhabitants

Source: Authors' own elaboration

---

[2] The Act of 11th January 2018 on the amendments to some acts to increase inhabitants' participation in the processes of selecting, functioning and supervising some public bodies (Journal of Laws 2018 item 130, n.d.), the Act of 8th March 1990 on the municipal self-government (Journal of Laws 2020 item 713, n.d.), the Act of 5th June 1998 on the county self-government (Journal of Laws 2020 item 920, n.d.), the Act of 5th June 1998 on the provincial self-government (Journal of Laws 2020 item 1668, n.d.).

of territorial self-government: municipality (the local level), county (the supra-local level) and province (the regional level). Implementation of participatory budgeting by self-government units is of optional nature with one exception. The statutory obligation of participatory budgeting has been imposed on one category of self-government units—cities with the county rights. These are the cities which simultaneously implement the tasks of a basic territorial self-government unit, namely a municipality and the tasks of a unit of a bigger spatial scale—a county.[3] Based on article 5a, item 5 of the Act of 2018, such municipalities are obliged to spend 0.5% of their expenditure on participation budgeting (before cities allocated from 0.2%—Kraków to 1.5%—Sopot to participatory budgeting, where it was implemented). One of the key criteria applied to evaluate the significance of participatory budgeting in the urban policy is the level of allocated funds. Eight years after the implementation of participatory budgeting in Sopot, the city still allocates much more funds per capita for PB than the richest cities in Poland: in 2018 the average amount per capita for the provinces was PLN 35.5 but for Sopot it was PLN 108 (Kempa & Kozłowski, 2020, pp. 69–70).

Implementing participatory budgeting in Poland, the above-mentioned act defines PB as a form of public consultation. However, considering the lack of any regulations which would specifically define the principles for the functioning of PB, the procedures of public consultations have been defined in a variety of ways by territorial self-government units. In accordance with article 5a, item 7 of the Act of 2018, it is indicated that relevant municipality councils, county councils or regional provincial parliaments will issue resolutions to define formal requirements for civil projects submitted by inhabitants for participatory budgeting. The maximal number of signatures required for a project to be processed has been also defined at the level not exceeding 0.1% of inhabitants in the area covered by participatory budgeting. In practice, trying to avoid inhabitants' discouragement, some cities have not implemented such a requirement at all. It can be considered as a positive solution which clears the way for individual single initiatives to be submitted without forcing their

---

[3] As a result of a self-government reform implemented in Poland in 1999, the status of a city with the county rights was given to the cities which (1) have over 100,000 inhabitants, (2) have lost the status of the provincial capital city as a result of the above-mentioned reform, and (3) are situated in large urban agglomerations (mainly in the Silesian conurbation). At present, there are 66 such entities in Poland.

originators to collect signatures. In accordance with the act, the above-mentioned bodies also have to define the principles for the evaluation of projects, voting standards, determining voting results and informing the public about them. While working on the budget, self-government authorities cannot remove or significantly change the projects which inhabitants have selected for the implementation through the voting.

All the above-mentioned regulations were implemented in 2018 and they have been binding since the start of the term of office of the self-government bodies appointed for the years 2018–2023. Before that there were no regulations in the Polish law which would directly regulate the issues of participatory budgeting.

In accordance with the current legal regulations, the role of self-government authorities is to organise the process of participatory budgeting in particular territorial units. The principles and procedures for holding public consultations for participatory budgeting are defined in relevant regulations which are accepted by the regulatory bodies of self-government units through resolutions. Considering the fact that legal requirements are of general nature, municipalities have some considerable freedom in organising participatory budgeting. As a result, the regulations defining the principles and procedures for establishing participatory budgets in the particular units differ from each other in terms of the specific elements in the process of participatory budgeting.

According to Polish law, the only entities who are allowed to submit projects for participatory budgeting are natural persons, that is inhabitants of particular territorial units. Project application forms cannot be submitted by inhabitant organisations, public institutions, associations and any other legal persons. It results from the above-mentioned legal status of participatory budgeting as a form of public consultation. In accordance with Polish law, such consultations can be carried out exclusively with natural persons, that is, namely, with inhabitants of a municipality.[4] Submitting projects is one of the consultation stages; hence they cannot be submitted by entities other than inhabitants of a particular self-government unit. Groups of inhabitants, organisations and other entities of social life can only provide their support to various activities related to the preparation of the projects and their promotion.

---

[4] The Act of 8th March 1990 on the municipal self-government, article 5a.1; the Act of 5th June 1998 on the county self-government, article 3d.1; the Act of 5th June 1998 on the provincial self-government, article 10a.1.

The government does not have any direct influence on the processes related to participatory budgeting. The only central authority which affects the above-mentioned processes is the legislative authority which defines the basic legal regulations for participatory budgeting in municipalities. Politicians who operate on the national scale rarely comment on participatory budgets. Their comments are rather more related to their election campaigns. Before the elections to the territorial self-governments in 2018, the Prime Minister of the Polish government announced a programme for self-governments which was referred to as *Self-government Five*. One of the promises listed in the programme was allocating PLN 300 million (€66 million) for the support to implement participatory budgeting in smaller self-government units—urban and urban-rural municipalities. This programme was called *You Reside—You Decide*.[5] In 2019, the Prime Minister obliged the Minister of Internal Affairs and Administration to prepare a programme project in cooperation with local self-governments. So far, the work on this project has been continued; however, it seems that the COVID-19 pandemic and related economic problems can result in the postponement of activities undertaken in this field.

Debate about participatory budgeting is not held on the national political scene. Considering Polish political conditions, the problem seems to be relatively insignificant. Most political parties represented in the Polish Parliament do not include the issues of participatory budgeting in their political programmes. The only exception here is Koalicja Obywatelska (Civic Coalition). In its programme entitled Your Poland there is a chapter *True Self-government*, where the following statement is found: *the Poles should be given as much power as possible at each level; therefore, without weakening self-governments, we declare to delegate some tasks to village councils, community councils and non-government organisations. It will strengthen inhabitants' empowerment and activities. We shall also increase the role of participatory budgeting, resolution-passing initiatives and municipal referendums in the matters which are most important for local communities* (Twoja Polska, 2019, p. 26). This is the only statement referring directly to the discussed problem which can be found in the programmes of large Polish political parties.

---

[5] https://www.gazetaprawna.pl/artykuly/1242604,wystapienie-morawieckiego-na-konwencji-pis-przez-wyborami-samorzadowymi.html (access: 9.11.2020).

Participatory budgeting is still a field reserved for politicians at the local and regional levels. Hence, debates do not refer to general systemic issues but to practical solutions applied in the particular regions and cities. The discussions are usually brought down to the reasonability of the submitted and selected projects, applied procedure mechanisms, voting principles and efficiency of implementing the winning projects. On the one hand, the discussions are attended by inhabitants and social organisations and their participation ensures the substantive value to the discourse. On the other hand, local politicians also participate in such debates, pushing them to the field of political fight for power.

During the initial stage of the development of participatory budgeting (2011–2014), it was possible to observe city authorities' less than positive attitudes towards this form of spending public funds. There are records of opinions given by important local politicians, indicating their scepticism towards participatory budgeting (Kowanda, 2014). The reason was probably their concern about the effectiveness of the discussed instrument, its economic efficiency and its social perception. At present, participatory budgeting is rather a generally accepted instrument for spending public funds, the validity and necessity of which is not questioned.

9.5   RESULTS

The report provided by the Supreme Audit Office indicates positive results of participatory budgeting implemented in the Polish self-government units. The authors of the document emphasise that the functioning of participatory budgeting has allowed inhabitants to directly participate in the decision-making process referring to the ways how a portion of the budget funds of their territorial self-government units should be spent. Due to such social participation in the power of municipal authorities, civil society is reinforced and the municipality inhabitants' trust in the self-government and its representatives is increased (Najwyższa Izba Kontroli, 2019, p. 9). As has already been indicated, this evaluation does not fully reflect the reality and it refers rather to a smaller but active part of Polish society.

Numerous scientific publications draw our attention to the efficiency of participatory budgeting implemented by Polish self-government units. Sobol emphasises that in most Polish cities, the experience with participatory budgeting is assessed in the category of success. Such evaluation results from the fact that even in the cities where inhabitants seem to be completely 'dormant' in terms of civil activities, it is possible to find some energy in them to act in favour of their local communities by using participatory budgeting (Sobol, 2017, p. 181). While analysing the implementation of participatory budgeting in Łódź, Rybińska concludes that it has significantly affected the development of the city, and it has allowed numerous permanent projects to be implemented in order to improve the quality in various aspects of the inhabitants' life (Rybińska, 2018, p. 63). While analysing the results of participatory budgeting in Jelenia Góra, Sempiak reaches some similar conclusions. Similar conclusions are also drawn by Rynio and Adamiczek who provide a research study on participatory budgeting in Wrocław (Sempiak, 2017, p. 90). A broad analysis of the influence exerted by participatory budgeting on the City of Lublin is provided by Kociuba and Rabczewska. The authors indicate three aspects in which the influence of participatory budgeting affects the city: (1) organisational and procedural (readiness for changes, flexible procedures, implementation of modifications); (2) activation of citizens and (3) implementation of investments (Kociuba & Rabczewska, 2019, p. 106).

The scientific research indicates that in Polish cities the following projects dominate among those which are submitted for participatory budgeting in the following categories: sport and recreation infrastructure, construction and retrofitting of public facilities and road infrastructure (Pistelok & Martela, 2019, pp. 16, 67).

9.6   Conclusions

In numerous municipalities, the implementation of participatory budgeting has provided an opportunity to obtain some new quality in the perception of self-government and the role of authorities, administration and inhabitants in the processes of social and economic development. It has allowed people to get a new look at the positions these entities take in the life of local communities and their mutual relationships. The processes of participatory budgeting have, to some limited extent, activated the needs and will in some parts of society to act for the common good. Among the most important advantages resulting from the implementation of participatory budgeting in Polish self-governments in which it is possible to observe a relatively high voter turnout and positive engagement of the authorities, the following merits should be mentioned:

- empowerment of inhabitants in decision-making processes implemented by the local self-government;
- closer relationships between the authorities and administration of a self-government unit and its inhabitants;
- developing civil attitudes in inhabitants;
- creating an image of the authority and administration which is open to society and transparency of local policy;
- implementing numerous projects which meet inhabitants' needs and improve the quality of their lives.

The dilemma whether PB comes as a complement to the municipal budget policy or rather delegates infrastructural solutions to inhabitants still remains unsolved. However, it is certain that it has some flaws. Hence, there is an important question; when the number of infrastructural projects decreases, will participatory budgeting be transformed into a forum for real exchange of thought about the city which can be institutionalised in the form of associations and foundations acting in favour of local development? Considering active citizens, it cannot be denied that the idea of participatory budgeting and participatory projects has some positive influence on the reinforcement of civil competences in various participants who take part in the process, including the authority representatives and officials who still follow the ideas of improving democracy during the implementation of PB.

References

Błaszak, M. (2019). Budżetobywatelski w Polsceidylematy z nimzwiązane. RuchPrawniczy, EkonomicznyiSocjologiczny, 81(3), 203–220. https://doi.org/10.14746/rpeis.2019.81.3.13

Bocatto, E., & Perez-De-Toledo, E. (2019). Citizenship knowledge acquisition in local governments: The participatory budgeting process. Proceedings of the European Conference on Knowledge Management, ECKM, 1, 142–150. https://doi.org/10.34190/KM.19.138

Bryer, A. R. (2011). Accounting as learnt social practice: The case of the empresas recuperadas in Argentina. Accounting, Organizations and Society, 36(8), 478–493. https://doi.org/10.1016/j.aos.2011.09.002

Bryer, A. R. (2014). Participation in budgeting: A critical anthropological approach. Accounting, Organizations and Society, 39(7), 511–530. https://doi.org/10.1016/j.aos.2014.07.001

Célérier, L., & Cuenca Botey, L. E. (2015). Participatory budgeting at a community level in Porto Alegre: A Bourdieusian interpretation. *Accounting, Auditing and Accountability Journal, 28*(5), 739–772. https://doi.org/10.1108/AAAJ-03-2013-1245

Filipiak, B. Z. (2017). Partnerstwopubliczno-prywatne w realizacjimałychprzedsię wzięć. *FinanseKomunalne, 10*, 36–49. https://sip.lex.pl/komentarze-i-publikacje/artykuly/partnerstwo-publiczno-prywatne-w-realizacji-malych-przedsiewziec-151320456

Filipiak, B. Z., & Dylewski, M. (2018). A real or a marginal trend in participatory budgets in local governments. *E-Finanse, 14*(4), 12–21. https://doi.org/10.2478/fiqf-2018-0024

Journal of Laws 2018 item 130. (n.d.).*Act of 11th January 2018 on the amendments to some acts to increase inhabitants' participation in the processes of selecting, functioning and supervising some public bodies.*

Journal of Laws 2020 item 1668. (n.d.).*Act of 5th June 1998 on the provincial self-government.*

Journal of Laws 2020 item 713. (n.d.).*Act of 8th March 1990 on the municipal self-government.*

Journal of Laws 2020 item 920. (n.d.).*Act of 5th June 1998 on the county self-government.*

Kempa, J., & Kozłowski, A. R. (2020). Participatory budget as a tool supporting the development of civil society in Poland. *NISPAcee Journal of Public Administration and Policy, 13*(1), 61–79. https://doi.org/10.2478/nispa-2020-0003

Kłucińska, P., & Sześciło, D. (2017). Miejskibudżetpartycypacyjny—w kierunkuw spółzarządzaniaczyfasadowejpartycypacji?(City participatory budget—towards governance or façade participation?). *PedagogikaSpołeczna, 65*(3), 103–118. http://cejsh.icm.edu.pl/cejsh/element/bwmeta1.element. desklight-ea01d2cf-8f9e-4112-8581-2d16a3727321

Kociuba, D., & Rabczewska, K. (2019). Rolabudżetówpartycypacyjnych w zagospodarowaniuprzestrzenipublicznychpolskichmiast—studiumprzypadkuLublina (The role of participatory budgets on the development of urban public spaces—the lublin case study). *StudiaRegionalneiLokalne, 76*(2), 82–109. https://doi.org/10.7366/1509499527605

Kowanda, C. (2014). Budżetobywatelski: dlakogo? Po co?*Polityka.Pl.* https://www.polityka.pl/tygodnikpolityka/rynek/1575151,1,budzet-obywatelski-dla-kogo-po-co.read

Kozłowski, A. R. (2019). Populism as a factor of destabilisation in consolidated democracies. *NISPAcee Journal of Public Administration and Policy, 12*(2), 81–108. https://ideas.repec.org/a/vrs/njopap/v12y2019i2p81-108n4.html

Lederman, S. (2015). Councils and revolution: Participatory democracy in anarchist thought and the new social movements. *Science and Society, 79*(2), 243–263. https://doi.org/10.1521/siso.2015.79.2.243

Leśniewska-Napierała, K. (2019). Budżetobywatelskijakonowy instrument partycypacjispołecznejnaobszarachwiejskich w Polsce = Participatory budgeting as a new instrument of social participation in Poland's rural areas. *StudiaObszarówWiejskich, 53,* 77–93. https://doi.org/10.7163/sow.53.6

Miasto 2077. (2019). *Raport: Budżetobywatelski w polskichmiastach.* http://www.miasto2077.pl/wp-content/uploads/2019/03/Raport-Budżety-Obywatelskie-w-polskich-miastach.pdf

Najwyższa Izba Kontroli. (2019). *Funkcjonowaniebudżetówpartycypacyjnych (obywatelskich).Lata 2016–2018.* https://www.nik.gov.pl/plik/id,21187,vp,23819.pdf

Naumiuk, A., & Bron, M., Jr. (2017). Budżetpartycypacyjny w kształtowaniuwspólnejprzestrzenilokalnej—potencjałedukacyjnyiinspiracjepedagogiczne (The role of the participatory budget in shaping a common local space—educational potential and pedagogical inspirations). *PedagogikaSpołeczna, 63*(3), 37–54.

Nykiel, K. (2020). *Budżetobywatelski—władza w ręceludu, czyułudasprawczości?*InstytutSprawObywatelskich. https://instytutsprawobywatelskich.pl/budzet-obywatelski-wladza-w-rece-ludu-czy-uluda-sprawczosci/

Pinnington, E., Lerner, J., & Schugurensky, D. (2009). Participatory budgeting in North America: The case of Guelph, Canada. *Journal of Public Budgeting, Accounting & Financial Management, 21*(3), 454–483. https://doi.org/10.1108/jpbafm-21-03-2009-b005

Pistelok, P., & Martela, B. (2019). *Raport o staniepolskichmiast.Partycypacjapubliczna.* InstytutRozwojuMiastiRegionów.

Polska, T. (2019). *Program KoalicjiObywatelskiej.* KoalicjaObywatelska. https://demagog.org.pl/wp-content/uploads/2019/10/Koalicja-Obywatelska-2019.pdf

Rodgers, D. (2010). Contingent democratisation? The rise and fall of participatory budgeting in Buenos Aires. *Journal of Latin American Studies, 42*(1), 1–27. https://doi.org/10.1017/S0022216X10000039

Rose, N. (1991). Governing by numbers: Figuring out democracy. *Accounting, Organizations and Society, 16*(7), 673–692. https://doi.org/10.1016/0361-3682(91)90019-B

Rybińska, D. (2018). Instytucjabudżetuobywatelskiegojakonarzędziarozwojusamorządulokalnego. *FinanseiPrawoFinansowe, 1*(17), 49–65. https://doi.org/10.18778/2391-6478.1.17.05

Sempiak, A. (2017). Budżetobywatelski, jako instrument partycypacjispołecznej w mieście Jelenia Góra. *PraceNaukoweWyższejSzkołyZarządzaniaiPrzedsiębiorczości z Siedzibą w Wałbrzychu, 40*(1), 139–152.

Smalec, A., Sadowska, B., &Wanagos, M. (2018).Participatory budgeting as a form of citizen involvement in codecision process. *Economic and social development: Book of proceedings*, pp. 48–56. https://search.proquest.com/docview/2139480817?pq-origsite=gscholar&fromopenview=true

Sobol, A. (2017). Budżetobywatelskijakonarzędzierozwojulokalnego. *StudiaEkono miczne, 316*, 172–182.

Suteu, S. (2019). The populist turn in Central and Eastern Europe: Is deliberative democracy part of the solution? *European Constitutional Law Review, 15*(3), 488–518. https://doi.org/10.1017/S1574019619000348

Żabka, A., & Łapińska, H. (2014). Budżetpartycypacyjny a rozwójlokalny (Participatory budget vs. local development). *ZeszytyNaukoweWyższejSzkołyFin ansówiPrawa w Bielsku-Białej, 4*, 36–65.

CHAPTER 10

Participatory Budgeting in Romania

Emil Boc and Dan-Tudor Lazăr

10.1 Introduction

Participatory budgeting (PB) is a democratic instrument that has many forms in the contemporary world and that has aroused many debates in the last 30 years. Considering the variety of the processes that self-identify as PB, the variety of the existing procedures and representations, formulating a definition is a challenge (Sintomer et al., 2008, p. 168). Indeed, there are different views, resulting in different processes, different expectations, and different outcome assessments. Although we cannot talk about a general definition, what emerges, though, are civic transactional engagement models (Sintomer et al., 2012, pp. 17–28) or collective decision and citizen empowerment models (He, 2011, pp. 122–133).

Considered by development agencies as a tool for economic and social development, and by local authorities as a tool for increasing their effectiveness, transparency, and administrative capacity, PB includes a political

---

E. Boc • D.-T. Lazăr (✉)
Faculty of Political, Administrative and Communication Sciences, Babeș-Bolyai University, Cluj-Napoca, Romania
e-mail: boc@fspac.ro; lazar@fspac.ro

© The Author(s), under exclusive license to Springer Nature Switzerland AG 2022
M. S. De Vries et al. (eds.), *International Trends in Participatory Budgeting*, Governance and Public Management,
https://doi.org/10.1007/978-3-030-79930-4_10

187

approach, which is often ignored even by the academic literature. The view behind the first processes in Brazil (at the end of the 1980s) is a radically democratic one, Gramsci-inspired. This normative approach and the liberal one are the most common. The liberal approach sees the PB only as a development tool, related to the idea of good governance. Both approaches are based on a series of common goals: extended and efficient public services, poverty alleviation, transparency, and accountability. Nevertheless, the differences can be easily noticeable in the way in which the two approaches define PB, since the radical democratic approach sees citizens' involvement in the decision and outcome monitoring as being a central focus whereas the liberal view includes various forms of cooperation between the citizens and the authorities, including citizen consultation (Goldfrank, 2007, pp. 94–97).

As for methodological definitions, there is also a relative diversity. In many of these definitions, the citizen decision-making process and the relationship between authority and the decisions concerned play a pivotal role; in other cases, the existence of a close connection to social justice is important, but, in substance, as in other participatory processes (Best et al., 2011, p. 7), there is no general recognition of what the PB praxis should be and no general agreement among the social actors on the regulatory grounds of an engagement or the expected impact. Although controversial up to this moment, the attempt to define certain ideal and generally applicable PB models exist (Sintomer et al., 2012, pp. 28–30), most of the studies are based on the PB comparative analysis at the local, national, and international level and good practice examples (Baiocchi & Lerner, 2007; Džinić, 2016; Herzberg, 2011; Pinnington et al., 2009).

As it has spread worldwide, PB has proven an extraordinary adaptive capacity, unfolding today in different forms and benefitting from the participation, in various roles, of certain social and political actors. Its global success is based precisely on the substantial split with the original model. A special view of the relationship between political society, civil society, and the state has been replaced by a set of procedures (also of great diversity) and the relationship between these procedures and the state or between the state and the civil society differ from one implementation to the other (Baiocchi & Ganuza, 2015, pp. 198–200). The PB process polymorphism does not represent a victory of any of the normative views, but it is an adaptation to the various political, economic, and social realities.

For a brief analysis of the participatory budgeting projects carried out in Romania, we will use the models proposed by Sintomer et al. (2008, pp. 169–174). In short, these models refer to the participatory budgeting processes carried out in Europe and they consider the following aspects: the origin of these processes, how the citizen meetings are organised, the type of deliberation, and civil society involvement in the processes. The six basic models are: Porto Alegre adapted for Europe; participation of organised interests; community funds at local and city level; a public/private negotiating table; proximity participation; and consultation on public finances and. In practice, mixed models are seen. These models, which have been detailed during the last years in the scientific literature (Herzberg, 2011; Krenjova & Raudla, 2013; Sintomer et al., 2013), provide the possibility to coherently describe the participatory budgeting processes carried out in Romania between 2013 and 2020. This chapter describes how PB took shape in Romania and mentions a number of factors explaining the emergence of this Romanian design of PB.

10.2   National Context of Participatory Budgeting Processes Development

Romania does not currently have legislation that refers to participatory budgeting, but it has a legal framework that refers to the information of and consultation by citizens and organised civil society and to take their proposals into consideration (Boc, 2019, p. 42). Such provisions have been included, starting with the 2000s, in the laws regulating local public administration, budgetary proceedings, and ensuring decisional transparency (Arpad & Pârvu, 2013, pp. 34–35). The law on decisional transparency within public administration (52/2003) provides opportunities for the citizens for "active participation", not only in administrative decision-making but also in drafting normative acts issued by the local public authorities with Law 242/2010 extending such an approach extensively also regarding drafting and adoption proceedings of public policy documents (Moldovan & Stan, 2013, pp. 50–59).

The new Administrative Code, which came out in 2019, states among the specific principles applicable to the local public administration "the principle of consulting citizens on special local interest issue solving". It is worth noting that in the Administrative Code (just like in the previous legislation) the term "consulting citizens" is used, implying that the decision-making on local budget remains the responsibility of the local authorities.

There are at least two background elements that do not favour the development of participatory budgeting in Romania, as it is the case in other ex-communist countries as well. Firstly, many times, local authorities have at their disposal limited funds as compared to the needs, while tax allocation is established at the national level (Fölscher, 2007, p. 130), and during Romania's recent history, such allocations have changed depending on the governing parties' interests, which are usually detrimental to the local authorities. Secondly, historical heritage, mainly the communist one, means that citizens have been kept at a distance from any decision regarding public life for more than 50 years, and have been treated by the authorities only as passive receivers, or as secondary resonators, at best, of decisions already made. Therefore, there is a distrust and a passivity background, which must be overcome (Krenjova & Raudla, 2013, p. 20).

10.3   PARTICIPATORY BUDGETING PROCESSES IN ROMANIA

10.3.1   The First Public Participation Projects

At the end of the 1990s and especially at the beginning of the 2000s, academic researchers, but also representatives of the organised civil society and politicians have become interested in public participation processes, given that they have made contact with public participation processes carried out in other European countries and the United States. Thus, they have become interested mainly in the PB, given also to the fact that the Brazilian model has been promoted within international development-dedicated events, which have been attended also by Romanian representatives (de Oliveira, 2017, pp. 154–155).

In the 2000s, the first public participation projects emerged. They had a significant impact on the communities and have been initiated in a few important cities, which are also academic centres such as Braşov (Fölscher, 2007, pp. 139–140; Serban, 2002), Timişoara (Radoslav et al., 2012, p. 54), and Cluj-Napoca. We need to see the participatory budgeting processes as a segment in a wider public participation picture because citizen participation is bound to a specific technique, but must be seen in the light of democracy development as a long-term process (Best et al., 2011, p. 95), which is an important aspect, especially in the ex-communist countries.

The process as it unfolded in Mănăştur, one of Cluj-Napoca's neighbourhoods, in 2013, was the first PB process. It had its achievements and limitations and has caused debates (Boc, 2019, pp. 43–45). It has been a project initiated and led by the local administration, which has been the "PB decision making body" (Krenjova & Raudla, 2013, p. 22) and which also controlled the project's implementation. The district citizens were invited to attend the meetings, utilising public announcements and announcements directed at the leaders of the homeowners'/inhabitants' associations. The five meetings were attended by over 600 citizens.

The process carried out in Mănăştur has been a "Proximity participation"-type process, with all the achievements and limitations possible within such a model. It has ensured a decent level of public debate and established a list of priorities for the neighbourhood investments, which the municipality has taken into consideration during the following years. The overall budget for the works performed at the citizens' proposals being approximately €4 million, for more than 50 projects carried out over three years (alleys and sidewalks, green areas, public lighting, etc.).

The process has been challenged by voices coming from civil society. The challenge origin comes, essentially, from the different views about what a PB process should be. The authorities have chosen a consultative model instead of the "Porto Alegre adapted for Europe" model (in which the citizens can make decisions and monitor project implementation). The administration has chosen a good governance tool, which could provide it with the possibility to prioritise the investment works in the neighbourhood. With the 2008–2010 economic crisis, a better public expenditure prioritisation has become a desideratum of public administrations in Romania (Mantescu & Lazar, 2014, p. 960).

This debate, between different views, is significant because it has occurred also during other participatory budgeting processes in Romania and is likely for it to occur under various forms also in the years to come. Under such circumstances, we must not confuse such an idea-related debate with the actual achievements improving citizens' life.

The pilot project carried out in Mănăştur district, with all its limits, managed to develop the participatory local governance. It increased decisional transparency, informed the citizens about the city's budget, and led to direct communication and actual collaboration between public servants within local administration and citizens. It has been a mutual learning process between citizens and public servants.

10.3.2   Youth-Oriented PB Processes: From Com'On Cluj-Napoca to Com'On Europe

In 2015, in Cluj-Napoca, a different pioneering PB process type was car-ried out, a youth-oriented one, briefly called Com'On Cluj-Napoca (Boc, 2019, pp. 45–47). This process has been initiated considering that, in 2015, Cluj-Napoca was a European Youth Capital. The model corre-sponding to the Com'On Cluj-Napoca is, mainly, the "Community funds at local and city level" model. Although part of the funding came from the local budget, the process has been proposed, managed, and monitored by an NGO (the Pont Group), in partnership with other NGOs, which have ensured part of the co-funding, got involved in media coverage actions, in facilitating initiatives and in the operational management. This was done with a partner from the business environment, Banca Comercială Română, which has ensured a credit line. Another part of the funding was obtained by the Pont Group utilising the European Economic Area Mechanism (strictly for 2015).

Before 2015, there had been a dialogue between the administration and the youth associations with the administration expressing its intention to support participatory processes for young people.

Com'On was focused on the participation of a target group consisting of informal groups each containing at least three young people aged between 14 and 35. The informal groups proposed initiatives that have subsequently been subject to a public vote. Com'On has been a support for the coagulation of the civil society (some of the groups that have pro-posed initiatives have joined later on certain NGOs or have created their youth associations). For organised civil society, there is a series of pro-grammes financed at the local, national, and European levels, but for the informal groups, such resources were rarely available. This project is one such example, although the financing value is a small one (a maximum of €2000 budget, €1000 of which were guaranteed through local budget contribution). Practically, we have seen small projects carried out by young people for their friends and colleagues, for their neighbours: cultural events, education campaigns for sustainable development and environ-mental protection, innovative use of certain spaces in the city for short periods, highlighting intercultural diversity and dialogue in the city, stu-dent contests, local sports events, and so on.

In 2015, 248 informal groups consisting of 744 people with an average age of 25 years submitted 451 initiatives. A total of 437 initiatives were considered eligible after an administrative check and received a total number of 48,609 votes, from 18,782 people. Every single voter could choose up to 10 projects. In total, 102 projects benefitted from financing and have been implemented in 2015.

The project was resumed in three other editions, 2016, 2018–2019, and 2020, but participation decreased from year to year, dropping in 2020 to only 71 initiatives from 191 young people, with only 4079 persons who voted (8426 votes), and with a decreasing number of funded projects (46 projects).

It should be noted that, since 2016, at the proposal of the municipality, there was a special section for young people from disadvantaged communities. And even if the processes have been online, the facilitators have provided assistance for the initiatives coming from those who do not have Internet access.

The Pont Group developed this PB youth-oriented model, in which there is a "co-governing partnership" (Krenjova & Raudla, 2013, p. 26), also applied outside the city of Cluj-Napoca, in Sfântu Gheorghe, and Timișoara.

The first PB initiative in Romania, dedicated exclusively to schools (2019–2020), came also from organised civil society (http://www.inova-republica.ro/bugetare-participativa-la-scoala) and is focused on financing certain educational activities, having as a basic model the 'Community funds at local and city level' model again.

At the youth participation project level, civil society has managed to propose projects and create partnerships that have managed to impose themselves as good practice models also at the national and European levels. The Pont Group carried out an Erasmus+ (2017–2019)—financed project, which accomplished an open-source framework and a toolkit for European cities regarding participatory budgeting for the youth, enhanced by practical examples of seven European cities (Cluj-Napoca, Turin, Braga, Cascais, Maribor, Thessaloniki, and Varna; http://www.comoneurope.org).

10.3.3   Online Participatory Budgeting in Romania: Potentials and Challenges

In 2017, the municipality of Cluj-Napoca initiated a new PB process, an online PB, according to a model it has continued to use in 2018 and 2019 (Boc, 2019, pp. 47–48). It is a process initiated and managed by the municipality. It addresses citizens, who make proposals and then vote on the projects. The implementation is done and monitored by the municipality, but the citizens are consulted to understand the actual needs and to streamline project implementation. The process is carried out online, but it also provides the possibility to participate for those people who do not have Internet access. There has been no formal debate forum within the process during the first two years, but there have been debates and mobilisation for certain projects on social networks, generated by the citizens who proposed projects. In 2019, two participatory workshops have been organised as the most desirable e-participation model combines the use of technology with meeting directly the citizens (cf. Cropf & Benton, 2019, p. 107).

It must be mentioned, though, that the vote is of great importance since the local administration has undertaken to implement the 15 most voted projects each year. This means citizen's empowerment, a *de facto* decision transferred to the citizens. This has been transposed in the budget of the following years, after each edition, although the formal decision on the project budgeting has been made within the local Council. It has given citizen involvement in the decision-making process an intrinsic value (Mansuri & Rao, 2013, p. 283).

The list of the projects put to vote refers to district investments (alleys, sidewalks, pedestrian areas; mobility, accessibility, traffic safety; green areas and playgrounds; educational infrastructure; urban furniture, public lighting, etc.), to which, an investment-assimilated digital city component is added.

The model adopted is a mixed one, essentially a "Proximity participation" model, which takes the voting element from the "Porto Alegre adapted for Europe" model, without making social justice its central goal (although the solidarity ideas can be present in certain projects). Basically, it is the outcome out of a liberal perspective and not the outcome out of a view that targets the renewal of politics.

The model implemented in Cluj-Napoca (https://bugetareparticipativa.ro) is not a novelty. It exists under various hybrid forms, relatively similar, in other European cities. After being implemented in Cluj-Napoca, it has spread rapidly to other Romanian cities. This success is explained by the fact that it is based on a relatively simple concept (it is desirable that the rules be simple and very clearly structured—(Boulding & Wampler, 2010, p. 275)), easy to accept and apply by the administrations, regardless of their political spectrum and, last but not least, open to experimentation and improvement. Any PB process contains an unpredictability element (Ganuza & Baiocchi, 2012, p. 8) because even when the scale is a small one, it provides the citizens with the possibility to express their needs and to propose innovative solutions to the problems they are facing daily. The openness to innovation is essential for the administrations to be able to deal with the challenges accompanying urban development (Vesnic-Alujevic et al., 2019, p. 88).

Following the model experienced in Cluj-Napoca, 10 county capital cities in Romania have carried out similar processes: Arad, Oradea, Târgovişte, Craiova, Deva, Suceava, Sibiu, Zalău, Baia Mare, and Iaşi. Added to these are the processes carried out in Bucharest: both across the entire capital, and in its districts: Bucharest—District 3 and Bucharest—District 1. Moreover, a series of towns organised PB processes, following the same model: Făgăraş, Dej, Turda, Roman. All in all, 16 cities and towns in Romania implemented such PB processes. Two cities can be added that have announced the organisation, in 2020, of actions using the same model, but which, because of the pandemic, had to delay their plans: Braşov and Hunedoara. Administrations in other cities and towns have expressed their intention to implement PB processes, although these intentions have not yet materialised.

It must also be mentioned that participatory budgeting has become an election campaign topic with opposition parties in several cities proposing the unfolding of such processes, for instance, in Bacău, Focşani, Râmnicu Vâlcea, Vaslui, Tulcea, Timişoara, Târgu Jiu, Constanţa, Satu Mare, or Câmpia Turzii. This has happened also in smaller localities, for instance in the commune of Sânpetru. The opposition parties themselves have been the ones to propose process changes/improvements in the cities where these processes have been implemented.

Organised civil society has been a constant supporter of the participatory budgeting where it has not yet been implemented (for instance, in Târgu Mureş), and a careful critic where such processes have been carried out (for instance, in Cluj-Napoca and Bucharest).

One of the visible shifts is seen in simplifying the voting procedure. In Cluj-Napoca and a few other cities (Sibiu, Iaşi, Bucharest—District 3) a two-round voting system has been adopted. One round for obtaining the first selection and then a second round for establishing the winning projects (a stage in which a small number of projects participated). This system provides an advantage when a large number of projects are proposed because it accomplishes a preliminary selection. All the other cities have adopted a single round voting system. The periods during which the voting takes place vary from one week to one month.

A significant change has also been made in Oradea, where a mixed voting system has been adopted. Meetings with the citizens have been organised, within the neighbourhoods, where eligible projects have been presented, and where the citizens have been able to debate and vote offline. The selection has been made by combining the online vote (50%) with the vote expressed within public meetings (50%). All the cities address citizens for the vote, but some of them capitalise the direct meetings because the real-life meeting is seen as an opportunity that triggers and supports civic participation (Brodach, 2019, p. 34).

The areas for which projects could be proposed have been, mostly, related to local investment projects, and the six areas proposed initially in Cluj-Napoca have been reformulated, but new areas have also been added, reaching 8, 9 even 10 areas of interest, depending on the community needs.

The estimated budget for one project has generally been between €50,000 and €200,000 (in Cluj-Napoca, it was €150,000), with the specification that in the smaller cities/towns, the estimated budget is reduced to €5000 or €10,000. The overall budget assigned varies from €25,000 for the towns and up to €4 million for Bucharest. Although the absolute amounts seem significant, especially in big cities, these amounts are percentage-wise around or less than 1% of the development budget. Related to this aspect, in the Romanian public space, both the representatives of opposition parties and parts of civil society have come with the idea to assign 5% of the local development budget to PB processes. Likewise, the number of projects varies from a small number in small towns to 15 projects in Cluj-Napoca or even 20, in Bucharest.

Regardless of the issues and limitations that have emerged, some cities have turned PB into a constant exercise. However, there are also cities where such continuity is absent. For these cities it seems that it has all been nothing but a "one-time" exercise (for instance, Baia Mare, Iași, or Bucharest). Of course, the 2020 pandemic has altered priorities and has postponed many of the actions that should have been initiated in 2020.

All the online processes that unfolded in Romania between 2017 and June 2020 address the citizens directly for project proposals, most of them focusing only on the citizens, but we also have examples where legal entities are allowed to submit projects (the business environment and the organised civil society), in Craiova, in Bucharest—District 3 and in Zalău.

To take part in the process, there is a registration procedure in all cities and the most common formula to delimit the participants refers to the people with permanent or temporary residence in the locality concerned. As for the participants' age, in most cases there is an age limit of 18, but in Iaşi and Bucharest—District 1, this age has been set to just 16 years.

10.3.4   Case Study: Cluj-Napoca Online PB

The most suitable city for studying the evolution of the participation process is Cluj-Napoca because it is the only city where three consecutive PB editions took place according to the online formula. In 2017, 338 proposals were submitted, 126 projects of which were declared eligible and put to a citizen vote. In 2018, 164 projects were submitted, 47 projects being put to a vote. In 2019, 199 projects were submitted and 40 projects were subject to deliberation. Each year, after the first voting stage, 30 projects have been selected, 15 of which have won, in the second voting stage. The number of projects submitted has dropped by half in the second year and it has increased slightly in the third year.

Each year, the number of the projects declared eligible becomes smaller (between 20% and 37%) compared to those submitted. The main reasons for rejecting certain projects are related to the phrasing. Some only enunciate certain ideas, others exceed the budget. For certain projects, problems related to land ownership arise, implying that any expropriation would bring the budget way over the limit assigned.

During the first edition, projects for which the implementation exceeds the level of €150,000 were accepted for the voting. Cluj-Napoca City Hall has accepted these projects to be put to vote, considering they are important for the community, and the amount assigned will be used to implement only one stage, implicitly accepting the additional financing. The best example is a new park in development, the East Park. After it was voted upon, a more serious study of the problem began and a public debate was organised of which the conclusion was that building the biggest park of the last 100 years in the city would need land expropriation and an international solution contest. In other words, an action spreading over several years and with much bigger costs as compared to the originally assigned amount.

At the first voting stage, every single citizen registered on the participatory budgeting platform could choose six projects, one for each of the six areas established. In 2017, 29,138 votes were recorded, from 8559 users, which is a 3.4 vote average out of the 6 possible. In the second voting stage, when every citizen could choose only one project, out of the 30 ranked highest at the first stage, a greater number of people casting their vote has been recorded, namely 11,499. The 34% growth of the voter number is due to the mobilisation concerning certain projects, which were related to school modernisation and the already-mentioned park. It is to be specified that Cluj-Napoca city has 324,576 inhabitants, according to the latest census. This means that the number of people who have voted is only 3.54% of the city's resident population, and a part of that 3.54% did not even need to have a permanent residence in the city, but only to study or work in the city.

In 2018, during the first voting stage, there have been 4342 voters supporting 3.43 projects on average, while in the second stage, there have been 4112 voters (a slightly smaller number).

In 2019, during the initial voting stage, there have been 3140 voters, supporting 4.55 projects on average, which is somewhat higher compared to the previous years, while in the second stage, 2877 voters had expressed their preferences.

A clear decrease in the number of people participating in the voting process can be seen, year by year. Among the possible reasons, one can mention that there is less media coverage compared to 2017 when the novelty caught media's attention. Furthermore, there is a lack of flagship projects as were there in 2017. The drop can be caused also by the fact that implementing most of the projects could not be done immediately, but over several years, because of the legal stages concerning public investment implementation.

As for the average age of those who voted, it was low in the first year, namely 21.7 years in 2017. It increased by almost 10 years, up to 32.2 years in 2018 and 31.5 years in 2019.

The number of voters taking part in both voting stages is decreasing. It is worth noting that each year, a considerable number of voters in the first round have given up voting in the second round, in 2017—4803 voters (56.11% of the voters in the first round); in 2018—2821 voters (64.97%); in 2019—2208 voters (70.31%). This could be an argument in favour of the cities that have implemented a single-round voting system. On the other hand, in the second round, people who have not participated in the first round can express their preferences (2017—7743 voters, 2018—2591 voters, and 2019—1945 voters).

Although the process has been an online one, the needs of the people without Internet access have been taken into account as well as of those people not knowing how to use technology (support was provided). E-participation needs public policies to assist citizens to acquire the necessary skills and to ensure access to technology (Novo Vázquez & Vicente, 2019, p. 172). In this regard, in Cluj-Napoca, in order to provide more access, the municipality ensures free Wi-Fi in an area where disadvantaged people live, and in 2020, 2098 tablets have been purchased for those students coming from families who do not own a computer, a laptop or tablets.

In 2020, out of the 45 projects declared winners in the previous three years, 22 have been completed. A total of 22 projects were in one of the various implementation stages and 1 project has been cancelled upon the request of the directly involved citizens. The decision to cancel the project concerned the building of a playground in a neighbourhood. This decision was made after a dialogue with the directly affected citizens who lived in the nearby apartment blocks, in which the residents expressed their opposition to the project, and told they wanted to keep the space as it was, that is, arranged as a small urban garden. This example shows that the administration manages the PB as a good local governance tool and not only as a mere project contest. Of course, if this consultation would have taken place before the voting process, the situation would have been avoided.

As for the already implemented projects, it can be noted that certain projects that started as pilot projects with a limited budget have been significantly extended with the subsequently assigned amounts being much larger. This shows the innovation potential that the citizens can bring to the city's life. The most exemplary, without being single examples, refer to the school buses and the smart units for waste selective collection, equipped with solar panels.

10.4   Conclusions

PB is an idea that is alive in Romania. There are many processes that have already been carried out in 16 cities, with accomplishments and limitations. Even if they started from a specific model, the actions tend to diversify and to adapt to the local needs. Two models dominate the current picture, both being hybrid models, copying elements from versions that unfolded globally and particularly, at the European level. One model addresses informal groups of young people, financing small cultural, educational, and social actions, which has, in its current shape, also a segment dedicated to the disadvantaged categories and which is managed by organised civil society. The other model targets mainly local investments (small and medium), being financed and carried out (design and implementation) by the administration and addressing citizens. This second model has proven its capacity to include social-economic issues and to be open to organised civil society participation. Although the unfolding method is online, there is also the possibility to attend meetings for those who do not have access or technological skills.

Even if the amounts allocated from local budgets are relatively small, around or less than 1% of the development budget, the outcomes of the implemented projects are visible within the communities, as they involve district investments, better public services, dialogue between citizens, and improved local administration. Indeed, they do not solve structural issues but concentrate on issues important for "the everyday-life of people" (Röcke, 2014, p. 176). At the "everyday-life of people" level, a city's administration is, first of all, a set of public policies provided, infrastructure maintenance and modernisation, placement of urban furniture, playground arrangements, planting trees, ensuring public safety, and so on. Even if the scale is small, for a former communist country like Romania, with a low level of decentralisation, with a legislative environment that only speaks about "citizen consultation", it is important to have such processes.

The processes that have been carried out in Romania did not emphasise social justice, even if there are elements that show a preoccupation for forms of social solidarity. Local administrations see these processes as an element for developing local communities and as a support factor for local good governance. PB can be considered to be a tool for modernising the Romanian administration, mainly through the learning process with which it is associated. At this moment it cannot be considered to be a means for structural reform.

The segments concerning proposal generation, development, and deliberation are elements that need a more consistent approach (Lerner, 2017, p. 158), even if the voting is important because it means that the *de facto* decision belongs to the citizens.

The issue of the reduced number of attending citizens and the drop of this number, in time, is an issue that will have to be tackled in the years to come if the cities want to use this tool at its maximum capacity. Local authorities must take the fact that people wait for actual and immediate results into account.

There is also the risk that the administration will abandon this idea and there are already examples of actions that have been conducted in a single edition in certain cities. It is a normal thing to say you are learning from mistakes, but only a few manage to do it. And even if they understand they have done it wrong, the governments, at any level, are rarely willing to admit it publicly.

The consultation of those who have proposed projects and the consultation of citizens who are directly affected by the project implementation is a good practice in need of generalisation. To make that happen, it needs legislation, regulation, and serious monitoring. PB could become exemplary for collaboration between administration and citizens, in terms of performance, co-design, and co-implementation.

Political pressure coming from the opposition, the media, and civil society can play an important part in starting participatory processes. The possibility to challenge public authorities is in dire need and any responsible administration must deal in earnest with such criticism, accepting criticism is the basis for dialogue. Public participation, mainly through PB, with approaches coming from different ideological backgrounds, implies aiming for consensus, not the disappearance of different views or their melting into a technocratic model. Even when all the actors attending a participatory process synchronise their actions, it is not certain that they do it based on the same normative grounds.

The basic ingredients of a successful PB process unfolding are found in political will to use this democratic tool and the availability of necessary resources: financial, but also human and time resources. To ensure the sustainability of this kind of participation process, political will must be based on the understanding that citizens are responsible people, who are capable of making decisions, who can provide new ideas and expertise, who are waiting to be asked about their needs, more often than once every four years during elections. Starting from here, participation tools can be built, including participatory budgeting, designed and carried out coherently and transparently, in an attempt to build an open and inclusive public sphere.

REFERENCES

Arpad, T., & Pârvu, S. (2013). *Manual de proceduri privind procesul de luare a deciziilor și elaborarea politicilor publice*. Asociația Pro Democrația. http:// www.apd.ro/wp-content/uploads/2015/07/Manualul-de-proceduri-cos-SMIS-40366.pdf

Baiocchi, G., & Ganuza, E. (2015). Becoming a best practice: Neoliberalism and the curious case of participatory budgeting. In C. W. Lee, M. McQuarrie, & E. T. Walker (Eds.), *Democratizing inequalities: Dilemmas of the new public participation* (pp. 187–203). NYU Press. https://doi.org/10.18574/ nyu/9781479847273.003.0010

Baiocchi, G., & Lerner, J. (2007). Could participatory budgeting work in the United States? *The Good Society, 16*(1), 8–13. https://www.jstor.org/ stable/20711245?seq=1#metadata_info_tab_contents

Best, E., Augustyn, M., & Lambermont, F. (2011). *Direct and participatory democracy at grassroots level: Levers for forging EU citizenship and identity?* European Institute of Public Administration. https://doi.org/10.2863/63437

Boc, E. (2019). The development of participatory budgeting processes in Cluj-Napoca. *Transylvanian Review of Administrative Sciences, 15*(58), 38–51. https://doi.org/10.24193/tras.58E.3

Boulding, C., & Wampler, B. (2010). Voice, votes, and resources: Evaluating the effect of participatory democracy on well-being. *World Development, 38*(1), 125–135. https://doi.org/10.1016/j.worlddev.2009.05.002

Brodach, A. (2019). Entrusting citizens with their city's budget: The participatory budget in Paris. In *From local to European: Putting citizens at the centre of the EU agenda* (pp. 31–34). European Committee of the Regions.

Cropf, R. A., & Benton, M. (2019). Towards a working model of e-participation in smart cities: What the research suggests. *Public Administration and Information Technology, 34*, 99–121. https://doi.org/10.1007/978-3-319-89474-4_6

de Oliveira, O. P. (2017). International policy diffusion and participatory budgeting—ambassadors of participation, international institutions and transnational networks. In *International policy diffusion and participatory budgeting*. Palgrave Macmillan. https://doi.org/10.1007/978-3-319-43337-0_1

Džinić, J. (2016). Komparativna iskustva upravljanja kvalitetom u javnoj upravi. In I. Koprić, J. Džinić, & R. Manojlović (Eds.), *Upravljanje kvalitetom i učinkovitošću u javnoj upravi* (pp. 129–157). Institut za javnu upravu. https:// www.bib.irb.hr/800523

Fölscher, A. (2007). Participatory budgeting in Central and Eastern Europe. In A. Shah (Ed.), *Participatory budgeting, public sector governance and accountability series* (pp. 127–156). World Bank.

Ganuza, E., & Baiocchi, G. (2012). The power of ambiguity: How participatory budgeting travels the globe. *Journal of Public Deliberation, 8*(2), 1–14. http://www.publicdeliberation.net/jpd/vol8/iss2/art8

Goldfrank, B. (2007). *Lessons from Latin America's experience with participatory budgeting.* Diplomacy Faculty Publications. https://scholarship.shu.edu/diplomacy-faculty/16

He, B. (2011). Civic engagement through participatory budgeting in China: Three different logics at work. *Public Administration and Development, 31*(2), 122–133. https://doi.org/10.1002/pad.598

Herzberg, C. (2011). Democratic innovation or symbolic participation? A case study of participatory budgeting in Germany. *6th ECPR general conference, panel 25, "democratic innovations in Europe: A comparative perspective", 25–27 August 2011,* Reykjavik, Iceland. https://ecpr.eu/Events/Event/PaperDetails/8236

Krenjova, J., & Raudla, R. (2013). Participatory budgeting at the local level: Challenges and opportunities for new democracies. *Halduskultuur, 14*(1), 18–46. http://halduskultuur.eu/journal/index.php/HKAC/article/view/78

Lerner, J. (2017). Conclusion: Time for participatory budgeting to grow up. *New Political Science, 39*(1), 156–160. https://doi.org/10.1080/07393148.2017.1278860

Mansuri, G., & Rao, V. (2013). Localizing development: Does participation work? In *Localizing development.* The World Bank. https://doi.org/10.1596/978-0-8213-8256-1

Mantescu, D., & Lazar, D.-T. (2014). Estimation of potential GDP and output gap. Comparative perspective. *The Amfiteatru Economic Journal, 16*(37), 951–951. https://ideas.repec.org/a/aes/amfeco/v37y2014i16p951.html

Moldovan, R., & Stan, V. (2013). *Parteneriat pentru guvernare—Manual de tehnici și proceduri de consultare intre autoritățile publice și organizațiile guvernamentale.* https://issuu.com/crjromania/docs/brosura_crj_mod_

Novo Vázquez, A., & Vicente, M. R. (2019). Exploring the determinants of e-participation in smart cities. *Public Administration and Information Technology, 34,* 157–178. https://doi.org/10.1007/978-3-319-89474-4_8

Pinnington, E., Lerner, J., & Schugurensky, D. (2009). Participatory budgeting in North America: The case of Guelph, Canada. *Journal of Public Budgeting, Accounting & Financial Management, 21*(3), 454–483. https://doi.org/10.1108/jpbafm-21-03-2009-b005

Radoslav, R., Stelian, M., Morar, T., Bdescu, T., & Brane, A.-M. (2012). Sustainable urban development through the empowering of local communities. In *Sustainable development—policy and urban development—tourism, life science, management and environment.* InTech. https://doi.org/10.5772/27324

Röcke, A. (2014). Framing citizen participation: Participatory budgeting in France, Germany and the United Kingdom. In *Framing citizen participation:*

Participatory budgeting in France, Germany and the United Kingdom. Palgrave Macmillan. https://doi.org/10.1057/9781137326669

Serban, D. (2002). Community involvement in public service delivery—a challenge for both local authorities and citizens: The Romanian experience. In J. Finlay & M. Debicki (Eds.), *Delivering public services in Central and Eastern Europe: Trends and developments. The NISPAcee 10th annual conference held in Cracow, Poland, April 25–27, 2002* (pp. 111–122). NISPAcee.

Sintomer, Y., Herzberg, C., Allegretti, G., Röcke, A., & Alves, M. L. (2013). *Dialog global. Participatory budgeting worldwide—Updated version. Study no. 25.* Engagement Global gGmbH.

Sintomer, Y., Herzberg, C., & Röcke, A. (2008). Participatory budgeting in Europe: Potentials and challenges. *International Journal of Urban and Regional Research, 32*(1), 164–178. https://doi.org/10.1111/j.1468-2427.2008.00777.x

Sintomer, Y., Herzberg, C., Röcke, A., & Allegretti, G. (2012). Transnational models of citizen participation: The case of participatory budgeting. *Journal of Deliberative Democracy, 8*(2), 9. https://doi.org/10.16997/jdd.141

Vesnic-Alujevic, L., Stroermer, E., Rudkin, J.-E., Scapolo, F., Kimbell, L., Scapolo, J.-E. R. F., & Kimbell, I. collaboration with L. (2019). *The future of government 2030+: A citizen centric perspective on new government models.* Publications Office of the European Union. https://doi.org/10.2760/145751

CHAPTER 11

Participatory (Initiative) Budgeting in the Russian Federation

Mstislav Afanasiev and Nataliya Shash

11.1 Introduction

In Russian practice, thanks to the Russian Ministry of Finance, the term "initiative" budget is used instead of its synonym "participatory" budget. This makes the term more understandable for the majority of the country's population. The results of the implementation of various practices of participatory budgeting in the budget process are examined as summarised in their works (Astuty, 2014; Craig et al., 2017; Godwin, 2018; Gonçalves,

M. Afanasiev (✉)
HSE University, Moscow, Russia

Institute of Economic Forecasting, Russian Academy of Sciences (Ecfor RAS), Moscow, Russia
e-mail: mstafan@hse.ru

N. Shash
Financial Management Department, Plekhanov Russian University of Economics, Moscow, Russia
e-mail: SHash.NN@rea.ru

© The Author(s), under exclusive license to Springer Nature Switzerland AG 2022
M. S. De Vries et al. (eds.), *International Trends in Participatory Budgeting*, Governance and Public Management,
https://doi.org/10.1007/978-3-030-79930-4_11

2014; O'Hagan et al., 2020; Shah, 2007; Shybalkina & Bifulco, 2019; Su, 2012). The current analysis focuses on the best practices of developing initiative budgeting in the federal subjects of Russia and in the municipal divisions (M.P. Afanasiev et al., 2020; M.P. Afanasiev & Shash, 2016; Mstislav Platonovich Afanasiev & Shash, 2017).

Initiative budgeting is the concept used in Russian practice to refer to a number of practices of involving citizens in the budgeting process who are joined in a common ideology of citizen participation, as well as to the area of government regulation of public participation in determining and selecting projects, which are funded with budget revenue, and in the subsequent control of carrying out the chosen projects (Shul'ga, 2017). Each year, initiative budgeting becomes a more and more popular economic and political action and, as a rule, is actively supported by the country's economic authorities.

The introduction of initiative budgeting in Russia is unique in that the country has a three-tier budget system: federal (federal budget—around 60% of all revenue), regional (budgets of federal subjects—around 35% of all revenue), and municipal (budgets of local government—around 5% of all revenue).

Furthermore, the country has a complicated administrative structure which includes federal (regional) subjects, each of which includes municipal divisions. In total the Russian Federation is made up of four types of subjects: 46 oblasts, 22 republics, 9 krais, 3 federal cities (Moscow, Saint Petersburg, Sevastopol), 4 autonomous okrugs (Nenets, Chukotka, Yamalo-Nenets, and Khanty-Mansiysk Autonomous Okrug—Yugra), and 1 autonomous oblast (Jewish Autonomous Oblast). In total there are 85 subjects of the Russian Federation. The Russian federal subjects are divided into municipal divisions, while under legislation, 7 different types of municipal divisions are defined such as municipal district, urban districts, intracity territory (or intracity municipal division) of federal cities (the aforementioned Moscow, Saint Petersburg, Sevastopol), urban district with intracity division, intracity district, urban settlement and rural settlement. As of January 1, 2020, there are 22,327 municipalities in Russia, including 567 urban districts, 1784 municipal districts, 19 city districts, 267 intracity territories of federal cities, 1589 urban settlements, and 18,101 rural settlements.

In Russia in 2019 "initiative budgeting" projects covered 4.7 million participants from the country's population of 144 million people. Almost 90,000 project ideas were put forward (Russian Ministry of Finance,

2020). Project activity covered 68 out of the 85 subjects of the Russian Federation. In the end, 18,700 winning projects were selected in 25 regional project centres for the amount of 19.3 billion rubles (or €233 million at an exchange rate of 83.5 rub./euro). Such initial quantitative characteristics of the subject are presented in this chapter.

The authors are grateful to Prof., Dr A. Barabashev (HSE University) and A. Belenchuk (Accounts Chamber of Russia) for recommendations for this research.

11.2 Chronology of the Development of Initiative Budgeting in Russia

The history of how initiative budgeting has developed in Russia spans almost 15 years. It all started in 2007 with the World Bank launching the project "Local Initiatives Support Programme" (LISP) in one of the federal subjects (Stavropol Krai), gaining active support from the Russian Ministry of Finance.

The year 2010 was marked by the launch of the LISP project on the territory of the Kirov Oblast, under which the conference "Project for support of local initiatives" began to take place, leading to initiatives being carried out annually in various municipalities.

In 2011, as part of the project, LISP was extended to all municipal divisions of the Kirov Oblast. That same year, "United Russia", the political party with the majority in the State Duma of the Russian Federation, initiated the implementation of its project "National Budget" on the whole territory of the country. "Participatory" procedures were used within the "National Budget" project, which involved the discussion of individual budgeting indicators at various levels of the Russian budget system (federal, regional, municipal). At the same time, another version of this project, under the title "National Initiatives", was being started in one of the federal subjects—Irkutsk Oblast.

In 2012, the government programmes of the Russian federal subjects continued to develop and improve in other regions, particularly, the launching of the "National Budget" project in the Tula Oblast and the beginning of the implementation of the "National Initiative" in municipal divisions of the Tambov Oblast (All-Russian conference on initiative budgeting, 2015).

In 2013, LISP projects began to be carried out in a number of Russian subjects, namely, in the municipal divisions of the Khabarovsk Krai as well as in the area of the Nizhny Novgorod and Tver Oblasts. For the purposes of this project, in the Tver region "LISP School" was created. Furthermore, in urban districts of the Kirov Oblast, internet voting technology was used in procedures for selecting local initiative projects for the first time in Russian budgeting practice. Participatory budgeting (PB) technologies are put into practice by the local government when realising the projects "National Budget" (Cherepovets city, Vologda Oblast) and "I plan the budget" (Sosnovy Bor, Leningrad Oblast). The area covered by the municipal divisions of the Tula Oblast is growing thanks to events of the "National Budget" project (Chulkov, 2016). It will continue to spread to all municipalities of the oblast, and new selective procedures are emerging.

In 2014, LISP started in the Republic of Bashkortostan. The pilot project for introducing the PB technology "National Budget" started to work in three urban settlements of the Kirov Oblast. The project for introducing PB technology "National Budget" continued to develop in the city of Cherepovets in the Vologda Oblast through local public self-government (LPS), and a separate programme "National Budget—LPS" was launched (Fedosov & Bogatchenko, 2019).

In the same year, the electronic system "LISP Tver" was put into action in the Tver Oblast and was made possible to automatise work with project applications. During the events of the Open Government of the Russian Federation, a working group was formed consisting of experts directly dealing with questions of participatory and extra budgeting. The participants of this group prepared a corresponding project of guidelines. Furthermore, under the auspices of the Russian Ministry of Finance and based on the initiative of the Open Government, the round table meeting "Civic initiatives and citizen involvement in the open budget" was organised.

In 2015, LISP started to be carried out in the Republic of North Ossetia—Alania. The introduction of PB technology continued to develop under the "National Budget" project in ten urban municipal divisions of Kirov Oblast. Along with the "standard" practices of PB and LISP, the Kirov region implements local initiatives on co-financing expenses within programmes for providing the population with medicines and developing educational services. In the Tula Oblast, while carrying out the "National Budget" project on the portal "Open region—71", services were launched which enable project participants and other interested parties to work online.

In July 2015, the Russian Ministry of Finance and the International Bank for Reconstruction and Development (IBRD) signed a memorandum, the text of which called for the further spread and development of LISP practices in the regions of the country. In October 2015, the All-Russian Conference on Initiative Budgeting took place in Moscow for the first time.

In 2016, projects aimed at developing initiative budgeting practices began to be realised in a number of federal subjects of Russia with the involvement of appropriate specialists from the World Bank (Afanasiev & Shash, 2017).

In 2017, with the involvement of the Russian Ministry of Finance, a programme for developing initiative budgeting in the Russian Federation was launched. This project united 43 subjects of Russia to work together on a common problem (Afanasiev et al., 2020). Twelve regions of Russia launched original initiative budgeting programmes for the first time, specifically the Altai, Perm, and Krasnoyarsk Krai, the Republic of Dagestan, Chuvashia Republic, and seven oblasts (Moscow, Murmansk, Novosibirsk, Volgograd, Ryazan, Yaroslavl, Sakhalin).

In 2018, initiative budgeting was included in the state programme "Management of state finances and regulation of financial markets" implemented and administered by the Russian Ministry of Finance.

In 2019, large-scale experiments of organising online voting on citizen initiatives were launched based on blockchain technology. Organisers of initiative budgeting (IB) in federal subjects of Russia (e.g., the Volgograd and Nizhny Novgorod oblasts) and municipalities came close to needing to expand the arsenal of digital technology used due to the increased coverage and the need to expand the audience of the IB development programme (Vagin et al., 2019).

These trends require existing experience to be studied and discussions of several technical and essential issues around the use of digital forms of citizen participation in initiative budgeting, the most relevant of which seem to be the development of new formats for participation and verification practices on integrated platforms for citizen participation when making decisions regarding IB projects.

In 2020, authorities of the Crimea Republic for the first time tested the mechanism of initiative budgeting. The construction of playgrounds and sports grounds in the municipalities of the region was chosen as the priority for initiative budgeting projects to be carried out (Vagin & Shapovalova, 2020).

Currently, the coordination and policy guidance on the development of initiative budgeting in the federal subjects of Russia is as a whole fulfilled by the Russian Ministry of Finance and its subordinate institutions.

11.3   Mechanisms for Implementing Initiative Budgeting in Russia

Within participatory (initiative) budgeting processes, conditions are stipulated for citizens to take initiative at all stages of solving issues of local importance. Residents have the chance to formulate a relevant agenda, participate in the development of solutions, and control competition procedures and the practical implementation of the projects. Thus, this provides the most rational choice of priorities for budget spending at the regional and local levels for solving regional and local problems.

Specific mechanisms for managing and tracking initiative budgeting practices currently used in the Russian Federation are to a large degree determined by the existing context, including the traditions in municipal government and the size and status of key participants of the projects being implemented. The main mechanisms for tracking initiative budgeting practices in Russia are traditionally the following:

- design development of initiative budgeting practices: determining the main parameters, developing methodology, preparing operational documentation and regulatory documents;
- training the main participants of the initiative budgeting projects, who include administration workers from the regions and municipalities, non-commercial, public, and volunteer organisations;
- informing and consulting key participants of the initiative budgeting projects at different stages of their implementation;
- gathering project ideas, organising and moderating their discussion;
- technical analysis and refinement of proposals (the so-called joint project design);
- organising and conducting various voting methods for citizens in order to carry out the initiative budgeting;
- automatisation of processes, including the development and support of information systems for managing practices of initiative budgeting,

as well as the development and tracking of a specialised portal dedicated to initiative budgeting;

- monitoring initiative budgeting projects being implemented in various regions and municipalities;
- analysing results, evaluating the social and economic effects of initiative budgeting.

A breakdown of the mechanisms described above between different structures when introducing and implementing initiative budgeting in the Russian Federation is given in Table 11.1.

Examples of the specific procedures used in the Russian federal subjects regarding mechanisms for gathering project ideas, organising and moderating their discussion, and organising and conducting a competitive selection of projects (voting) are given in Tables 11.2 and 11.3.

According to the data of the Russian Ministry of Finance, the number of project ideas from citizens equalled 88,874 proposals in 2019. The number of applications claimed by the population which passed technical analysis and were registered for participation in the competition procedures was 23,420. The number of winning applications passing the competitive selection equalled 18,725 (Russian Ministry of Finance, 2020).

While introducing the mechanisms for implementing initiative budgeting in Russia in the Russian federal subjects, three main models for organising project activities within initiative budgeting practices were formed: centralised model (Model 1), budget model (Model 2), consulting model (Model 3).

Model 1 (centralised). Executive government bodies of the Russian federal subject (local government body of the municipality) carry out the functions of managing and tracking initiative budgeting practices independently.

Model 2 (budget). Executive government bodies of the Russian federal subject (local government body of the municipality) completely or partially delegate the functions of tracking the practice to government (municipal) institutions or non-commercial organisations, the founders of which are municipal authorities.

Model 3 (consulting). Executive government bodies of the Russian federal subject (local government body of the municipality) completely or partially delegate the functions of tracking the practice to outside consulting organisations.

Table 11.1   Mechanisms for tracking existing initiative budgeting practices in Russia

p/p	Types of tracking mechanisms	Structures implementing tracking mechanisms for initiative budgeting practices
1	Practice design	• World Bank • Administrations of the regions • Project centres
2	Training of main participants	• Russian Ministry of Finance and its institutions • World Bank
3	Informing	• Russian Ministry of Finance and its institutions • World Bank • Administrations of the regions • Project centres
4	Gathering of project ideas, organising and moderating their discussion	• Administrations of the municipalities • Project centres
5	Technical analysis and refinement of project proposals	• Municipalities
6	Organising and conducting a competitive selection of projects/voting	• Administrations of the regions • Municipalities
7	Automatising processes (development and support of the information system for project management)	• Administrations of the regions • Municipalities
8	Monitoring	• Administrations of the municipalities • Project centres
9	Analysing results and evaluating effectiveness	• Russian Ministry of Finance and its institutions • World Bank

Source: Authors, based on data from www.minfin.ru

Analysis shows that in 40% of the federal subjects of Russia where initiative budgeting projects are being carried out, the functions of managing the initiative budgeting practice and its tracking are fulfilled by executive authorities with their structural subdivisions. This is option **Model 1**.

Thus, for example, in the Orenburg and Tver oblasts the management and tracking of initiative budgeting practices are handled by the subdivisions of the regional ministries of Finance. In Leningrad Oblast it is

Table 11.2 Procedures used in subjects of the Russian Federation for gathering project proposals from citizens and the number of acts of citizen participation within the framework of these procedures in 2019

% p/p	Types of procedures	Number of subjects	Number of acts
1.	In-person meetings and discussions	53	2,434,343
2.	Questionnaire	33	966,186
3.	Sharing project ideas over the internet	19	20,682
4.	Collection box for ideas	12	105,580
5.	Public offices	10	2205
6.	Other procedures	24	420,221

Source: Authors, based on data from www.minfin.ru

Table 11.3 Procedures used in Russian federal subjects for selecting winning projects and the number of acts of citizen participation in these procedures in 2019

% p/p	Types of procedures	Number of subjects	Number of acts
1.	Commissions of authority representatives	46	0
2.	In-person voting at assemblies and meetings	41	1,260,482
3.	Internet voting for projects	15	726,171
4.	Citizen commissions	8	20,769
5.	Referendum	3	1,128,567
6.	Other procedures	20	1,545,240

Source: Authors, based on data from www.minfin.ru

handled by the department "Committee for local government, transnational and interfaith relations".

In the Leningrad, Kirov, and Vologda oblasts, and in the federal city of Saint Petersburg, the practice used involves allocating the given budget amount based on the decisions of the budget commission, which is made up of citizens and municipal representatives selected through sortition.

Any resident has the right to file an application and be chosen through sortition to participate in the budget commission and receive the chance to see their initiative through. These commissions can put forward budget initiatives under the authority of the municipality where they function. One of the tasks fulfilled in such practice is immersing residents in budget procedures and first-hand training in the basics of local government. This model of management is in many ways similar to that used in smaller municipal divisions of European countries where practically all functions of practice management are carried out by one or another of the subdivisions of the municipal administration.

A significant drawback of this model is the great amount of additional work placed on the workers of the administration, or related to this, refusal of certain important tracking functions, primarily, those concerning the practical work of involving citizens in implementing initiative budgeting practices.

The model of the first type is described in more detail using the example of the Orenburg Oblast, where initiative budgeting practices are tracked by nine workers from the Regional Ministry of Finance, which organises a competitive selection and develops and refines the methodology and regulatory acts, trains participants, processes applications and conducts a competitive selection.

Participants in initiative budgeting projects in municipalities are trained through the following two kinds of training events: field training events with methodological support and "area-based" seminars. The collection and processing of bids for the competitive selection of initiative budgeting projects is carried out using an automated management system. The advisory and tracking function of the initiative budgeting process is fulfilled by a public council at the Regional Ministry of Finance. About 2–3 municipalities are assigned to each member of the council, which comprises 15 people. When the next cycle of implementing the initiative budgeting projects is first launched, members of the public council visit field training events and then consult with municipalities about all issues concerning participation in the initiative budgeting programme. If necessary, members of the public council go directly to the municipalities to assist with organising and holding public assemblies or during the monitoring stage. Services rendered by members of the public council are free of charge.

The specifics of **Model 2** are looked at using the example of the Krasnoyarsk Krai, where a project centre for initiative budgeting was created based on the Regional Ministry of Finance and local institute of state and municipal government of the Krasnoyarsk Krai government. Applications of initiative budgeting projects are first received at this centre. This *project centre* in the initiative budgeting system is a structure whose function includes providing methodological, analytical, advisory support during the preparation and tracking of implementing initiative budgeting practices, including training services. Furthermore, project centres monitor the results of implementing IB practices.

The current municipal counselling involves monitoring of work of municipal divisions with documents on granting subsidies for implementing a programme for developing initiative budgeting practices, and the processing and preparation of applications to hold a review commission. All this falls on specialists of the region's Ministry of Finance.

Workers from the Institute of State and Municipal Government are assigned the following functions of training:

- in-person training and consultation at all stages of implementing each initiative budgeting project;
- developing methodological recommendations;
- monitoring the participation of municipal divisions in the initiative budgeting programme;
- receiving and reviewing bids, as well as preparing rating tables for the competitive selection;
- preparing proposals on improving the initiative budgeting practice in the region.

Furthermore, the institute monitors assemblies, participation of initiative groups, gathers information on the results of the selected projects, and compiles a statistical report. The next cycle of launching initiative budgeting projects starts with training participants. This is carried out separately for different participant groups: those new to the practice and experienced municipal divisions. During the preparation stage and holding of the final meetings, project participants pass remote training and receive consultation from the project centre, the workers of which oversee several municipalities each. According to the results of the competitive selection, work is carried out with the territories on implementing the projects.

Research shows that in 50% of the Russian federal subjects, separate functions of tracking initiative budgeting projects are carried out by various state (municipal) institutions. Some regions (e.g., Altai Krai, Stavropol Krai) change over to this model of management after having used Model 1, where all of the managerial functions are fulfilled by the executive authorities of the region and municipality. It should be noted that similar models are not used in practice abroad.

Model 3 is examined using the example of the Kirov Oblast, where the management and tracking of the initiative budgeting practice is carried out by workers of the development programme department of the Ministry of Social Development. The initiative budgeting cycle, which includes the editing and refinement of methodological recommendations, receiving bids, and competitive selection, is launched by workers of the ministry. Project participants are trained through three types of events: conferencing facilities and holding ten-day "cluster" workshops and field events. The training carried out in all of the initiative budgeting models implemented cover the following issues:

- involving citizens and organisations in the decision-making process regarding the distribution of public finances (14%),
- calling citizens to control the results of budget spending and how well the initiative budgeting projects are implemented (13%),
- procurement procedures (12%),
- organising and holding public assemblies (12%).

At the same time, when training project participants the most effective turned out to be training workshops, exchanging the best practices, and interactive, in-person classes.

The role of consultants is to complete two tasks: train curators of initiative budgeting projects in municipalities and consult them at all stages of implementing the initiative budgeting project. Thus, in 2019 consultants helped organise and hold 530 assemblies of residents in various municipalities of the Kirov Oblast.

Model 3 is currently used in two regions (Kirov Oblast and Saint Petersburg), where individual functions of tracking initiative budgeting projects are given to the winning outside independent organisation. In particular, during the implementation of the project "Your Budget", consultants from the local university are actively involved in the Finance Committee of Saint Petersburg.

One of the important differences between Models 2 and 3 is that the tracking of initiative budgeting projects is often handled by a subordinate structure created by authorities. An outside consultant organisation acts as a contractor for carrying out a limited number of tasks such as, for instance, holding public assemblies and training project participants. At the same time, an outside organisation can provide consultation services for other regions and municipal divisions as well.

As concerns municipalities, in many cases they independently develop and launch initiative budgeting projects and organise their tracking. A similar approach is taken in the Yamalo-Nenets and Khanty-Mansiysk autonomous okrugs.

In separate municipalities (e.g., in the city of Cherepovets in the Vologda Oblast) initiative budgeting projects are carried out through local public self-government (LPS) and the launching of a separate programme "National Budget—LPS". In essence, LPS acts as a tool for the people to self-organise according to their area of residence in a specific territory: intracity (federal cities), intracity districts, rural and urban settlements. This is used by the local population to implement their initiatives within the municipal authorities.

Diverse practices of initiative budgeting, which allow citizen initiatives to be put forward have been developed in parallel. This has led to a growth in interest among citizens towards mechanisms for determining budget spending, primarily at the municipal level. Moreover, it is the possibility to influence the redistribution of budget expenditures in favour of solving the pressing problems of residents of a specific municipality which has become the "launcher" for spreading these practices in other local authorities. People's interest in initiative budgeting practices can be explained by a number of reasons:

- Firstly, IB was an important resource for developing local government in urban and rural municipal divisions, which received resources for solving the most important problems for the people of that area.
- Secondly, IB turned out to be an important tool in improving the effectiveness of budget spending.
- Thirdly, the procedures for citizens to take part in the selection and implementation of projects makes it possible to receive a whole array of additional social, economic, and management effects.

Research shows that the main factor for the successful development of a sophisticated IB set in the Russian Federation can be seen as the joint efforts of all participants: state authorities, municipalities, citizens, non-commercial organisations, local business communities. By using an initiative budgeting mechanism in Russia, the principle of a government-citizen partnership, which takes into account the interests of all (mentioned above) parties concerned, is realised.

11.4   FINANCING INITIATIVE BUDGETING PROJECTS

In most cases, the financial resources for initiative budgeting projects are planned within regional state programmes and are annually approved in the budgets adopted (see Table 11.4).

In individual cases, projects are co-financed from other sources. For example, in the Tambov Oblast, the development programme for initiative budgeting was financed with means from a federal grant from the Russian government.

In a number of regions, participatory (initiative) budgeting projects are tracked with means from private organisations to support citizen initiatives. It should also be noted that in addition to regional-level programmes, municipal initiative budgeting programmes financed exclusively from local budgets have started to appear.

Co-financing projects at the municipal level is one of the key elements for supporting local initiatives since the level of co-financing. On the one hand, it shows a degree of trust of the programme participants and, on the other hand, serves as an indicator of how effectively the selection mechanism works and the priorities of the tasks, completed during the launch of the initiative budgeting programmes, are determined. Local co-financing

Table 11.4 Dynamics of financial indicators of practices in federal subjects of Russia for 2015–2018, millions/rubles

Parameter	2015	2016	2017	2018
Overall cost of projects, including:	2395.0	6995.6	14,501.7	19,314.3
Budget spending of Russian subjects for implementing projects	1375.8	5132.6	7678.9	10,499.3
Overall amount of financing from other sources, including:	1019.2	1863.0	6822.9	8815.0
Spending of federal budget	n/a	22.3	3782.7	3907.3
Budget spending of municipalities	614.9	1137.0	1910.9	2964.6
Co-financing means from the population	205.5	478.1	776.6 1	123.1
Co-financing means from legal entities	182.1	218.9	344.5	714.6
Other forms of co-financing	16.7	6.7	8.2	105.4
Overall amount of extra-budgetary funding (means from the population, legal entities, other forms)	404.3	703.7	1129.3	1943.1

Source: Authors, based on data from www.minfin.ru

includes three main sources of co-financing (Russian Ministry of Finance, 2019):

- from local budgets;
- from local businesses (sponsors);
- from the people—project beneficiaries (the so-called self-taxation mechanism is used).

Means of self-taxation of citizens is understood under current Russian legislation as lump-sum payments by citizens for the purpose of solving specific problems of local significance. The amount of the payments for the self-taxation of citizens is established as an absolute value as equal for all residents of the municipal division, with the exception of individual categories of citizens, the number of which cannot exceed 30% of the total number of residents of the municipal division and for whom the payment amount can be reduced.

The contribution of the population and municipality is decided on in a public assembly. Financial means collected by the population or provided by sponsors are put into the appropriate municipal budget as targeted voluntary donations. Financial means collected by the population or provided by sponsors are taken into the appropriate municipal budget as targeted voluntary donations.

Other sources of local co-financing are also possible. For example, in several rural settlements in the Tver Oblast co-financing was provided by deputies from their own funds for the development of the municipalities. In the Kirov Oblast the means used were received as self-taxation from the population. An interesting experience is that of one of the rural settlements of Bashkiria, where a special charity lottery was organised and held in order to collect funds for renovating the House of Culture.

At the same time, it should be noted that contributions from the population and sponsors can be given not only in the form of money but can also be in the form of completing, free of charge, part of the work expected in the technical documentation of the project, as well as by providing the equipment or materials necessary for its implementation.

At the same time, when implementing initiative budgeting projects, the goal of the co-financing is not so much in attracting extra-budgetary sources of funding, as much as in creating motivation for the community: the contribution of the population is evidence of how ready they are to participate in solving selected problems. Practice shows that resident contribution is only possible in cases when there is a need for the project to be implemented immediately.

Co-financing indicators from all sources of the local level (settlement budget, citizen contribution, support from local businesses) increase from year to year. The minimal contribution from the municipal budget, which gives entry to participate in the competition of initiative budgeting projects, makes up in most federal subjects of Russia from 5% to 10% of the requested regional subsidy. Here, the required level of co-financing from the residents usually does not exceed 3–5% of the total budget of the project.

However, research shows that from 2015 to 2018 the actual portion of the contribution from the municipal budget reached on average 20% of the project cost; the portion of the contribution from the population equalled 12% and from businesses—8%. Thus, the regional component of the project cost equalled on average 60%, while in individual regions this indicator is even smaller. For example, in the Tver and Nizhny Novgorod Oblasts, the portion of means of the regional subsidy in the cost of the initiative budgeting projects came to 49% for the period of 2015–2018 (Russian Ministry of Finance, 2018).

Of even bigger interest is the project for creating a ski track in the city of Uchaly (Bashkiria), the overall budget of which equalled 7.5 million rubles, where 20% was allocated from the budget of the Republic, 13.5% from the budget of the municipality of Uchaly, 11.5% from the financial contribution of the public, and a share of sponsor support equalling 55%.

Thus, the contribution from the local communities made it possible to attract additional significant financial resources for implementing the project (in some cases—up to 50% of the amount of the subsidy received from the budget above). In conditions of a deficit of financial resources in the municipal budgets, this is a very significant factor.

Self-taxation or the practice of volunteer public participation in financing expenditures is used in municipal activities for replenishing the revenue of local budgets, predominantly rural ones. The question of introducing payments is decided on at a local gathering (assembly) and is subject to mandatory execution on the territory of the appropriate municipal divisions. In a number of subjects—Republic of Tatarstan, Perm Krai, Kirov Oblast—incentive co-financing mechanisms were developed, where for each ruble collected from the population, 3–5 rubles are received from the regional budgets as a mechanism of self-taxation of the municipality.

At the same time, carrying out self-taxation procedures on the whole territory of the municipality is complicated and lengthy and likewise requires the involvement of significant organisational and financial resources. Furthermore, constructing any kind of infrastructure facilities, organising the provision of specific public services within the framework of the initiative budgeting project is not always of equal importance to the whole population of the respective territory. These and other difficulties of implementing a self-taxation mechanism have led to the use of this practice remaining quite limited.

Despite this, the involvement of extra-budgetary funding from the public and businesses makes it possible to carry out more large-scale projects for relatively small sums allocated from the regional budget. In individual cases, the overall sum of the projects is a few times higher than the subsidy from the region's budget. At the same time, as trust grows as a result of the joint implementation initiative budgeting projects, the possibilities of attracting extra-budgetary funding increase with time.

At the same time, attention should be drawn to the fact that the existing system of formal criteria for selecting initiative budgeting projects motivates participants of the competition to ensure the biggest contribution they can, since the higher the share of financing from the local community, the more points the presented application will receive and, thereby, the chances for their project winning and receiving a regional subsidy to realise its increase.

However, the high level of co-financing in itself does not guarantee victory in the competition and subsequent funding:

- firstly, the criteria for co-financing are balanced by more than 10 other competitive criteria for evaluating a filed application;
- secondly, a threshold was set whereby, when exceeded, additional points for co-financing are not counted.

As a rule, the maximum possible point for co-financing is awarded to the application when its level reaches 10–20% of the total project cost. The established criteria motivate project participants to not only increase their own contribution but also search for ways to attract financial resources from local business communities, often leading to effective, mutually beneficial partnerships between the population and businesses.

The community benefits from attracting additional resources for implementing socially significant projects, while businesses are ready to invest their money into projects which receive real support from the people of the area the former is located in. The widespread awareness of these projects and positive attitude towards them from the public contribute to forming a positive image of the entrepreneurs that participate in funding initiative budgeting projects.

The following evaluation and selection criteria were developed, based on which the project applications are assessed and ranked:

- public participation in identifying and selecting a project (35–40%): the level of participation is evaluated both in preparatory events as well as in general public assemblies;
- the level of project co-financing from all interested parties (35–40%): population, municipal budget, private business, and other sponsors (whereby not only monetary but all other types of contributions are assessed);
- social and economic effects (10–15%): for example, the percentage of beneficiaries in the overall population; workplaces created or preserved; impact on the environment; materials and mechanisms available for effectively tracking and operating the project;
- degree of openness and transparency of decisions made during the project (5–10%), including the use of media for informing the public of the respective territory.

Thus, the evaluation criteria used in assessing and ranking project applications are mainly countable, in other words, they involve using simple calculation algorithms for scoring a project.

At the same time, there are practices in Russia which involve other mechanisms for funding initiative budgeting projects. Starting in 2016, an initiative budgeting project was carried out in Saint Petersburg as part of the government programme "Creating conditions for ensuring social harmony in Saint Petersburg". The winning initiatives of the project "Your Budget" were financed on account of the corresponding targeted sections of the budget of Saint Petersburg. Thus, the amount of funds for realising project initiatives in 2017 was set at 0.01% of budget revenues, in 2018—0.16% and in 2019—0.16% of budget revenues.

Projects carried out within regional initiative budgeting programmes at this stage are mostly related to the condition and development of the social infrastructure which includes utilities, engineering, and road infrastructures, as well as facilities of education, healthcare, social protection, and the cultural sphere. Table 11.5 presents a typology of the projects carried out in the subjects of the Russian Federation for 2016–2018. All types of initiative budgeting projects are represented. This typology as a whole reflects a spectrum of "typical" problems of small Russian municipalities, especially of rural settlements. It is these problems of developing a basic infrastructure which are most keenly perceived by the people and have public resonance, and solving them directly contributes to strengthening public trust of municipal authorities.

In conclusion, it should be noted that the model emerging in Russia for tracking initiative budgeting is characterised by a number of features, particularly:

Table 11.5 Typology of all types of IB projects carried out in Russian federal subjects in 2016–2018 (%)

		2016	2017	2018
1.	Water supply, drainage	11.0	9.7	8.5
2.	Roadways, sidewalks, crosswalks, stops	14.5	13.0	15.1
3.	Street lighting	8.7	7.2	8.4
4.	Fire safety	2.8	2.7	2.7
5.	Provision of utilities for residents	0.2	0.2	0.1
6.	Cultural heritage (monuments, museums)	2.1	2.2	2.2
7.	Projects in education	–	–	5.6
8.	Realms of culture, library science, renovation of palaces of culture	11.7	10.1	7.7
9.	Physical education and mass sports	4.6	4.6	5.3
10.	Projects for improving courtyards	–	–	8.4
11.	Playgrounds	8.8	8.1	7.8
12.	Places of mass recreation for the public/improvement of public services	18.1	17.9	9.4
13.	Burial sites	3.7	3.8	4.8
14.	Solid/household waste and trash collection	5.3	3.0	3.1
15.	Event projects (celebrations, festivals)	4.5	3.8	3.0
16.	Housing and communal services (repairment of facades and roofing), organisation of heating, sewers, gas pipelines	–	1.3	1.9
17.	Large-scale infrastructure projects (bridges, dams)	–	0.3	0.2
18.	Purchasing of equipment and technology	–	4.1	1.6
19.	Vulnerable social groups and citizens with disabilities	–	–	3.0
20.	Other projects	4.0	8.0	1.2
	Total	100.0	100.0	100.0

Source: Authors, based on data from www.minfin.ru

- the weak role of public organisations and volunteers;
- lack of specialisation on the consulting services market (the project centres created fulfil various kinds of roles: developing methodology, informational support, moderating discussions, monitoring, the realisation of all of which is traditionally divided between different executors in international practice);
- "fall out" of individual tracking tasks (particularly noted is the weak execution or practically complete lack of tasks related to (a) analysing results and evaluating the effects of implementing various types of projects; (b) organising joint project design; (c) leading in-depth work when gathering, discussing, and selecting projects during participation of individual targeted groups of the population).

When researching mechanisms and results of carrying out initiative budgeting practices, it should be taken into account that the Russian model currently prevailing was formed under the influence of the following three factors.

Firstly, the initiative budgeting practices analysed were initially formed at the regional level, which naturally suggested the management, administration, and monitoring from the regional centre when directly organising and holding events at the level of specific municipalities. Secondly, at different stages of developing initiative budgeting in Russia there lacked specially prepared independent consultants (methodologists, moderators, trainers) and public organisations having the necessary knowledge in the area of participatory budgeting. In connection with this, the competencies of the project participants were built practically "from scratch". Furthermore, at the beginning stage of introducing initiative budgeting mechanisms into Russian budgeting practice, workers of the regional administration lacked both specialised knowledge in this realm and organisational opportunities, which required reinforced outside consulting support.

An analysis of the particularity of forming and implementing the Russian initiative budgeting model shows that the following factors can have a serious impact on its sustainability in the long run:

- emergence and development of municipal (as opposed to regional) initiative budgeting models;
- rate of building expertise and new competencies relating to initiative budgeting for external (relative to the administrations and project

centres) structures such as non-commercial, public, and volunteer organisations;

- developing and strengthening specialisation on the consulting services market in the area of introducing and implementing initiative budgeting practices.

Over the 10 years from the launch of the first projects with public participation in solving issues of local importance, and support of local initiatives, significant experience has been gained under the initiative budgeting mechanism in Russia. At the same time, analysis shows that there is currently a need to pay greater attention to initiative budgeting as a tool for introducing a project approach to managing at the regional and municipal levels since successfully solving local problems has shown great project potential when carrying out initiative budgeting practices.

The current situation identifies risks occurring as regional IB programmes scale up and new practices arise when quality professional tracking is lacking. Monitoring the development of IB annually records an increase in the number of practices, a growth in funding, an expansion of coverage area, and an increase in the number of participants in IB events.

One of the most important areas of development for initiative budgeting is urban practices. Involving citizens in initiative budgeting is a strong trend of urban development. In Russian cities, for now only in fragments, elements of ecosystems of civic participation, appearing primarily in a variety of forms of citizen participation in managing cities and settlements, are starting to emerge.

Since the use of the initiative budgeting mechanism has demonstrated its effectiveness in regions and municipal divisions of the Russian Federation, there needs to be an intensification of its furtherance and development by developing and actively introducing tools for monitoring and evaluating based on conducting a comparative analysis of various existing practices under the corresponding programmes in the Russian regions.

11.5   Conclusions

In 2019, the Russian Federation continued to implement the Programme for the Development of Initiative Budgeting, which is included in the activities of the federal state programme "Public Finance Management and Regulation of Financial Markets". Initiative budgeting has been actively developed in terms of legislative consolidation at the federal level. On July 15, 2020, important draft laws on initiative budgeting were adopted. As part of the implementation of the Concept of Improving the Efficiency of Budget Expenditures in 2019–2024, the Ministry of Finance of the Russian Federation is working to integrate the mechanism of initiative budgeting into federal and national projects and state programmes.

By the end of 2019, the development of information security at the regional and municipal levels was intensified, including projects that involve the organisation and financing exclusively at the expense of local budgets. In 2019, information security projects were implemented in 69 regions, the number of which reached 21,841 (+13% by 2018).

In the same year, the total amount of funding for initiative projects increased significantly, which amounted to 24.1 billion rubles (+25% by 2018). Financial support from budgets at all levels is still the most important resource for the implementation of civil initiatives and accounts for 91% of the total cost of projects. In the structure of budget sources of project financing, the contribution of the budgets of the constituent entities of the Russian Federation is fundamental—54.5%. The highest indicators of financial support for initiative budgeting projects at the expense of the regional budget in 2019 were found in the Sakhalin, Tula, Novgorod, Volgograd, Sverdlovsk Regions, Stavropol, Altai Territories, and the Republic of Bashkortostan.

The total cost of all implemented projects at the municipal level was 934.1 million rubles, including 736.4 million rubles at the expense of municipal budgets. The average cost of one project has increased: if in 2018 this indicator was equal to 1.02 million rubles, then in 2019 it was 1.1 million rubles. Municipal support for citizens' projects has increased both in absolute terms (by 1 billion rubles) and in relative terms (by 1%). This approach is typical for most countries of the world, where municipalities are the most interested party in the practices of citizens' participation in budget decision-making. In 2019, 5,170,000 people participated in information security projects, with the total contribution of citizens exceeding RUB 2 billion, which accounted for 10% of the total funding.

The participation of the population in the launch and implementation of TB projects allowed to solve the primary problems of the territories, increased the transparency of budget management, and its effective distribution. The share of beneficiaries in 69 regions of Russia from all information security projects implemented in 2019 increased to 34.3% of the total population of these regions (+11.0% by 2018), which is 30.8% of the total population of the country (almost every third Russian). As the main social effects can be noted: the involvement of citizens in the process of budget management, higher levels of trust in government; engaging citizens to participate in the life and development of the region and, as a consequence, the reduction of the dependency; and increasing literacy of the population in matters of budget allocation.

According to the Report on the best practices in the development of initiative budgeting in the subjects of the Russian Federation and Municipalities of the Ministry of Finance of the Russian Federation (Russian Ministry of Finance, 2020), in 2019, the International Monetary Fund, as part of the assessment of the transparency of the budget and tax sphere, noted the achievements of the experience of initiative budgeting in Russia at the international level.

REFERENCES

Afanasiev, M. P., Belenchuk, A. A., & Krivogov, I. V. (2020). *Byudzhet i byudzhet- naya sistema (Budget and budget system)* (6th ed.). Yurait.

Afanasiev, M. P., & Shash, N. N. (2016). Byudzhet goroda Moskvy i rost effek- tivnosti gosudarstvennykh finansov (Budget of Moscow and growth of effec- tiveness of government finances). *Voprosy Gosudarstvennogo i Munitsipal'nogo Upravleniya (Issue of State and Municipal Government), 2*, 72–95.

Afanasiev, M. P., & Shash, N. N. (2017). The crisis of public finances and the detachment of budgetary reform (2011–2015 years in Russia). *Information, 20*(9), 6339–6350.

All-Russian conference on initiative budgeting. (2015). *Initiative budgeting in the Russian Federation. Issue 1*. World Bank.

Astuty, W. (2014). An analysis on the impact of participatory budgeting and pro- cedural fairness toward manager's commitment and performance. *International Journal of Academic Research in Accounting, Finance and Management Sciences, 4*(4), 191–204. https://doi.org/10.6007/IJARAFMS/v4-i4/1321

Chulkov, A. S. (2016). Opyt i perspektivy primeneniya v Rossii initsiativnogo byudzhetirovaniya (Experience and future of using initiative budgeting in Russia). *Finansy i Kredit (Finances and Credit), 22*(8), 10–21.

Craig, P., Campbell, M., & Escobar, O. (2017). The impact of participatory bud- geting: A systematic scoping review of evaluations and outcomes. *European Journal of Public Health, 27*(suppl_3), 185. https://doi.org/10.1093/eur- pub/ckx187.185

Fedosov, V. A., & Bogatchenko, V. V. (2019). Financial mechanism of participatory budgeting in the Russian Federation. *Financial Journal, 3*, 117–127. https://doi.org/10.31107/2075-1990-2019-3-117-127

Godwin, M. L. (2018). Studying participatory budgeting. *State and Local Government Review, 50*(2), 132–144. https://doi.org/10.117 7/0160323X18784333

Gonçalves, S. (2014). The effects of participatory budgeting on municipal expenditures and infant mortality in Brazil. *World Development, 53*, 94–110. https://doi.org/10.1016/j.worlddev.2013.01.009

O'Hagan, A., MacRae, C., O'Connor, C. H., & Teedon, P. (2020). Participatory budgeting, community engagement and impact on public services in Scotland. *Public Money & Management, 40*(6), 446–456. https://doi.org/10.108 0/09540962.2019.1678250

Russian Ministry of Finance. (2018). *Report on the best practice for developing initiative budgeting in subjects of the Russian Federation and in municipal divisions.* Ministry of Finance.

Russian Ministry of Finance. (2019). *Report on the best practice for developing initiative budgeting in subjects of the Russian Federation and in municipal divisions.* Ministry of Finance.

Russian Ministry of Finance. (2020). *Report on the best practice for developing initiative budgeting in subjects of the Russian Federation and in municipal divisions.* Ministry of Finance.

Shah, A. (Ed.). (2007). *Participatory budgeting.* The World Bank.

Shul'ga, I. Y. (2017). *Initsiativnoe byudzhetirovanie. Rossiyskiy opyt v oblasti uchastiya grazhdan v reshenii voprosov mestnogo znacheniye (Initiative budgeting. Russian experience in citizen participation in solving issue of local importance).* Aleks.

Shybalkina, I., & Bifulco, R. (2019). Does participatory budgeting change the share of public funding to low income neighborhoods? *Public Budgeting & Finance, 39*(1), 45–66. https://doi.org/10.1111/pbaf.12212

Su, C. (2012). Whose budget? Our budget? Broadening political stakeholdership via participatory budgeting. *Journal of Deliberative Democracy, 8*(2), 1. https://doi.org/10.16997/jdd.149

Vagin, V. v., & Shapovalova, N. A. (2020). Challenges and issues of initiative budgeting development. *Financial Journal, 12*(1), 9–26. https://doi.org/1 0.31107/2075-1990-2020-1-9-26

Vagin, V. V., Shapovalova, N. A., & Gavrilova, N. V. (2019). The monitoring of initiative budgeting development in Russian regions: Methodology and practice of organization. *Financial Journal, 2*, 51–64. https://doi.org/10.3110 7/2075-1990-2019-2-51-64

CHAPTER 12

Participatory Budgeting in Serbia

Miloš Milosavljević, Željko Spasenić, and Slađana Benković

12.1 Introduction

Recently, almost all European countries have to some extent embraced the concept of direct citizen participation in the public administration decision-making process (Michels & de Graaf, 2017). Participation in financial decision-making has surprisingly attracted immense attention from both practice and academia (Wampler, 2007; Weber et al., 2019). A myriad of theories such as agonistic pluralism (as opposed to liberal democracy) has been developing since the early introduction of the term 'participatory budgeting' in the 1960s (Mouffe, 2018; Pateman, 2012). Although it has been quite some time since the introduction of the term, and the first successful implementation in the Brazilian city of Porto Alegre, the phenomenon of participatory budgeting remains amorphous. Recently, participation in financial decision-making has become a cornerstone of collaborative public management (Fung, 2006).

M. Milosavljević (✉) • Ž. Spasenić • S. Benković
Faculty of Organizational Sciences, University of Belgrade, Belgrade, Serbia
e-mail: milos.milosavljevic@fon.bg.ac.rs; zeljko.spasenic@fon.bg.ac.rs; sladjana.benkovic@fon.bg.ac.rs

M. S. De Vries et al. (eds.), *International Trends in Participatory Budgeting*, Governance and Public Management, https://doi.org/10.1007/978-3-030-79930-4_12

229

Following the flux of novel theories, scholars have depicted several 'ideal' procedures of public budgeting in the Old Continent (Sintomer et al., 2008). Since participatory budgeting remains an ambiguous phenomenon, these procedures have been widely used in the concurrent literature to describe the type of participatory budgeting used by an administrative entity (i.e. Džinić et al., 2016). In this chapter, we will refer to these procedures as participatory budgeting (PB) models and will focus on their application in Serbia.

Leaving the theory aside, participatory budgeting in Serbia has been off the scholarly research radars. Only a fistful of studies have tackled this phenomenon. For instance, in an abstract political manner, it has been mentioned as a form of participative innovation (Damnjanović, 2018). Other studies have examined PB in Serbia through the lens of lessons learned from current externally funded projects (Milosavljević et al., 2020).

This chapter aims to add to the body of knowledge on participatory budgeting in Serbia. Specific goals of the chapter are to analyse contextual factors of participatory budgeting, explain the modus operandi, analyse the funds used for the PB programmes, analyse the processes conducted to date and delineate the main outcomes. To the best of our knowledge, a study of this kind has never been conducted in the aforementioned geographical region.

The remainder of the chapter is organised in the following order. Section 12.2 reviews related works and thoroughly examines the lessons learned from the extant worldwide experiments related to participative budgeting. In the same section, we provide a business case for Serbia by delineating the political, economic, social, and technological context for the Serbian public budgeting system. Section 12.3 elaborates on the methodology used in the study. Section 12.4 depicts the research results, and accordingly contextualises the results, and explains key findings. The last section is reserved for the concluding remarks.

12.2   The Contextual Analysis of the Serbian Public Budgetary System

12.2.1   Local Administration in Serbia

The Law on Territorial Organisation of the Republic of Serbia defines municipalities, cities, the city of Belgrade, and autonomous provinces with territorial units (§2). The city can, but does not necessarily have to, have municipalities. The Constitution defines two autonomous provinces— Vojvodina and Kosovo with Metohija being under dispute. The central government, autonomous provinces, and local governmental units (LGUs) have their own budgets to finance their administrative services (§92, Constitution). In 2020, Serbia had 150 municipalities (§16), and 28 cities (§20). The largest municipality is Novi Sad with 358,572 citizens and the smallest one is Crna Trava with only 1219 citizens. In total, 18 municipalities had less than 10,000 citizens.

12.2.2 Contextual Analysis for Participatory Budgeting in Serbia

Serbia has passed through several development stages of the budgeting process. These transitions were affected by the political, economic, social, technological, and other contextual factors briefly described below.

Political factors. Serbia is seldom loosely clustered as a country 'from the other side of the Iron Curtain'. Unlike other post-communist countries, direct participation of citizens in the financial decision-making process is not unfamiliar to Serbia. The self-management doctrine of former Yugoslavia is a form of quasi-direct democracy (Trpin, 2003). The first multi-party elections were held in 1990 and they were envisaged as an initial step towards parliamentary democracy. However, Serbia once again did not fit into the mould of 'colour revolutions' of the other East European countries (Stewart, 2009). Instead of a relatively smooth transition towards democracy, throughout the last decade of the twentieth century, Serbia was directly or indirectly involved in three wars, faced international sanctions, an embargo, and had multiple other political, societal, and economic turmoil. After the political roller coaster at the end of the millennium and the 'bulldozer revolution', Serbia saw the first democratically elected government after 5 October 2000. The newly elected and all consecutive governments have seldom emphasised democracy, transparency, citizen participation, and decentralisation of fiscal decision-making as one of the focal points of their governance. When thoroughly scrutinised, these processes were sometimes even adverse (Bartlet et al., 2020).

Economic factors. According to the research of the Centre for Applied European Studies (CPES, 2012), before the adoption of the Law on Financing of Local Self-Government of 2007, the system of financing of local self-government had been strongly influenced by the discretionary political power at the national level. Serbia has a long tradition of heavy centralisation in terms of public finance (Jovanović et al., 2013), and a general lack of transparency, particularly when it comes to the disclosure of financial data (Milosavljević et al., 2017). The main weakness of that system arises from unclearly defined types of public fund transfers and the lack of a unified methodology for calculating the amount that should be transferred to individual local governments. Even the new legislature has not significantly improved the fiscal autonomy of local governments, as reported in Alibegović et al. (2019).

Based on the current Law on Financing of Local Self-Government (Zakon o finansiranju lokalne samouprave, 2006), the revenue of the local government units can be divided into the following: (1) own sources of revenue, which are defined by a local government unit. However, the general tax rate or the minimum and maximum tax payable can be limited by state law. (2) Shared revenues, which are defined by state law. More specifically, the state law defines the tax base, tax rate, and how the revenue will be calculated. The revenue realised within the local government unit territory is partly or wholly transferred to the local government unit. (3) Transfers from the state budget can represent block transfers, which are defined yearly and are transferred to all local government units, except for the city of Belgrade; and earmarked transfers, which are used for specific needs or projects of local government units. Local government units can borrow funds at the market as defined by the law. The Republic of Serbia is obliged to provide sufficient funds for the local government unit each time a new service is transferred or delegated to them.

Social factors. When it comes to the public financial decision-making process, Serbia is characterised by weak institutional mechanisms combined with the silence and inertness of professional circles to participate in public debates (Kostić & Vuković, 2019). Also, the system of watchdog institutions has been poorly developed (Benković et al., 2015). From a social point of view, civil society organisations play a pivotal role in fostering government accountability in Serbia. However, recent studies find that the Serbian 'NGOs follow policy-not-politics, that is, a depoliticised approach. They target individual citizens and not social groups and nurture relationships with state institutions and public officials with whom they cooperate' (Vukovic, 2015). As such, they have a limited capacity to initiate wider civic mobilisations—an important precondition for participative budgeting.

Technological factors. Technology is a key enabler of participatory budgeting and has accordingly attracted immense scholarly attention (Omar et al., 2017). As for Serbia, citizens are not generally satisfied with the e-government services offered by local administrations (Kostic et al., 2013). Improving the quality of public administration, through the process of digitalisation and introduction of e-services, using IT technologies has become a strategic goal of Serbia since 2007, when the first strategy for the development of eGovernment was adopted, followed by an action plan for its implementation (Milanovic et al., 2019; Radonić & Milosavljević, 2019). A comparative analysis, conducted by the Swiss Agency for Development and Cooperation (SDC) in 2019, shows that local self-governments (LG) in northern and central Serbia achieve better results than municipalities in southern and eastern Serbia, which is positively correlated with the level of their economic development. The most successful municipality achieved 68% of the criteria used in the research, from which it can be concluded that eGovernment, at the local level, is still in the development phase.

The availability of e-services is still at a very low level. According to the aforementioned research done by the Swiss Agency for Development and Cooperation (SDC), only 24 out of 60 LGs that were included in the research sample (60%) have published a service on the e-government web portal but only a small portion of them can be fully executed electronically. Due to the outdated databases, the quality of e-services and the accuracy of their execution are quite questionable.

12.3 Methods

This chapter aims to analyse the use and outcomes of participatory budgeting in Serbia. The specific goals of the chapter are to explain the modus operandi, analyse the funds used for the PB programmes, analyse the processes conducted to date and delineate the main outcomes.

For this purpose, we followed the analytical framework developed by Džinić et al. (2016) and adapted it for this study by the authors. The analytical framework is presented in Table 12.1.

The main materials used in this chapter are secondary sources and include data from municipality websites, press, and official reports. The main documents analysed in this study include Local Finance Reform (2020), and BIRN (2016) reports, and websites of LGUs that have implemented participatory budgeting projects in the last five years (Pirot,

Table 12.1   Analytical framework for the chapter

Dimension	Criteria for case study
Model	• Form of PB implemented in different LGUs
Budget	• Initiation of PB
	• Governmental level for PB implementation
	• Specific policy areas
	• Sources of funding and response to austerity measures
	• Sustainability
Participation	• Rules of participation
	• Participants (citizens and NGOs)
	• Selection of participants
	• Advertising plan and implementation
	• Selection of projects
	• Actual number of participants
Process	• How PB is administered and organised
	• The public discussions on proposed projects
	• The mechanics of decision-making
	• The voting organisation
Outcome	• Acceptance of proposals by local governments
	• The actual effects of PB on public budgets
	• How innovative were proposals
	• Lessons learnt from the PB projects

Source: Authors, inspired by Džinić et al. (2016)

Sremska Mitrovica, Sabac, Vracar, Pancevo, Sombor, Trstenik, Ruma, Zrenjanin, and Knjazevac).

12.4   RESULTS

12.4.1   Analysis of Participatory Budgeting Models

Participatory budgeting in Serbia has been actively developed through several externally financed projects centred around Local Finance Reform. The projects were initiated by the civil society organisations that partnered with Serbian LGUs and were financed externally (for instance, EU funds, USAID, Norwegian, and Swiss development agencies). As the idea has not been indigenous, the models implemented have been 'imported' from the Western European local governments.

The most common model, according to which local governments implement the participatory budgeting process in Serbia, is described as follows. First, citizens of a particular municipality are informed about the participatory budgeting process through local media, the municipality's website, and local forums. Second, local administrations do not typically disclose the amount of budget which will be allocated for projects selected in the participatory budgeting process. Based on previous experiences, only a small and relatively insignificant portion of LGUs' funds have been allocated for participatory budgeting. Third, the right to propose a project financed through participatory budgeting is a general right and any citizen can practice it. The exception from this rule is the city of Sabac, where the right to propose projects is conditioned by duly paid property tax. Fourth, after the initial proposals are analysed, they are shortlisted—usually 5–10 are selected as a subject of further direct voting of the citizens in a specific LGU. The final selection encompasses the projects that get the most votes at direct elections. The project that wins the most votes is implemented and becomes a binding budget item. Dependent on the size of the municipal budget, it is possible to implement a larger number of projects in the same budget cycle. Accordingly, the participatory budgeting in Serbia is characterised by: (1) individual citizens as participants, (2) concrete investments as the scope of projects, (3) detailed suggestions as a decision paradigm, (4) financing from the municipal budget and (5) the legal obligation of LGUs to implement the projects. Seen through the lense of the main categories of participatory budgeting given in Sintomer et al. (2008), the system of participatory budgeting in Serbia can be described as the 'Porto Alegre adapted for Europe' type.

12.4.2 Analysis of the Budgets for Participatory Purposes

To enhance the public finance administration, the Swiss Secretariat for Economic Affairs has initiated a Local Government Finance Reforms (RELOF) project. The project takes into account eight high-priority reform areas including the preparation of the first participative budgets in the Republic of Serbia. PB was initiated in 2016 in six different city-municipalities (Pirot, Sremska Mitrovica, Sabac, Pancevo, Sombor, and Zrenjanin), three municipalities (Trstenik, Ruma, and Knjazevac), and one city municipality, that is of the city of Belgrade (Vracar). The local government units, which have been included in this project, consist of 28,000–120,000 citizens and represent 11% of the total population in Serbia. The results from the first cycle of participative budgeting have been outlined in Table 12.2.

Table 12.2 Financial and other outcomes and results for the first participatory budgeting cycle

LGU	Citizens with voting rights	Citizens who voted		LGU budget (millions of RSD)	Allocated to PB projects (millions of RSD)	% of the total budget
Sombor	76,742	1096	1.42%	2737	100	0.04
Ruma	47,293	1228	2.60%	1993	380	0.19
Trstenik	37,363	346	0.93%	1140	250	0.22
Knjazevac	26,523	832	3.14%	934	1000	2.14
Pirot	49,126	522	1.06%	1637	0.75	0.05
Zrenjanin	106,692	–	–	5585	3200	0.57
Sabac	104,179	463	0.44%	3305	1000	0.30
Pancevo	112,200	903	0.80%	5600	500	0.09
S. Mitrovica	70,562	595	0.84%	3150	500	0.16
Vracar	63,948	–	–	394	3350	8.50
Total	733,396	5985		26,475	103,550	0.39

Source: Authors

As shown in Table 12.2, the main features of the first cycle of participatory budgeting processes are (i) lack of interest and, consequently, poor participation of citizens in the process of the final selection of projects and (ii) the small amount of funds for the implementation of PB projects. The relatively insignificant involvement of citizens in the selection of projects whose financing will be provided from the budget is not a consequence of their aversion to the election processes as such. This can be confirmed by the turnout of citizens in the last local elections held in 2016, where the lowest turnout was in Zrenjanin (51.8%) and the highest in Trstenik (62.8%). The main reason for the low turnout is the symbolic amount of funds allocated for projects.

The practice of participatory budgeting continued in the following budget cycles, but the number of new municipalities, which started PB, is still relatively small. According to publicly available data, participatory budgeting is applied in only 10% of the total number of local self-government units. In 2020, the city of Belgrade (the capital city) flagged the introduction of the participatory budgeting process. Nonetheless, it was merely an invitation for the citizens of the capital city to propose projects, which could be financed in FY2021 from the city budget. The PB process remains relatively unnoticed and beyond the interest of citizens while the participation of participatory budgeting projects in the local budget is negligible. The exception is the city of Sabac, which has significantly improved the PB process compared to other local self-government units.

12.4.3   Analysis of the Participatory Budgeting Processes

The participatory budgeting process in Serbia is relatively complex and is implemented through several successive and interconnected activities as presented in Fig. 12.1.

The decision on the implementation of participatory budgeting is made by the local government assembly that aims to start the process. This decision is the legal basis for the initiation of the process. To ensure the continuity and development of participatory budgeting, the decision should be valid for more than one year and should not be subject to significant changes in subsequent budget cycles. The decision defines the activities by which the citizens are involved in the process of participatory budgeting and determines the professional services that will carry this process. Since this is a new process, it is necessary to prepare and submit to the broad audience the timeline and the description of the planned activities. The

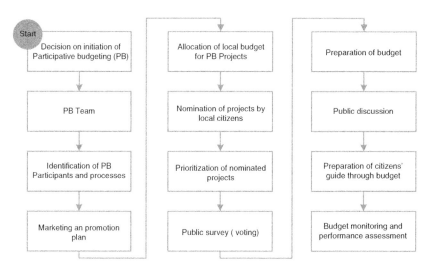

Fig. 12.1   Participatory budgeting process in Serbia. (Source: Authors, based on Local Finance Reform (2020))

delegation of activities that make up the participatory budgeting process is formalised through the decision on the formation of a Participatory Budgeting Team. The number of team members and their structure depends on the size of the municipality, human resources, and the complexity of the process to be implemented. The team must be multidisciplinary for competent individuals to be in charge of various activities.

Informing the public about the participatory budgeting process is done through an appropriate media promotion plan that aims to encourage citizens to be actively involved in the local budget decision-making process. The marketing plan is to be supported by an appropriate budget that enables the implementation of appropriate marketing activities. The marketing budget is prepared separately and is not an integral part of the budget allocated for the implementation of participatory budgeting projects. The budget is proposed by the PB team and approved by the assembly so that the funds provided can be included in the draft budget decision. Local governments are expected to focus on those marketing activities that can give good results and are aligned with the available budget. Depending on the specific situation, it is not necessary to use expensive communication channels (i.e. television) to achieve a satisfactory level of information for citizens.

The PB team has to initiate a budget proposal to fund participatory budgeting projects. There is no binding amount of funds, for example, in the form of a certain percentage of the budget, which the local self-government must allocate. PB is already being implemented in accordance with the possibilities of the municipality. The amount of funds is determined through consultations with budget users and can, but does not have to, be communicated to citizens during the implementation of the marketing plan. PB can be implemented through the cooperation between local government and the private sector. This is, however, only a legal possibility as it has not been implemented hitherto.

The public survey represents an important activity to collect project proposals. The survey can be realised using different forms: printed questionnaires that are delivered through utility bills, online questionnaires, and questionnaires published in local newspapers. The project proposals can be limited to certain areas, which are considered as important for the development of the local government. The implementation of the proposed infrastructural projects has to be exclusively within the competence of local self-government.

After collecting the proposals from the citizens, which can be numerous, it is necessary to prioritise them and then organise the voting which is the final ranking and selection of projects. Selected projects are included in the draft budget decision, which should be made available to the public in a way that citizens understand the structure of the budget. The draft decision of the budget is subject to changes, during the process of public debate, which can be proposed by interested citizens.

The last step represents the adoption of the budget and the preparation of a citizen's guide through the budget, which aims to present, in a simple way, the structure of the adopted budget. The Citizens' Budget Guide is intended for all citizens, the media, and other interested individuals and organisations. The guide aims to increase transparency and promote the budget process. The budget item intended for financing participatory budgeting projects should be presented independently with an indication that it is participatory budgeting.

12.4.4   Analysis of Participatory Budgeting Outcomes

The aforementioned guidelines for LGUs that initiate PB processes are only considered as a good practice. As LGUs in Serbia vary extensively in size, wealth, and services they provide—PB will also vary. The differences in processes, as well as the differences in outcomes, are delineated below.

The Municipality of Pirot implements participatory budgeting for four consecutive years following the above-mentioned model. The submission of citizens' proposals takes two weeks by the city service centre, local communities, and electronically via e-mail, or by using a form on a municipal website. For instance, in 2016 citizens proposed 107 projects, but the number has been decreasing ever since. Last year, only 44 proposals were submitted. The number of citizens who vote has not been significantly changing (the number is roughly around 1000), and the budget has been the same over a four-year period. In total, the funds granted to the participatory budgeting process were one million RSD which roughly makes only 0.06% of the total municipal budget. Due to the small amount of funds intended for participatory budgeting, only non-capital-intensive infrastructure projects have been implemented so far: refurbishment of rural roads, restoration of local riverbeds, and renovation of parks.

The Municipality of Ruma collects citizens' proposals through questionnaires that can be filled out in the premises of local communities or two buildings of the town hall, whereas the electronic version can be downloaded from the Municipality's website and sent to the e-mail address dedicated specifically for this purpose. The collection of proposals is open for 10 days, and they are submitted a month before final voting. Citizens are informed about the PB process through the local media and the official website of the municipality. The municipality of Ruma records a positive trend in the involvement of citizens as the number of citizens who voted has increased from 1228 in 2016 to 3531 in 2019. Nevertheless, the turnout is still insignificant. Alongside the number of voters, the budget has increased from RSD 3,800,000 to RSD 36,500,000, reaching 1.6% of the total municipal budget. The main outcomes of the participatory budgeting are renovated city parks, installation of elevators for the disabled in the city health centre, an arrangement of a local picnic area and children's playground, and so on. The number of projects has been steadily growing over time.

The city of Sombor organises PB following a similar model. Citizens propose projects in the premises of the City Hall, local communities, and electronically. In 2019, for the first time, voting was organised in the city's secondary schools, where students voted on the projects relating to the improvement of the quality of schools. Completed and printed questionnaires are submitted at the City Service Center, local community premises, and other locations where ballot boxes are placed. The questionnaires are distributed through local newspapers and at all polling stations. The questionnaires can also be sent electronically. Citizens' proposals are submitted within 10 days, a month before the final vote. The final voting is realised by filling in the ballot which is distributed to the citizens along with the utility bills. The ballots are available at the polling stations and the citizens can vote for one of the proposals that entered the final selection process. The questionnaires can also be sent electronically to the municipal e-mail used for these purposes. Unlike the municipality of Ruma, the City of Sombor has decided to implement one project per year. This approach enabled the arrangement of the centre of the village that belongs to the city of Sombor, the arrangement of a local picnic area and swimming pool, as well as the renovation of a kindergarten.

The government of the city of Sabac has been the most diligent in developing and advancing the process of participatory budgeting in Serbia. The participatory budgeting in this city presents an aspirational model of a more democratic relationship between residents and the city as depicted in Petite (2020). The main feature of PB in this city is the ultimate decentralisation, where funds are allocated to the local communities (apart from the city or a village within the municipality) where the tax has been collected in that particular fiscal year. This is the only municipality in Serbia that has been applying this model of participatory budgeting since 2017. Depending on the amount of collected property tax revenue, the amount of the participatory budget is determined in advance, individually, for each of the 60 local communities. Another interesting feature is the voting right—unlike other local governments, the city of Sabac grants the voting right only to taxpayers (minors are by general rule not included). Voting is organised in the premises of the local community and citizens vote in the territory of the local community where they reside. The described PB process had good outcomes in overcoming the above-mentioned limitations: (i) over 40% of citizens participated in the process of the final selection of projects by direct vote whilst this percentage is over 60% in some local communities and (ii) participatory budget is approximately 5% of the total city budget and reached the amount of 200 million RSD, which is far above the amount allocated by other municipalities. The improvement of the PB process was realised within four years. The entire PB process and selected projects are promoted through the local media. The projects voted upon are available on the website of the municipality, bulletin boards of local communities, and in the media, making the process transparent and efficient. A significant amount of funds enabled the realisation of large-scale investment projects—the construction of a suburban ambulance, the construction of a small indoor sports hall, the beginning of the construction of a suburban house of culture, the construction of irrigation wells, and the purchase of livestock scales for local green markets.

12.5   DISCUSSION AND CONCLUSION

This chapter aimed to depict participatory budgeting in Serbia—particularly the model used, funds allocated, and processes implemented, together with the main outcomes and outputs. In this section, we contextualise the findings of the participatory budgeting experiences in Serbia. In specific, we delineated the international development context, scale and forms, design of the process and outcomes, and results.

As for the international dimension, participatory budgeting has not been an indigenous phenomenon of Serbian local communities. Rather the idea and applicative forms have been 'imported' via the international donors (particularly the EU funds). In general, participatory budgeting is still in the earliest phase of development in Serbia. The initial participatory budgeting projects were externally funded and the sustainability of these projects is still questionable. Hitherto, other elements of participative democracy, such as participative urban planning, have received greater attention, especially in large urban areas. Nonetheless, a handful of local communities demonstrated the capability to utilise a good international practice and in FY2020 some local self-governments have announced their will to implement participatory budgeting in the FY2021.

Citizens who voted in participatory budgeting processes prioritised basic infrastructure projects. The most important outcome of participatory budgeting is seen in hard infrastructure. Roads, paving of streets, reconstruction of parks, and renovation of local schools and ambulances are by far the most frequent projects funded through participatory budgeting. In most cases, the size and value of those projects were not significant, but they were important for small communities that had no investment into local infrastructure for many years. The participatory budgeting failed to mobilise financial and non-financial resources beyond the devoted local budget. Also, no projects were financed from international aid or international financing including resources from central government programmes.

Participatory budgeting has been reserved for smaller local communities. The experiences of herein isolated local governments can serve as a role model for further development and proliferation of participatory budgeting. It should, however, be noted that, given that the amount of funds allocated for participative budgeting to local governments is limited, the discontinuity incentives are rather too small. Keeping this in mind, the processes flagged as 'participatory budgeting' still lack a uniform design. There is no legal obligation or any kind of universal practice guide for the preparation and implementation of participatory budgeting. The processes dissected in this chapter serve as a good practice, rather than the ruling cast in stone.

The process of participatory budgeting in Serbia is characterised as follows: (a) participants are individual citizens rather than civil society organisations, (b) scope of projects is reserved for particular projects (most of them based on hard infrastructure), (c) the decision is made on a two-tier selection process, (d) funding is provided by municipalities rather than from independent sources or self-made contributions, and (e) local governments have a legal obligation to execute selected projects. Accordingly, participatory budgeting in Serbia is of a 'Porto Alegre adapted for Europe' type (for the specific classification of participatory budgeting types, see Sintomer et al. (2008)).

The outcomes that emerge from participatory budgeting in Serbia are below initial expectations and it cannot be concluded that the purpose and goals of this process are met. The proposals of citizens were included in the local budgets and were delivered within an agreed timeframe, but those projects captured only a small portion of the municipal budget that is far from actual needs. The city of Sabac is an exception and a positive example that where the process is implemented well it becomes popular among citizens as it can address their needs and priorities. Participatory budgeting contributed, to a limited extent, to the democratisation and modernisation of local government.

Despite the myriad of different constraints and limitations, the pioneering participative budgeting projects might be used as a good vehicle for fostering participative and direct democracy in Serbia. Next to the hard or social infrastructure financed from PB projects, an important outcome is educational. Citizens can learn how to generate ideas and directly participate in the development of the local financial system, all of which is highly appreciated in Serbia.

References

Alibegović, D. J., Hodžić, S., & Bečić, E. (2019). The level of fiscal autonomy: Evidence from Croatia, Serbia and Bosnia and Herzegovina. *NISPAcee Journal of Public Administration and Policy, 12*(1), 91–112. https://doi.org/10.2478/nispa-2019-0004

Bartlet, W., Đulić, K., & Kmezić, S. (2020). The impact of fiscal decentralisation on local economic development in Serbia. *Lex Localis, 18*(1), 143–163. https://doi.org/10.4335/18.1.143-163(2020)

Benković, S., Krivokapić, J., & Milosavljević, M. (2015). Application of the public-private partnership organizational structure in the improvement of business operations of public sector enterprises in Serbia. *Lex Localis, 13*(3), 397–417. https://doi.org/10.4335/13.3.397-417(2015)

BIRN. (2016, April 28). *Prvi Gradanski vodiči kroz budžet u 10 lokalnih zajednica u Srbiji.* http://birnsrbija.rs/prvi-gradanski-vodici-kroz-budzet-u-10-lokalnih-zajednica-u-srbiji/

Centre for Applied European Studies (CPES). (2012). *Finansiranje lokalne samouprave u Srbiji i uticaj političke veze lokalne i republičke vlasti.* https://www.cpes.org.rs/Downloads/Analize/Finansiranjelokalnesamouprave.pdf

Damnjanović, I. (2018). Participative experiments in Serbia: Democratic innovations? (text in Serbian). *Srpska Politička Misao, 2*, 27–43. http://www.ips.ac.rs/publications/participativni-eksperimenti-u-srbiji-demokratske-inovacije

Džinić, J., Svidroňová, M. M., & Markowska-Bzducha, E. (2016). Participatory budgeting: A comparative study of Croatia, Poland and Slovakia. *NISPAcee Journal of Public Administration and Policy*, 9(1), 31–56. https://ideas.repec. org/a/vrs/njopap/v9y2016i1p31-56n2.html

Fung, A. (2006). Varieties of participation in complex governance. *Public Administration Review*, 66(s1), 66–75. https://doi.org/10.1111/ j.1540-6210.2006.00667.x

Jovanović, P., Joksimović, N. Ž., & Milosavljević, M. (2013). The efficiency of public procurement centralization: Empirical evidence from Serbian local self-governments. *Lex Localis*, 11(4), 883–899. https://doi.org/10.4335/11. 4.883-899(2013)

Kostić, S., & Vuković, D. (2019). The perfect silence: An empirical study on how ignorance and lack of critical debate effect the process of enacting tax legislation in Serbia. *Anali Pravnog Fakulteta u Beogradu*, 67(1), 67–92. https:// doi.org/10.5937/analipfb1901069k

Kostic, S. C., Okanovic, M., Milosavljevic, M., & Vukmirović, J. (2013). Antecedents of citizens' satisfaction with local administration in Serbia. *Transylvanian Review of Administrative Sciences*, 9(40), 22–34. https://rtsa. ro/tras/index.php/tras/article/view/141

Local Finance Reform. (2020). *Aktivnosti u procesu realizacije participativnog budžetiranja*. http://lokalnefinansije.rs/pbvodic/aktivnosti_u_procesu_pb.php

Michels, A., & de Graaf, L. (2017). Examining citizen participation: Local participatory policymaking and democracy revisited. *Local Government Studies*, 43(6), 875–881. https://doi.org/10.1080/03003930.2017.1365712

Milanovic, N., Milosavljevic, M., & Milosevic, N. (2019). Failure management approaches and public service quality: Empirical evidence from Serbia. *Lex Localis*, 17(3), 417–433. https://doi.org/10.4335/17.3.417-433(2019)

Milosavljević, M., Milanović, N., & Benković, S. (2017). Waiting for Godot: Testing transparency, responsiveness and interactivity of Serbian local governments. *Lex Localis*, 15(3), 513–528. https://doi.org/10.4335/15. 3.513-528(2017)

Milosavljević, M., Spasenić, Ž., Benković, S., & Dmitrović, V. (2020). Participatory budgeting in Serbia: Lessons learnt from pilot projects. *Lex Localis—Journal of Local Self-Government*, 18(4), 999–1021. https://doi.org/10.4335/ 18.3.999-1021(2020)

Mouffe, C. (2018). Democracy as agonistic pluralism. In *Rewriting democracy* (pp. 35–45). Routledge. https://doi.org/10.4324/9781315244167-3

Omar, A., Weerakkody, V., & Sivarajah, U. (2017). *Developing criteria for evaluating a multi-channel digitally enabled participatory budgeting platform* (Lecture Notes in Computer Science (Including Subseries Lecture Notes in Artificial Intelligence and Lecture Notes in Bioinformatics)) (Vol. 10429, pp. 3–11). LNCS. https://doi.org/10.1007/978-3-319-64322-9_1

Pateman, C. (2012). Participatory democracy revisited. In *Perspectives on politics* (Vol. 10, pp. 7–19). Cambridge University Press. https://doi.org/10.1017/S1537592711004877

Petite, W. (2020). The promise and limitations of participatory budgeting. *Canadian Public Administration, 63*(3), 522–527. https://doi.org/10.1111/capa.12385

Radonić, M., & Milosavljević, M. (2019). Human resource practices, failure management approaches and innovations in Serbian public administration. *Transylvanian Review of Administrative Sciences, 15*(Special Issue), 77–93. https://doi.org/10.24193/tras.SI2019.5

Sintomer, Y., Herzberg, C., & Röcke, A. (2008). Participatory budgeting in Europe: Potentials and challenges. *International Journal of Urban and Regional Research, 32*(1), 164–178. https://doi.org/10.1111/j.1468-2427.2008.00777.x

Stewart, S. (2009). Democracy promotion before and after the 'colour revolutions'. *Democratization, 16*(4), 645–660. https://doi.org/10.1080/13510340903082978

Trpin, G. (2003). Local government reform in Slovenia. From socialist self-management to local self-government. In *Local democracy in post-communist Europe* (pp. 157–180). VS Verlag für Sozialwissenschaften. https://doi.org/10.1007/978-3-663-10677-7_6

Vukovic, D. (2015). The role of civil society in fostering government accountability in contemporary Serbia: On the limits of depoliticized social activism. *Sociologija, 57*(4), 637–661. https://search.proquest.com/docview/1771455503?pq-origsite=gscholar&fromopenview=true

Wampler, B. (2007). *Participatory budgeting in Brazil: Contestation, cooperation, and accountability.* Penn State Press. https://www.psupress.org/books/titles/978-0-271-03252-8.html

Weber, H. I., Vogt, S., Eberz-Weber, L.-M., Steinmetz, H., Wagner, S. A., Walther, F., Weber, P., & Kabst, R. (2019). Participatory budgeting: Findings from Germany. In *Civic engagement and politics: Concepts, methodologies, tools, and applications* (pp. 1087–1107). IGI Global. https://doi.org/10.4018/978-1-5225-7669-3.ch054

Zakon o finansiranju lokalne samouprave. (2006). ("Sl. glasnik RS", br. 62/2006, 47/2011, 93/2012, 99/2013—usklađeni din. izn., 125/2014—usklađeni din. izn., 95/2015—usklađeni din. izn., 83/2016, 91/2016—usklađeni din. izn., 104/2016—dr. zakon, 96/2017—usklađeni din. izn., 89/2018—usklađeni din. izn., 95/2018—dr. zakon i 86/2019—usklađeni din. izn.) (text in Serbian).

CHAPTER 13

Participatory Budgeting in Slovakia: Recent Development, Present State, and Interesting Cases

Mária Murray Svidroňová and Daniel Klimovský

13.1 INTRODUCTION

The models of participatory budgeting (PB) in Europe vary a lot (e.g. Krenjova & Raudla, 2013; Sintomer et al., 2013), but every model enables citizens to participate in passing the budget of the local government either

M. Murray Svidroňová (✉)
Faculty of Economics, Matej Bel University in Banská Bystrica,
Banská Bystrica, Slovakia

Faculty of Economics and Administration, Masaryk University in Brno,
Brno, Czechia
e-mail: maria.murraysvidronova@umb.sk

D. Klimovský
Faculty of Arts, Comenius University in Bratislava, Bratislava, Slovakia

Faculty of Economics and Administration, Science and Research Centre,
University of Pardubice, Pardubice, Czechia
e-mail: daniel.klimovsky@uniba.sk

© The Author(s), under exclusive license to Springer Nature
Switzerland AG 2022
M. S. De Vries et al. (eds.), *International Trends in Participatory Budgeting*, Governance and Public Management,
https://doi.org/10.1007/978-3-030-79930-4_13

247

directly or in a mediated way by various representatives (non-governmental organisations [NGOs], community groups). Direct participation or participatory democracy is very important as it means that associations of non-elected citizens are involved in the decision-making process (although deliberative democracy is identified in only few models by Sintomer et al. (2008)) and thus in public services delivery. In that sense, the existing models of PB in Slovakia will be analysed hereafter.

The aim of this chapter is to review participatory budgeting in Slovakia in terms of implementation, rules, process, and objectives in order to identify examples of good practice and point out obstacles that limit the broader use of PB in the country. Slovakia is an interesting case thanks to an extreme level of local fragmentation (Csachová & Nestorová-Dická, 2011). While the largest city is the capital city, Bratislava (approx. 437,800 inhabitants), only 12 inhabitants have permanent residence in a rural municipality of Príkra. The arithmetic average size of the municipalities in Slovakia is 1870 inhabitants. Using the median instead, the municipal structure of Slovakia would have looked much fragmented and the original number would have fallen to 642 inhabitants (Klobučník & Bačík, 2016). From the perspective of the local government system, a strong mayor form is used (Heinelt et al., 2018). The local as well as regional governments deliver a wide range of public services, and according to the multi-level governance typology (Hooghe & Marks, 2001), a multipurpose model or type I of multi-level governance is applied. According to the Local Autonomy Index recently developed by Ladner et al. (2019), Slovakia's total score for the period of 2010–2014 is 60.9; it belongs to the Type III of local autonomy that is equal to a medium level of political discretion accompanied with a medium level of financial autonomy. Although the self-government system at the local level was renewed in 1990, one of the most important reforms was implemented in the first decade of the 2000s. It consisted of a wide devolution, establishment of regional governments with directly elected political representatives, fiscal decentralisation, and introduction of performance-based programme budgeting (Daniel Klimovský et al., 2019).

13.2   First Participatory Budgets in Slovakia

So far, there are quite a few municipalities that have implemented participatory budgeting. The first three municipalities were the city of Bratislava in 2011, followed in 2013 by the town of Ružomberok and the city of

Banská Bystrica in 2014. In all of the three municipalities, the process of PB was started by a local NGO initiative and the work of volunteers (Džinić et al., 2016; Székely, 2014).

The case of Bratislava was specific—in the first year (2011), the money for PB (€15,000) was obtained from sponsors, not from the public budget. The process of implementing PB was started in a bottom-up way where active citizens and the NGO Utopia raised the money, established cooperation with the city council, and involved other citizens. Approximately 200 citizens participated in 5 thematic communities ((1) Youth, (2) Senior citizens, (3) Culture, (4) Green town, (5) Cycle–transport) whereby up to 3 projects were selected for each community. The winning projects were approved in a deliberation process. In the next year, Bratislava City Council allocated €29,975 from its budget and for 2013 it was €46,000. However, the problem was that the city had promised the amount for PB would be 1% of total costs which should have been around €2 mil. This was highly demotivating for those volunteers who had devoted their free time and work on the projects but lacked the funding. The city of Bratislava was challenged by other problems: low publicity of PB, delayed tranches for some projects, non-transparent process of drawing money, and the quality of deliberation. These challenges led to the division of PB in Bratislava to local districts; in 2013, it was Bratislava and Petržalka, and in 2014, Bratislava, Petržalka and Bratislava-Nové mesto (BA-NM).

Petržalka has implemented a different model of PB—projects were presented by the municipality in three categories and citizens could only vote which one will be realised in each category. These categories were: (1) new greenery, (2) stairs (public spaces), and (3) sport (renovation of sport areas, gyms, playgrounds). This is the so-called model of Consultation on public finances.

BA-NM adapted the "Porto Alegre for Europe model", with public deliberation and voting system where votes cast at the deliberation have 50% weightage, online voting has 20% weightage, and voting at 11 designated points has 30% weightage. Priorities for projects were chosen at the first open discussion forum by citizens as follows: (1) youth, (2) senior citizens, (3) green town, and (4) public spaces and urbanism.

In Ružomberok, PB was implemented in 2013 thanks to the NGO Tvorivý Rozvoj (Creative Development) in cooperation with the NGO Utopia which had also helped to implement PB in Bratislava. The first thematic communities were (1) green town and (2) Youth. Out of 7 submitted projects 6 were approved in the election which consisted of public deliberation (90% weightage) and on-line voting (10% weightage). A step to increase the civic participation was that projects can be submitted only by citizens who actively met during the year at the thematic assemblies. As for voting, anybody with permanent residence in the town and over the age of 18 was eligible to vote. In the following years, the initiating NGO could not persuade the town council to increase the amount of money allocated for PB and the process was terminated in 2015.

Banská Bystrica (BB) started with PB in 2014. The initiators were the NGO Via Altera, again in cooperation with NGO Utopia, and one town councillor. This fact is worthy of notice as there were local elections in Slovakia in 2014 and the step of supporting PB was aimed at getting some extra votes from those activists who appreciate that they can decide on public spending. Despite the support of the councillor, which enabled the smooth passage of PB in the town council, there were several problems in the pilot year. First of all, the money allocated for PB was taken from so-called civic councils. These councils were assigned €1.5 per citizen living in the district of each council from collected local taxes. In 2014, it was only €1.25 per citizen and the rest of the amount (€0.25 × 77,820 citizens) was assigned to PB. This minor drop in funding for civic councils evoked a large wave of disagreement. The members of civic councils complained that they were elected to decide how to spend public money in their districts and they wanted to disrupt the process of PB. Their protests stopped when they discovered they can also submit projects, this time as citizens, not as elected bodies. Indeed, 2 out of 4 approved projects were submitted by citizens from these civic councils. The second problem is the low level of interest of public servants to cooperate. Whereas the councillors are in favour of PB, the public servants see it as another burden when they have to deal with project documentation and monitor financial reports. Despite the problems, PB continued in 2015 with the amount of €19,343 which increased in the following years up to €40,000 in 2020. During those years there were several changes in the statute of PB, mostly on eligibility to submit a project, to vote (who, where, for how many projects, the weight of voting), and maximum amount for one project. Since this is the only town where PB has continued since its introduction, we describe the current conditions in more detail: all citizens over the age of 15 with permanent residence in the town and also students with temporary residence in BB are eligible to vote; this also empowers young people to decide and increases their participation. Project submission is open to all citizens over the age of 18 with permanent or temporary residence, or if a younger citizen over the age of 15 wants to submit their project he/she must be under the approval of their lawful guardian. In BB there is no online voting. Citizens can vote either at the public forum after the deliberation process or in the Information Centre or the client zone at the town hall by casting their votes after having their residency validated. It is possible to vote for 1–4 proposals. The maximum amount per project is €10,000 (Table 13.1).

The objectives of PB in Banská Bystrica are:

- democratic, open, and shared use of public resources to create and implement one's ideas for improving the city, self-government, and community;
- enabling the participation of as many inhabitants of Banská Bystrica as possible;
- more flexible response to the needs and requirements of the city's inhabitants;
- increasing the transparency of self-government (PB statute in Banská Bystrica, 2019).

Table 13.1 Development of participatory budget in Banská Bystrica, 2014–2020

Year	Number of projects	Number of approved projects	Number of voters	Share of voters on the population (%)	Participatory budget in €	Share of PB on total town expenditure (%)
2014	31	4	382	0.48	19,455	0.04
2015	20	5	512	0.65	19,343	0.04
2016	12	4	505	0.64	20,000	0.04
2017	18	6	740	0.94	30,000	0.05
2018	8	8	434	0.55	40,000	0.05
2019	16	4	737	0.94	40,000	0.06
2020	9	4	–	–		0.06

Source: Authors, based on www.utopia.sk

13.3   Participatory Budgeting in Slovakia

At present, local governments in Slovakia are historically the "most open" to civic participation in deciding on sections of the budget. While according to Transparency International Slovakia, a participatory budget was used by 17 of the 100 largest municipalities in 2018, it can be stated that the total number of local governments offering participatory budgeting for their citizens has been growing in a significant way since 2015 (Table 13.2). A clear majority of them have implemented the so-called Porto Alegre for Europe model. Local governments that have adopted a participatory budget can therefore "flourish" in redistributing part of the public money in favour of implementing the ideas and thoughts of citizens, whom they jointly believe will improve the quality of life in the city (G. Brutovská & Marošiová, 2019). There are also unsuccessful attempts in the short history of the PB in Slovakia. For example, the local council of Detva entitled the head of the town office to elaborate a draft of the bylaw of a PB in Detva but this initiative did not lead to the introduction of a PB in 2015. Even more paradoxical situation happened in Zlaté Moravce in 2017. An idea of a PB was presented by one of the local councillors of this town, but his proposal was rejected by the inhabitants of Zlaté Moravce during a public gathering where this issue was discussed.

Based on the available resources, it can be stated that 53 local governments declared at least the idea of a participatory budget at the beginning of 2020 (Table 13.2). However, the unexpected COVID-19 pandemic has become a real turning point. More precisely, total revenues of the local governments have dropped, new expenditures have occurred, the level of uncertainty has become too high from the decision-makers' point of view, and various governmental restrictions have significantly limited options for active public participation since February/March 2020. A majority of the local governments with the PBs have either temporarily suspended or completely cancelled the processes of participatory budgeting under these conditions. In addition, some of those to be introduced in 2020 have never begun. Due to a suspension or cancellation of the PBs, some local governments (Lučenec, Svidník, etc.) have decided that the funds earmarked for the PBs would be used for unexpected or urgent expenditures related to unfavourable situation caused by the pandemic.

On the other hand, only nine local governments had already decided to terminate participatory budgeting before 2020 (Table 13.3). Reasons for termination were different and they include a lack of funding for projects,

Table 13.2 Overview of municipalities according to the year of introduction of the PB (January 2020)

Municipality	Year of introduction of the PB	Number of inhabitants	Own revenues (2018) in EUR
Banská Bystrica	2014	78,100	73,193,623
Bratislava-Nové Mesto	2014	39,600	23,357,308
Senica	2015	20,300	19,263,901
Svätý Jur	2015	5700	9,847,370
Šaľa	2015	21,700	23,180,399
Hlohovec	2016	21,300	22,929,269
Liptovský Mikuláš	2016	31,000	32,965,737
Partizánske	2016	22,300	17,188,223
Poltár	2016	5600	5,976,091
Trnava	2016	65,000	62,805,934
Vranov nad Topľou	2016	22,200	23,196,747
Bratislava-Rusovce	2017	4100	4,029,485
Bratislava-Vajnory	2017	6000	4,559,425
Bratislava-Vrakuňa	2017	20,100	9,059,402
Kežmarok	2017	16,300	24,453,157
Nové Mesto nad Váhom	2017	20,100	18,144,756
Prievidza	2017	45,000	37,968,882
Rožňava	2017	19,000	17,742,026
Spišská Belá	2017	6700	7,882,065
Topoľčany	2017	24,800	27,998,720
Trstená	2017	7400	7,204,359
Nitra	2018	76,500	80,284,423
Poniky	2018	1600	2,096,577
Bratislava–Lamač	2019	7300	4,172,385
Chorvátsky Grob	2019	6300	3,572,530
Ivanka pri Dunaji	2019	6800	7,919,651
Košice-Západ	2019	39,700	2,257,220
Krásno nad Kysucou	2019	6800	7,582,201
Lučenec	2019	27,700	25,991,285
Modra	2019	9000	8,216,301
Nové Zámky	2019	37,500	31,787,710
Pezinok	2019	23,000	20,018,773
Považská Bystrica	2019	39,300	30,933,160
Stará Ľubovňa	2019	16,300	14,209,482
Svidník	2019	10,800	11,712,401
Trebišov	2019	24,600	19,165,020

(continued)

Table 13.2 (continued)

Municipality	Year of introduction of the PB	Number of inhabitants	Own revenues (2018) in EUR
Veľký Šariš	2019	6400	5,554,384
Vysoké Tatry	2019	4000	7,386,857
Zálesie	2019	2100	863,531
Košice-Sídlisko KVP	2019/2020	23,500	0
Bánovce nad Bebravou	2020	17,800	16,805,570
Hnúšťa	2020	7400	6,942,336
Hruštín	2020	3100	2,546,623
Humenné	2020	32,800	29,647,615
Jelšava	2020	3300	3,868,055
Levice	2020	32,700	28,418,378
Martin	2020	54,200	46,730,009
Nová Baňa	2020	7300	5,578,935
Púchov	2020	17,600	18,025,391
Rimavská Sobota	2020	23,800	18,082,388
Rovinka	2020	4700	4,966,868
Snina	2020	19,500	15,843,455
Stará Turá	2020	8800	7,169,559

Sources: Authors based on MV SR—ÚSV ROS, Príjmy, výdavky a dlh obcí

Table 13.3 Overview of municipalities that terminated their PBs (December 2019)

Municipality	Period of use of the PB	Number of inhabitants	Own revenues (2018) in EUR
Bratislava	2011–2014	437,800	339,434,372
Bratislava-Petržalka	2013–2015	104,100	40,206,473
Bratislava-Záhorská Bystrica	2017	6000	4,140,786
Košice-Nad Jazerom	2014	24,400	1,452,633
Lozorno	2016–2017	3100	2,686,973
Piešťany	2016–2019	27,300	26,720,491
Ružomberok	2013–2016	26,600	28,156,371
Sološnica	2018–2019	1600	1,677,014
Žabokreky	2018	1200	871,692

Sources: Authors based on MV SR—ÚSV ROS, Príjmy, výdavky a dlh obcí

volunteer burnout, success of newly elected councillors in the 2018 local elections who were not in favour of PB, and so on. This group of the local governments is not very numerous but it is a much more heterogeneous group in terms of a PB model. For instance, both Ružomberok and Bratislava used the "Porto Alegre for Europe" model. But Lozorno used the "Representation of organized interests" model and the "Consultation of public finance" model was used in Bratislava-Petržalka.

The following text presents interesting highlights on PBs' process in selected local governments.

BA-NM has a special method of voting: the information leaflets include ballots and are distributed to the citizens' mailboxes, which also increases awareness of PB. Internet voting has a control mechanism consisting of the control of IP addresses. The voter is also to provide personal data (name, surname, residence, and contact) in accordance with GDPR (www. banm.sk). In this way, the abuse of online voting is prevented as can happen when people share the call to vote with their acquaintances throughout Slovakia in order to get as many votes as possible and thus the idea of active civic participation in the town disappears. Despite this way of distributing ballots in combination with online voting, BA-NM did not achieve a much higher participation in PB (on average 3.76%).

The town of Prievidza (PB statute in Prievidza, 2019; PB statute in Prievidza, 2019) has a similar voting method, where ballots are distributed to citizens' mailboxes, or they can be downloaded from the town's website. Physical voting has a weightage of 50%, electronic voting has a weightage of 10%, and deliberation has 40%. These steps led to a higher participation in PB (on average 10.17%). Compared to BA-NM, there are differences in the possibility to download the ballot paper online and in the fact that Prievidza also offers public consideration. These are possible factors that may have influenced the fact that the participation of citizens in BA-NM was not so greatly influenced, while in Prievidza such voting increased participation in PB. The factors would need to be analysed in more depth, so we take these only as assumptions.

In cooperation between the city of Nitra and the Nitra Community Foundation, a participatory budget was implemented in 2018, which citizens know under the name Mením moje mesto (Changing My City). The programme is being run in cooperation with the NGO WellGiving thanks to the support of the European Social Fund. The city invites citizens to participate in civic projects through a grant call. The first project categories were focused on IT solutions and public spaces. In the following years, other thematic areas were added, such as education, social and health protection, activation of youth and seniors, culture, environmental protection, tourism development, and sports activities for the public. The city council allocates a percentage amount of the total city budget from which Changing My City projects (participatory budget) are financed. The role of the Nitra Community Foundation is to acquaint citizens with a participatory budget through a marketing campaign (PB statute in Nitra, 2019).

The town of Partizánske has a specific voting system via SMS, which has the form PROJEKT gap project number according to the table of projects, the price of a return SMS is €0.50. It is possible to vote for a specific project only once from one telephone number, but it is also possible to vote for all projects. The first 10 projects with the highest number of votes are supported. In order for a project to be supported, it must receive at least 50 SMS votes (PB statute in Partizánske, 2019).

In the town of Rožňava there was the condition that the maximum financial framework for one submitted project may not exceed 15% of the total approved budget for the PB for the relevant year. In 2018, this amount could not exceed €7500 per project (the total amount of money for PB was €50,000). Based on the experience from the pilot year, the time for project implementation was adjusted from one to two years. The financial support of the town makes up 70% of the project price; the remaining 30% is the contribution of the implementers, for example in the form of time worked on the project itself. Rožňava also has a specific electronic voting, where you need to log in via the city website, click on the vote icon, and then you need to log into your Google account. Physical voting takes place at designated places: the municipal office, a kindergarten, primary school, and community centre (PB statute in Rožňava, 2019). This makes it more accessible for citizens than just town hall like it is in most municipalities.

Compared to other towns, Trebišov has a very specific requirement for applicants from the town: each project must have a drawing of the location where it will be implemented. The project can have the character of a simple intervention in a public space or can support the following areas: culture, sports, social events and activities, or services for town residents. The voting conditions have the following steps:

- it is necessary to choose 3 projects, each project receives only 1 vote;
- after filling in the form, the voter enters their mobile phone number and then receives a verification code;

- the code is added to the form which can only then be sent, the SMS is free. (https://www.trebisov.sk/hlasobcanov).
- In the town of Veľký Šariš the submitter of an idea can be:
- town resident or group of town residents over 15 years of age,
- a legal person operating in the territory of the town,
- unspecified submitter, if the idea arises in a public meeting. (PB statute in Veľký Šariš, 2019)

Each resident can vote once and can support a minimum of one and a maximum of three ideas from the area of the town where they reside. Voting is possible physically at designated places, electronically by e-mail, or by sending a ballot paper by post to the municipal office.

In the town of Svidník (PB statute in Svidník, 2019), an amount of €5000 was set aside for the purposes of implementing the participatory budget. Of this amount, €300 was set aside for kindergartens with low-cost projects. Despite this low amount, 7 projects were submitted and implemented (budgets did not exceed the allocated amount of €5000).

The process of PB can be in general described as shown in Fig. 13.1:

The main objectives for which local governments are implementing PB can be summarised as follows:

- enabling the widest possible participation of as many citizens as possible;
- create space for activities and interests of residents aimed at improving life in the town;
- modernisation and streamlining of self-government so that it can respond as flexibly as possible to the needs and requirements of the citizens and at the same time implement public projects with them for the benefit of the entire town;
- improve the fulfilment of the needs and priorities of the population;
- increase the efficiency, legitimacy, credibility, and transparency of public decision-making and reduce clientelism and corruption;
- create a new relationship between self-government and citizens, which in practice means the formation of a new, more democratic form of management and decision-making of the city's inhabitants;
- bring the functioning of self-government closer to the general public;
- increase interest in public affairs, promoting an active civic approach—redirecting public resources to the benefit of the most affected and to projects that are a priority for the town's residents;

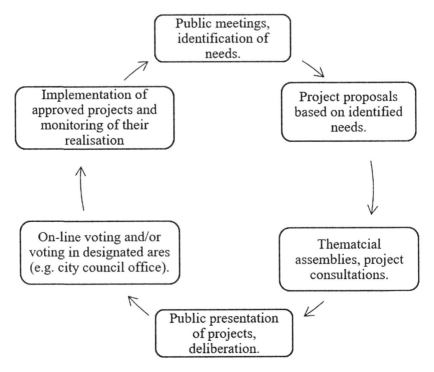

Fig. 13.1   Process of participatory budgeting in most of the Slovak local governments. (Source: Authors)

- enable the inhabitants of the town (possibly also NGOs) to propose
  the redistribution of the allocated funds from the town budget on
  the basis of the submitted projects and to involve them in setting the
  priorities of public expenditures;
- re-establish broken social ties;
- democratic, open, and shared use of public funds for the creation
  and implementation of ideas for improving the quality of life
  in the town.

For the selected municipalities that had available all data, we prepared
an overview of PB. Table 13.4 documents the different conditions for PB
in the given municipalities.

Table 13.4 Overview of selected local governments and their development of participatory budget

Self-government	Year of implementation	Total number of projects submitted	Total number of projects implemented	Eligible submitters	Average participation (% share of voting)	Methods of voting	Eligibility to vote	Average % of the amount of PB from the total expenditure	Initiator
BB	2013	105	40	PE—15 years of age, permanent, temporary residence in BB, students on the basis of confirmation of study	0.70%	P	PE—15 years of age, permanent, temporary residence in BB, student provides proof of studying in BB	0.05%	NGO in cooperation with 1 councillor
BA-NM	2013	87	65	PE—18 years of age, permanent residence	3.76%	P, O	PE 18 years of age, permanent PE	0.18%	Town (mayor)

(continued)

Table 13.4 (continued)

Self-government	Year of implementation	Total number of projects submitted	Total number of projects implemented	Eligible submitters	Average participation (% share of voting)	Methods of voting	Eligibility to vote	Average % of the amount of PB from the total expenditure	Initiator
BA-Rusovce	2016	11	7	PE, CA	6.95%	P, O	PE 15 years of age, permanent residence	0.13%	Town (2 councillors)
HC	2015	28	22	PE, CA	3.91%	P, O	PE	0.09%	Town (mayor)
HE	2020	9	1	PE— permanent residence	2.95%	P, O	PE permanent residence	0.04%	Town
LM	2016	152	72	PE— permanent residence	–	P, PD	PE permanent residence 18 years of age	0.12%	Town
LC	2019	11	6	PE—18 years of age, NGOs	–	P, O	PE 15 years of age	0.12%	Town (mayor)
NR	2018	110	33	PE—18 years of age, CA	12.71%	O	PE 18 years of age	0.08%	Town in cooperation with NGOs
PE	2016	63	39	PE, OZ	6.33%	SMS	PE	0.13%	Town

PD	2017	34	24	PE—18 years of age, CA	10.17%	P, O	PE 15 years of age, permanent, temporary residence	0.12%	Town
RV	2017	24	20	PE—16 years of age, CA	13.51%	P, O	PE	0.24%	NGO a Town
SK	2019	7	7	PE—18 years of age or FO 15–17 years of age with guarantor	5.21%	P	PE 15 years of age with permanent residence	0.39%	Town
TV	2018	16	10	PE—18 years of age, CA	19.92%	O	PE 18 years of age	0.22%	Town
TT	2016	69	50	PE, OZ	3.20%	O, PD	PE 15 years of age, permanent residence	0.07%	Town (mayor) in cooperation with NGO
VŠ	2019	65	13	PE—15 years of age, PO	5.21%	P, O	PE 15 years of age	0.39%	Town (mayor)

Source: Authors

Abbreviations: BB—Banská Bystrica, BA NM—Bratislava-Nové Mesto, BA—Bratislava, HC—Hlohovec, HE—Humenné, LM—Liptovský Mikuláš, LC—Lučenec, NR—Nitra, PE—Partizánske, PD—Prievidza, RV—Rožňava, SK—Svidník, TV—Trebišov, TT—Trnava, VŠ—Veľký Šariš, PE—physical entity, CA—civic association. O—online voting, P—physical voting, PD—public deliberation

13.3.1   Participatory Budgeting at Regional Level

The Trenčín self-governing region joined the participatory–community budget based on the model of democratic participation in 2017. The amount of €99,000 was distributed evenly among 9 districts. The process began after an extensive information campaign called Rozhodni (Decide). The projects were from areas such as transport and roads, environment, leisure time, culture, sport, social assistance, and social services. A maximum of €2200 is for one project which had to be based on the needs of the population, involve the public, be innovative, original, and understandable. A summary is given in Table 13.5; in 2020 the PB was suspended due to the COVID-19.

In 2018, the Bratislava region also implemented PB. The amount of €255,880 was distributed among 8 districts based on the population. The maximum amount for one project is €3500 but only municipalities and legal entities (i.e. companies and NGOs) can apply. Voting is online only on the dedicated website (www.rozhodni-bsk.sk). In the first year, 150 projects were submitted; in 2019 the number dropped to 106. In 2020 the participatory budgeting was suspended due to the COVID-19.

In 2019, the Trnava region started with PB with the following criteria for the projects: sustainability, inclusion, innovativeness, environment, and community collaboration. The total amount for PB is €250,000, the amount of one project is €5000, and citizens and NGOs were eligible to apply. The voting has an online form (50% weightage) and deliberation (50% weightage). In the first year, 56 projects were submitted, in 2020 154. In 2020 due to the COVID-19, the regions decided to prolong the cycle for 2 years (www.tvorimekraj.sk).

An interesting initiative had Stanislav Mičev as a candidate for the Banská Bystrica regional governor. He dedicated €13,000 from his

Table 13.5 Participatory budget in the Trenčín self-governing region, 2017–2019

	2017	2018	2019
Allocated sum (€)	99,000	99,000	200,000
Number of submitted projects	35	80	85
Number of approved projects	29	41	78
Number of voters	2196	15,320	10,754

Source: Authors based on www.tsk.sk

election campaign (2017) to participatory budgeting for the Banská Bystrica region with a promise if he gets elected, he would establish the PB at the regional level. He was not elected, so the PB was not implemented in the end.

13.3.2 Participatory Budgeting at Schools

Schools in the Trenčín Region in Slovakia also took part in the participatory budget project. In the 2018/2019 school year, secondary and grammar schools in this region participated in the project prepared by the Trenčín Region and the Office of the Government Plenipotentiary for the Development of Civil Society (USV ROS). The Trenčín region has allocated funds from its budget, which have been transferred to the budget of pilot schools (a total of 16 schools), each school received €1000 from the budget.

The condition for schools to enter the pilot year of implementing PB was the application of innovative educational tools and methods to the teaching process which were focused on participation and participatory budgeting.

In the PB, pupils decide for themselves how to spend the allocated part of the funds from the school budget. They offer solutions developed into specific projects, vote on their order, and implement the best projects. They learn to think about their surroundings and take concrete steps to help the development of the school (or town district or the town itself).

Objectives of the pilot project:

- pilot testing and implementation of participatory budgets and the PB process in an environment of sixteen pilot secondary schools;
- promote active citizenship and participation of young people;
- participation as a new topic of education in secondary schools;
- create a methodology aimed at raising awareness of the importance of participation.

The result of this process of involving schools in the participatory budget process is:

- professional training for teachers and school heads and the possibility of ongoing consultations;

- free access to educational materials and methodologies that introduce the theme of participation in teaching and learning;
- a support package that includes an educational aid: free access to an
  electronic application that guides schools safely through the budget
  implementation process, as well as ensuring transparent voting on
  the best projects in each school;
- a social game developed by USV ROS as an informal tool for introducing participatory budgets and educating young people for active
  citizenship and participation. (NP Participation).

In the school year 2019/2020 the PB at schools were supposed to
continue not only in the Trenčín Region but also in the Trnava and
Bratislava regions, but due to the COVID-19 it was suspended. (www.
participacia.eu).

13.4   Conclusion

The benefits of a participatory budget cannot be generalised. They depend
on the use of individual models. Most of the local governments with PBs
in Slovakia use the "Porto Alegre for Europe" model with a strong civil
society. Only a few other local governments have introduced different
models as defined by Sintomer et al. (2008).

The aim of a PB is, in addition to focusing on the needs of citizens, the
efficient use of funds and more transparency in budgeting and the elimina-
tion of bureaucratic decisions. In Slovakia, PB is no longer understood as
an experiment and is becoming an important part of modern democracy.

It is very difficult to provide any deeper assessment or to point out
some general effects of the PBs, which have been already implemented in
Slovakia. There are two crucial reasons for this statement. Firstly, no PB
has been implemented for two completed continual electoral periods, and
the clear majority of PBs has been implemented just for few years before a
suspension of the PBs due to the COVID-19. Secondly, many PBs have
been implemented as rather experiment-like local initiatives without any
long-term strategy-based vision.

Diffusion of the PB concept has been a heterogeneous process in
Slovakia since the early 2010s. In the very beginning, it could be described
as a fragmented group of policy attempts consisting of few cases (namely
Banská Bystrica, Bratislava, and Ružomberok) with contradictory experiences. These first three attempts were (co)initiated by Utopia, the NGO

that brought the PB concept to the local governments in Slovakia. Despite initial high expectations from the public and local politicians, the implementation of the first PBs did not avoid confusion, disappointments, and disarrays. Later, PBs were initiated by local activists or NGOs, but usually in collaboration with local politicians. The local governments with the PB had to improvise because the PB has not been explicitly regulated by law in Slovakia yet. Their decisions were not illegal but they did not have sufficient support in the existing legal regulation. On this matter Čunderlík (2015) pointed out that in some cases the subsidies for collaborating NGOs were granted in a legally disputed manner.

The PB concept was "discovered" by the state, or more precisely by the USV ROS, in 2017–2020 thanks to the implementation of the national project called "Promoting Partnership and Dialogue in the Field of Participatory Policy Making". This state agency-like institution has become a key policy entrepreneur in the process of further diffusion of the PBs in the conditions of a few regional governments and secondary schools, which are in the founding competence of the mentioned regional governments. As it has been already stated, the pandemic has led to a temporary suspension of majority of the PBs in Slovakia, including those that were implemented by means of this top-down initiative. Regardless of these events, approximately at the same time the USV ROS declared its intention to begin a series of public discussions on the need for either legal regulation or methodological guidance of the PB for the governments at various political levels. The first of these events was held as a virtual meeting in December 2020, and the established working group consisting of various experts and experienced or interested policymakers has had regular meetings since this first meeting.

Analysis of the existing data allows us to point out only case-based effects. From a procedural perspective, it is interesting that the majority of the PBs have been implemented in compliance with the requirements of the Porto Alegre model for Europe, but the local governments have prioritised neither social issues nor inclusion of marginalised groups (Gašparík, 2021), and thematic budget constraints were used only by the regional governments (Novák, 2021). In addition, many local governments open their PBs as much as possible also from a procedural point of view. Such unspecified conditions for project proposals and lack of assessment criteria could lead according to Koštial (2020) to serious difficulties for those who were entitled to evaluate those proposals.

Problems that occurred during the implementation (including voting stage) led in some cases to distrust and adversarial relations between the involved inhabitants and the local politicians as well as public servants. For instance, in Hlohovec, such a problem was used by the opponents of the mayor, who had co-approved the implementation of the PB in the town, in the 2018 local election campaign, and it became an important public issue that influenced the behaviour of some voters (Hrabinová, 2020). But in some other cases (e.g., Banská Bystrica, Veľký Šariš) the PB led to both higher popularity of the local politicians, who had introduced the PB in their towns, and improvement of relations between them and their voters. It can be said, there is a political motivation behind implementing PB—it was either the mayor or councillors in at least seven analysed cases who promoted PB in order to gain more popularity and be re-elected. These mayors and councillors were inspired by other towns, and so while in the early years the approach of introducing PB was bottom-up (from citizens or NGOs), later a top-down approach prevailed.

There are several obstacles that limit the broader use of PB in Slovakia. One of the biggest challenges is how to involve more citizens in PB processes since the share of participating citizens who voted for the projects varies between 0.7% and 19.92%; however, in general, it is rather low. To raise this low measure, the use of online voting and good PB campaigns has helped. Although it is debatable whether voting for projects means active citizen involvement, it is at least a tool that increases the interest of citizens in public services provision in terms of deciding on public spending. Within this context, it is important to point out the relatively low interest of local governments in Slovakia in outsourcing of e-tools facilitating organisation of virtual meetings, submission, and promotion of proposed projects, online voting, and so on. For instance, if one compares the Slovak experience with the experience of local governments in the Czech Republic, differences are clear. The majority of the Czech local governments which introduced PBs also use some outsourced e-tools in this field and there are several providers of the mentioned e-tools; such an approach is not so common in Slovakia, and only several local governments with introduced PBs use outsourced e-tools (NGO WellGiving is the usual provider).

Concerning the economic effects, the local activists as well as inhabitants of several towns perceived negatively that only very limited funds were earmarked for the PBs. A greater concern is the really low amount allocated for PB (between 0.04% and 0.39%): the budgets for citizens' projects do not even reach 0.5% of the total municipality budget. Another issue is the sustainability of the approved projects and their outputs. Many project promoters have underestimated a dimension of sustainability, and it is nothing rare to see the closure of projects (regardless of achieved outcomes) at the same time as the end of their funding. Taking into account experience from some Slovak cases, Brutovská and Hrehová (2019) have stressed that successful and meaningful implementation of the PB requires collaboration between the engaged local activists (sometimes associated in some NGOs) and both the local politicians and public servants.

On the other hand, the question that requires an answer is what the costs of PB implementation are and whether the benefits of PB are higher than these costs. In Slovakia, very little is known about the expense side of this process due to the fact that local governments do not track the administrative and transaction costs of PB. This is a field of further research, together with analysing and measuring the outcomes of PB and the risks inherent in the process.

Acknowledgement This research is equally supported by "APVV-18-0435 Behavioral interventions in local governments: increase of local public policies effectiveness" and "APVV-19-0108 Innovations in Local Government Budgeting in Slovakia".

REFERENCES

Brutovská, G., & Marošiová, L. (2019). *Participatory budgets in practice.* Report paper from project: Civic participation at the local level.

Brutovská, G., & Hrehová, D. (2019). Participatívne rozpočtovanie na lokálnej úrovni (prípadové štúdie). In D. Rovenská & E. Župová (Eds.), *Byrokracia verzus vedomostná organizácia v prostredí verejnej správy.Zborník z vedeckej konferencie* (pp. 22–49). FVS UPJŠ.

Csachová, S., & Nestorová-Dická, J. (2011). Territorial structure of local government in the Slovak Republic, the Czech Republic and the Hungarian Republica comparative view. *Geografický Časopis, 63*(3), 209–225.

Čunderlík, Ľ. (2015). Participatívne financovanie na úrovni územnej samosprávy. Participatívna demokracia v 21. storočí. In D. Čičkánová, I. Hapčová, & V. Mičátek (Eds.), *Bratislavské právnické fórum 2015. Proceedings of an international conference* (pp. 1029–1036). PrF UK.

Džinić, J., Svidroňová, M. M., & Markowska-Bzducha, E. (2016). Participatory budgeting: A comparative study of Croatia, Poland and Slovakia. *NISPAcee Journal of Public Administration and Policy, 9*(1), 31–56. https://ideas.repec.org/a/vrs/njopap/v9y2016i1p31-56n2.html

Gašparík, J. (2021). Diverzita participatívneho rozpočtovania v teórii a praxi. In A. Čajková, D. Klimovský, & N. B. Mulinová (Eds.), *Sociálne vedy z perspektívy mladých vedeckých pracovníkov V* (pp. 10–21). FSV UCM.

Heinelt, H., Magnier, A., Cabria, M., & Reynaert, H. (Eds.). (2018). *Political leaders and changing local democracy—The European mayor.* Palgrave Macmillan and Springer International Publishing. https://doi.org/10.1007/978-3-319-67410-0

Hooghe, L., & Marks, G. (2001). *Multi-level governance and European integration.* Rowman & Littlefield. https://rowman.com/ISBN/9780585381664/Multi-Level-Governance-and-European-Integration

Hrabinová, A. (2020). PP VIII. Transparentnosť výkonu samosprávy a otvorené dáta. In D. Klimovský (Ed.), *Participatívne procesy v praxi. Čítanka participatívnej tvorby verejných politík* (pp. 203–247). MV SR/ÚSV ROS.

Klimovský, D., Pinterič, U., & Jüptner, P. (2019). Path dependence and local (self-) government systems: A comparison of three CEE countries. *Politics in Central Europe, 15*(2), 193–218. https://doi.org/10.2478/pce-2019-0015

Klobučník, M., & Bačík, V. (2016). Local self-government structure in the EU member states in 2011. *Journal of Maps, 12*(4), 671–675. https://doi.org/10.1080/17445647.2015.1060181

Koštial, L. (2020). Implementácia participatívneho rozpočtu v meste Trnava. In K. Hoghová, D. Klimovský, & B. Kolman (Eds.), *Sociálne vedy z perspektívy mladých vedeckých pracovníkov IV. Conference proceedings* (pp. 188–193). FSV UCM.

Krenjova, J., & Raudla, R. (2013). Participatory budgeting at the local level: Challenges and opportunities for new democracies. *Halduskultuur, 14*(1), 18–46. http://halduskultuur.eu/journal/index.php/HKAC/article/view/78

Ladner, A., Keuffer, N., Baldersheim, H., Hlepas, N., Swianiewicz, P., Steyvers, K., & Navarro, C. (2019). *Patterns of local autonomy in Europe.* Springer International Publishing. https://doi.org/10.1007/978-3-319-95642-8

Novák, M. (2021). Participatívne rozpočtovanie samosprávnych krajov v podmienkach Slovenskej republiky. In A. Čajková, D. Klimovský, & N. B. Mulinová (Eds.), *Sociálne vedy z perspektívy mladých vedeckých pracovníkov V* (pp. 31–43). FSV UCM.

PB statute in Banská Bystrica. (2019). *PB statute in Banská Bystrica.* https://cdn.banskabystrica.sk/2019/05/Štatút-participatívnehorozpočtu-Mesta-Banská-Bystrica.pdf

PB statute in Nitra. (2019). *Mením Moje Mesto 2019.* https://www.nitra.sk/zobraz/obsah/31102

PB statute in Partizánske. (2019). *Komunitné projekty 2018—výsledky hlasovania.* https://www.partizanske.sk/index.php?id_menu=136968

PB statute in Prievidza. (2019). *IS-103 Pravidlá participatívneho rozpočtu mesta Prievidza.pdf.*

PB statute in Rožňava. (2019). *Návrh Zásad participatívneho rozpočtu.* https://www.roznava.sk/uploads/files/návrhPR-1.pdf

PB statute in Svidník. (2019). *PRAVIDLÁ—participatívneho rozpočtu mesta Svidník na rok 2019.* https://www.svidnik.sk/download_file_f.php?id=1103066

PB statute in Veľký Šariš. (2019). *Štatút participatívneho rozpočtu Veľký Šariš.*

Sintomer, Y., Herzberg, C., & Röcke, A. (2008). Participatory budgeting in Europe: Potentials and challenges. *International Journal of Urban and Regional Research, 32*(1), 164–178. https://doi.org/10.1111/j.1468-2427.2008.00777.x

Sintomer, Y., Herzberg, C., & Röcke, A. (2013). *Participatory budgeting in Europe. Democracy and public service in the 21st century.* Ashgate.

Székely, G. (2014). Participatívny rozpočet v podmienkach verejnej správy na Slovensku. In I. Dudinský, M. Cirner, & G. Székely (Eds.), *Súčasné reformy verejnej správy na Slovensku a ich politologické aspekty* (pp. 65–82). Vydavateľstvo Prešovskej univerzity.

CHAPTER 14

Participatory Budgeting in Slovenia

Maja Klun and Jože Benčina

14.1 INTRODUCTION

Participatory budgeting (PB) has a forty-year tradition worldwide. It is an innovative approach to citizen participation in the use of public money. Participation is predominantly oriented towards the use of budgetary resources for investments. PB Network (2019) states that there are more than 11,000 examples of participatory budgeting implementation worldwide, most of which are focused at the local level. There are several studies on the positive and negative effects of participatory budgeting in the literature. The most commonly mentioned positive effects are improved transparency, greater citizen satisfaction, and better service to citizens (e.g. Allegretti et al., 2004; Birskyte, 2013; Gilman, 2016; Radu, 2019; Shah, 2007; Wampler, 2007). The criticism of participation is mainly related to the reduced power of elected representatives in decision-making bodies (Allegretti et al., 2004; Memeti & Kreci, 2016). Moreover, the most common obstacles in introducing participatory budgeting in

M. Klun (✉) • J. Benčina
Faculty of Public Administration, University of Ljubljana, Ljubljana, Slovenia
e-mail: maja.klun@fu.uni-lj.si; joze.bencina@fu.uni-lj.si

© The Author(s), under exclusive license to Springer Nature Switzerland AG 2022
M. S. De Vries et al. (eds.), *International Trends in Participatory Budgeting*, Governance and Public Management,
https://Doi.org/10.1007/978-3-030-79930-4_14

practice are the disinterested public, the lack of understanding of the overall financial framework, proposals focusing on the fulfilment of individual wishes, exploitation by powerful stakeholders to achieve their proposals, and so on.

At the state level, participatory budgeting initiatives mostly comprise the publication of the draft budget and the public adoption process. In doing so, the state is to specify the period during which the public is to submit proposals for amendment of the draft budget. The study conducted among the members of the Council of Europe (Vodušek & Biefnost, 2011) shows that, at the time of the study, nine out of 24 countries had adopted regulations that enable public participation in the budgetary process at various levels. Most of those put the focus on the local level, comprising participatory budgeting as a tool for decision-making on public spending.

In Slovenia, the legislation on access to public information stipulates that municipalities are to submit a draft budget to citizens for public discussion and take a stand on the submitted proposals. In this context, the participatory budgeting implementation process is set out in the municipal charters and instructions for drawing up the municipal budget.

In this chapter, the term participatory budgeting is used in its most specific definition. That involves an established process of public participation, with defined criteria for selecting citizens' proposals, and a predefined amount of funds subject to the co-decision, and last but not least, that the selected proposals are implemented in the adopted budget.

The chapter initially presents the evaluation of participation in Slovenia and the legislative framework for participatory budgeting. In continuation, it provides a historical overview of the introduction of participatory budgeting in Slovenian municipalities, the characteristics of procedures in Slovenia, and the amount of funds that municipalities allocate for citizen decision-making, as well as a presentation of an example of the implementation of participatory budgeting in a selected municipality in Slovenia.

14.2   PARTICIPATION AND BUDGET IN SLOVENIA

14.2.1   *Participation Index in Slovenia at the State Level*

The International Budget Partnership (IBP) has conducted the most extensive research in the open budget field since 2006. The Open Budget Survey (OBS) assesses the three dimensions of a budget accountability system: transparency, public participation, and budget oversight. The latest data has been published for 2019 (International Budget Partnership (IBP), 2019). Slovenia ranks high for transparency (open budget index) with 68 points out of 100 and for budget oversight with 82 out of 100 points.

The score for public participation is less agreeable. Slovenia has obtained 11 points (out of 100), which is below the average of all analysed states (14 points). Detailed examination of the assessment of participation reveals that the draft state budget is only formally available to the public and the public can implement its opinion through elected representatives in the parliament only. Moreover, the public plays no role in controlling the budget, but may only propose control to the supervisory authorities. Slovenia has obtained the points for public participation only because the public is allowed to participate in the legislation adoption process in the field of the budget process (International Budget Partnership (IBP), 2019).

According to the OBS results, the public participation dimension is rated low for all countries in the survey. Even OECD countries, which reach an average of 24 points out of 100, experience a relatively low level of public participation in the budget process.

Participatory budgeting, however, has been much more closely linked to the local environment since its 'introduction'. The evidence reported in the literature demonstrates participatory budgeting being focused mainly on local budgets, which holds for the case of Slovenia too.

14.2.2   Legislative Framework of Participatory Budgeting in Slovenia

As indicated above, the legislation in Slovenia enables the public to participate in the local budget adoption process. The legislation governing local self-government stipulates that the municipal charter may grant the village or district committee the right to propose decisions relating to the narrower units of the municipality. The Public Information Access Act stipulates that municipalities are to publish the draft budget, that is, inform the public about the envisaged public spending and enable them to provide an opinion in this respect. Hence, the legislative framework fails to set out specific procedures or obligations in taking public opinion into account and consequently provides only a vague background for participatory budgeting.

Nevertheless, despite the lack of specific regulations, the initial steps of participatory budgeting in Slovenia were made. In 2017, Global Initiative for Fiscal Transparency (GIFT) network and the Court of Audit of the Republic of Slovenia organised a regional seminar on participatory budgeting. All Slovenian associations of municipalities participated in the event and indicated a high interest in participatory budgeting. The purpose of the consultation was to present the principles of participation and motivate municipalities for the implementation of participatory budgeting processes. At the same time, the good practices from other countries were presented as possible raw models for Slovenian municipalities. The Slovenian Government responded to this event by amending the Local Self-Government Act in 2018 (Article 48.a), which stipulated that the municipality is to determine the amount of fund dedicated to financing projects proposed by citizens in drawing up a municipal budget proposal. It imposed municipality implementing participatory budgeting to determine the share of resources intended for projects by a budget ordinance. Furthermore, it charged it to consult with members of the public before submitting the budget to the municipal council for adoption.

Still, the amendment to the legislation introduces a principled approach only, that is, the legislation enables participatory budgeting; however, each municipality may decide whether or not, and in what way, it is to implement the participatory budgeting. Hence municipalities decide autonomously on whether they are to introduce participatory budgeting in the municipal charter or not.

In introducing a participatory budget, the municipalities opt for different approaches. Some apply several process phases; some of them determine the amount of funds for the narrower units, which then freely dispose of; some distribute questionnaires throughout households (Petrovčič, 2018). However, only a small share of Slovenian municipalities has opted for the implementation of the participatory budget. At the same time, the vast majority of them continue merely to inform the public about the draft budget. According to the research in the years 2017–2019, almost 90% of municipalities publish a draft budget for public debate on their websites (Maja Klun et al., 2019).

Since the law obligates the municipalities for doing that, the percentage is not surprising. As the legislation does not stipulate, taking into account public proposals and comments when adopting the budget, they follow merely the principle of transparency while do not decide on the introduction of public participation in budget adoption.

In any case, the trend of participatory budgeting at the local level in Slovenia is positive. In 2019 and 2020, an increasing number of municipalities joined participatory budgeting due to the implemented consultation of municipalities, the amendment to the legislation, and probably partly due to local elections, which is presented in more detail hereunder.

14.3   Development of Participatory Budgeting at the Local Level in Slovenia

In Slovenia, there are 212 municipalities, of which 11 are urban municipalities. They differ a lot according to several criteria. First of all, they vary substantially in absolute measures, area, and population, and variables correlated with the latter. Moreover, the municipalities differ in relative indicators too. For instance, the budget revenues and expenditures per capita deviate from the average by more than 20%. Hence Slovenian municipalities are hardly comparable, neither by the financial or socio-economic capacity nor by the complexity of management and cooperation with citizens.

One of the most critical conditions in implementing participatory budgeting is the budget framework. Municipalities have to finance several obligations determined by legislation. Accordingly, a high proportion of local public expenditure is predetermined. Only a small portion of it is available to be spent according to the needs of the municipality or citizens. Consequently, the 'proportion' of the budget at hand for participatory budgeting is small or neglected. By that, in the vast majority of cases, participatory budgeting in Slovenia comprises small investments.

14.3.1   Participatory Budgeting Practices

As already mentioned in the introduction, our analysis took participatory budgeting as a process with determined steps: getting proposals, selection of proposals according to clear criteria, and implementation of selected projects. The first attempt in this respect was carried out in the municipality of Maribor in 2015. Despite the exact determined steps and criteria, the unresponsiveness of citizens caused the attempt to fail. Thereupon, the idea was put aside until 2019, when the municipality attempted to implement participatory budgeting for 2020. They opted for a different approach implementing the initiative in a narrower sense in a single district community. As the municipality of Maribor is the second largest in

Slovenia, the approach of gradual implementation of participatory budgeting significantly reduces the complexity of the project. Accordingly, the positive story from the project in the first district community could facilitate raising the awareness and motivation of citizens and contribute substantially to the further successful development of the participatory budget in Maribor.

As the first effort failed, we can count the first successful participatory budget at the local level in Slovenia to be initiated in the year 2016 in the municipalities of Ajdovščina and Komen when they started the process of participatory budgeting for the fiscal years 2018 and 2019. The municipality of Ajdovščina, in particular, began the process with great local and nationwide promotion. They invited citizens to participate in the process employing several promotion channels (radio, local newspaper and district meetings). Moreover, to inform the citizens about the exact processes and rules of submission of the initiative, the municipal authorities organised several workshops.

Citizens submitted their ideas on a prescribed form. They had to take into account the predetermined maximum worth of project proposals. The received proposals were evaluated according to predefined criteria by a specially appointed independent committee. The selected proposals were then put to the vote. The proposals voted out were included in the draft budget, and in the adopted budget (Municipality of Ajdovščina, 2020).

A similar approach was employed in the municipalities' of Komen participation budget initiative, presented as a case study in the next section.

The first two successful attempts brought 43 citizens projects in the total value of €420,000, with 31 projects in the total value of €360,000 in the Ajdovščina municipality, and 12 projects in the total value of €120,000 in the Komen municipality. Both have continued the practice of participatory budgeting in all subsequent years, with some modifications (i.e. the municipality of Ajdovščina has introduced a so-called youth section of participatory budgeting).

After the first two attempts and changed regulation in 2018, several new cases of participatory budgeting have been introduced, especially from 2019 onwards. In Slovenia, there is no general platform for following the progress in the field of participatory budgeting at the local level in place. In the absence of any other common source of information, we collected the data by checking the websites of all the municipalities in Slovenia. Since a lot of municipalities' websites are not easy to follow, as they do not include subpages on a budget or participatory budgeting, or they present the process and information on 'news' sites, which are continually changing, we decided to utilise the search engine as well. For this mean, we employed the Google search engine by typing in the keywords 'participatory budgeting of the municipality'.

The results of the review demonstrated that participatory budgeting in Slovenia is in its growth stage. The number of municipalities with participatory budgeting grew from 13 cases in the year 2018 to 21 cases in 2019 and finally to 26% or 12% of all Slovenian municipalities in the year 2020.

On average, municipalities allocated 0.4% of budgetary resources for the participatory part of the budget. If we take into account that the part of budget expenditure on free will disposal of municipalities presented between 5% and 10%, then on average, municipalities dedicated around 3% of budget resources to participatory budgeting. According to research in 2019 (M. Klun & Stare, 2020), the municipalities that performed participatory budgeting had a higher number of inhabitants and higher budget revenues. In reviewing the processes of participatory budgeting at the local level in Slovenia, we can find some common features, which are following those presented by World Bank:

- All municipalities publish a call for proposals, rules for submitting initiatives, and a set of other conditions (e.g. that the initiator can only be a citizen of the municipality or district). Criteria in municipalities differ from cases with stringent criteria (determination of projects that can be included) to instances with more generalised ones.
- Proposals that are collected, and fulfil the criteria, are assessed at the local community or by an especially appointed independent commission.
- All municipalities limit the total amount earmarked for the participatory budget; many of them restrict the value of the individual initiative within that amount too; some of them determined an amount for each district inside the municipality.
- All municipalities collect proposals for investment spending.
- All of them utilise some kind of voting through online applications and/or through the published forms.

In light of the common features of participatory budgeting processes in Slovenian local self-government, we can conclude that the processes meet the criteria or steps foreseen by the World Bank (2013), and those introduced in other countries.

In addition to common practices and rules in all municipalities that implemented participatory budgeting, we can also find some specialties in some municipalities:

- Two municipalities focused on the young population, which means that only citizens in a certain age group could submit proposals, and the voting was only open for this group.
- One municipality introduced a special youth section and determined a separate part of the amount for young citizens within a larger budget for all inhabitants.
- One municipality ran the whole process online, through its web page.
- The promotion of participatory budgeting differed as well. Some of the municipalities prepared special pamphlets, and distributed them to every household in the municipality; others organised meetings and workshops in community districts.

Within the positive trend and many success stories, we can also report a few unsuccessful attempts. We can highlight two interesting cases. In a municipality, the municipality council for two consecutive years opened a debate on introducing participatory budgeting and would like to support it. However, the mayor did not support the idea. The opposite situation occurred in the other municipality, where the mayor introduced participatory budgeting according to common practice, but the municipality council did not support it and stopped the implementation.

We should also grant attention to another practice that is common in several municipalities in Slovenia. According to the definition, we could not take them as participatory budgeting. Nevertheless, they include some kind of participation that influences budget spending. Several municipalities including the City of Ljubljana (the capital and the biggest municipality in Slovenia), promote web portals or social media channels that allow citizens to submit initiatives—not necessarily related to the budget alone— at any time. The initiatives are reviewed by the representatives of the district communities, municipality council, or municipality administration, and considered for realisation. However, as the portals for the submission of citizen's initiatives are not linked to the budget adoption process, and they do not include the rules for the evaluation and implementation of proposals, we cannot consider them participatory budgeting initiatives.

14.3.2   Case Study of the Municipality of Komen

Below, we present a detailed description of the process of the implementation of participatory budgeting in the municipality of Komen, which was one of the first to implement it in practice successfully. Komen is a small municipality with 3536 inhabitants, which combines 35 settlements and 20 village communities. The budget for 2020 amounts to €5.9 million, of which 3% was earmarked for the participatory budget. Every year, since its introduction in 2016, the municipality earmarks the same amount of €120,000 for participatory budgeting. It supports the initiative by strong promotion through leaflets, publications on their website. Additionally, at the workshops and presentations at various locations throughout the municipality municipal representatives explain the participatory budgeting process and rules of submitting proposals and voting to the citizens. The municipality of Komen applies a similar approach as used by the majority of municipalities in Slovenia.

The project selection criteria have been clearly defined upon the first implementation in 2016. Firstly, the criteria stipulate that the context of the proposal must be within the competence of the municipality. Secondly, the investment must be placed within the municipality, and the proposal must not break the legislation and ordinances. Finally, the purpose of the proposal must contribute to the protection of the environment or economic development of the municipality, or promote cultural activities, or create conditions for sport and recreation development, or contribute to the orderliness of settlements and villages. Also, the proposals have to correspond to certain restrictions. The value of project proposals is limited to between €2000 and €6000. Only citizens with permanent residence in the municipality who are older than 15 years could submit a project proposal.

Citizens could submit proposals in different ways: by filling out a form via a webpage, via a web application, by mail, or in-person (Municipality of Komen, 2016). An independent commission is appointed to evaluate the proposals. It adds all the proposals, which comply with the criteria, to the voting list.

Municipality appoints an independent commission to evaluate the proposals. It adds all the proposals which comply with the criteria to the voting list. In the case of the sum value of all eligible proposals failing to reach the maximum value set out, all proposals are to be included in the budget. Otherwise, voting takes place on a specific day, where each citizen could vote for a maximum of five proposals, whereby he/she could only cast a vote for one project within the individual village community. The projects that received the most votes are included in the budget, of course, limited by the maximum sum value of the participatory budget. If two projects in the same village community receive the same number of votes, the project is selected through a drawing of lots.

In the first attempt of the participatory budget initiative in 2016 for the fiscal years 2018 and 2019, a total of 158 proposals were submitted, of which 68 proposals complied with the criteria and were added to the voting list. Of the total population of the municipality, 2940 inhabitants were entitled to vote, of whom 608 people, that is, 21% of citizens cast a vote; 10% of ballot papers were invalid. The projects that received the most votes, that is, a total of 12 projects, were included in the budget. The realisation of the voted projects took two years. Projects related to the arrangement of the village centre, car parking, and bus stops, and the renewal of sports fields, were the best evaluated and realised (Municipality of Komen, 2016).

The following participatory budgeting process for the financial years 2020 and 2021 was carried out in 2019. With a new mayor appointed after the local elections in 2018, the approach changed remarkably. Over this period the submission of proposals was limited to the narrower units in the municipality. This meant the proposals to be submitted by the citizens of an individual village community for their community only, and only community members could vote for the proposals of their community. The funds were the same as in the year before; however, another €10,000 was added for projects targeting young people. The submitting procedure remained the same, except for the submission through the web application.

The evaluation process was supplemented by a previous review of the compliance of the proposals with the legal conditions. Hence the two-step evaluation included the legal conditions check, done by municipal administration followed by a criterion review of an appointed independent commission. The criteria for the selection of projects were changed. On the one hand, they were expanded with the area of tourism development, and greater involvement of young people in society, as the priorities. On the other hand, the construction of new sports and recreation fields, as well as children's playgrounds, was excluded from the participatory budgeting. The limitation of the proposals to individual village communities implicated the change in the voting process as well. The voting was carried out at the assembly of villagers. The citizens voted for a single project whereby young people could also vote for one joint 'youth' project.

In the municipality, the new approach to the participatory budgeting process resulted in a significant decline in participation. The number of proposals dropped sharply to 30. The majority of communities submitted a single proposal only, two of them proposed two projects each, while four communities did not join the initiative. The commission considered 22 proposals as appropriate for inclusion in the budget. As the vote on the projects of the individual village community was to be implemented in only two communities, the number of voting participants was very low—only 45 participants (Municipality of Komen, 2016).

A comparison of the two time periods shows that the approach to participatory budgeting significantly depends on the elected mayors and representatives in the municipal council, who freely develop and implement different approaches to participatory budgeting.

14.4   CONCLUSION

In conclusion, we evaluate participatory budgeting in Slovenian municipalities applying an evaluation scheme based on three dimensions: context, process, and outcomes with impact. The context includes contextual factors affecting participatory budgeting initiatives (socio-political, institutional, issue-related, etc.). The process dimension comprehends organisational context, participation, and procedural output as success factors and measures of efficiency linked to the outcomes. Finally, the outcome dimension covers the fulfilment of set goals and criteria proposed by democratic theory (Schneider & Busse, 2019).

In the Slovenian case, the context is not very favourable to participatory budgeting. The vague legislative framework and the small portion of the municipality's budget leeway provide only a weak ground for developing the participatory budgeting initiative. Because of the Government's fragmented structure, the majority of municipalities face low financial and human resource capacity. Accordingly, participatory budgeting projects considerably depend on the harmonised support of mayors and municipal councils. Moreover, the studies on transparency and participation at the state and local level demonstrate high awareness of transparency and a low level of public participation in Slovenia. The variances of the population over groups of municipalities exercising and not exercising public budgeting are equal. Hence, we could conclude that smaller, as well as larger, municipalities introduce participatory budgeting. Notwithstanding, the average population of municipalities conducting participatory budgeting is significantly higher than in the remaining municipalities. Non-parliamentary parties or independent mayors rule the majority of Slovenian municipalities. Accordingly, they contribute the majority of public budgeting initiatives as well. In line with previous research (Schneider & Busse, 2019), only 5% of right-wing ruled municipalities exercise public participation.

Considering Slovenian municipalities' low capacity within the process dimension, we should expose a weak organisational context in most municipalities. Previous research shows that larger municipalities more often perform participatory budgeting (M. Klun & Stare, 2020), which indicates low financial and administrative capacity a vital obstacle. However, some cases of best practices show that strong leadership results in a sound organisational approach. The implementations are managed and carried out by public servants while for the assessment of project proposals, special commissions are appointed.

The municipalities try to be inclusive in making it possible to submit project proposals for all municipal districts. In two cases, they have addressed youth needs only; an additional case comprised a specific youth category, while other socio-demographic groups have got no special attention. The municipalities implement processes differently. Still, they mostly follow the recommendations of the World Bank. The goals of participatory initiatives are defined and communicated to the public in the form of a value framework and a list of the proposed projects' eligible contributions. According to some published results, around 20% of citizens participate in the processes. Since debates at smaller communities are well conducted, webpage news is transparent, and the citizens can vote through different channels, we can evaluate mobilisation, communication, and inclusiveness relatively high.

Procedures are detailed and explained through meetings and webpages in all municipalities. They are implemented in a user-friendly and barrier-free manner. Participants are well informed about the goals and rules in most cases. Hence, we evaluate the quality of deliberation as high. The fulfilment of the participatory budget goals is assured by independent commissions, which consider the objects of participation and approve voting for only the relevant ones (according to the law and procedure determined).

As already mentioned, the Slovenian municipalities dispose freely of a small portion of the budget and opt only for a small percentage of it for participatory budget projects. Accordingly, the impact and outcomes of participatory initiatives in Slovenia are low. There are no citizens' satisfaction measurements in place. Consequently, it is challenging to evaluate empowerment. Nevertheless, considering the procedure steps, rich communication, and meetings with participants at least gains in knowledge can be confirmed.

The general context in Slovenia is relatively weak. The financial and human resource capacities are in the majority of municipalities low. The broadness of participation depends substantially on the effort put in promotion and motivation of citizens. The municipalities deliver sound procedures of implementation. However, they do not put enough attention to the ex-post evaluation of the outcomes. Besides, it seems the higher legitimacy of the political representatives to be the single outcome expected. Anyway, the small portion of the budget disposed of participatory budgeting initiatives supports the communities' development only marginally.

To conclude, we would like to stress that experience with participatory budgeting gained in Slovenia so far is limited both in time and in terms of presence in the local environment. Although the legislation opens space for the introduction of participatory budgeting in local communities, it appears that it only opens the door to individual experiments in particular municipalities and cannot incite the establishment of common practice. Hence, we conclude that Slovenia's participatory budgeting is a local community domain, whereby it is only declarative at the national level. Despite a brief history of participatory budgeting in Slovenia, we observe, similar to countries with a long-standing tradition, that participatory budgeting is becoming less important in the initially introduced locations, and is transforming into looser approaches with reduced citizen participation. Slovenian evidence shows that it is unlikely that legal provisions and more binding legislation will bring the desired effects. We observe that participatory budgeting can only be successful if at least four preconditions are met: the political will to implement participatory budgeting, successful promotion to and motivation of citizens, and so on, development of stakeholders' importance or influence, and last but not least provision of projects challenging important issues of specific target groups.

Acknowledgement The authors acknowledge the financial support received from the Slovenian Research Agency (research core funding no. P5-0093). We also thank anonymous referees and the editor for their useful comments and suggestions for improvement.

References

Allegretti, G., Sobrero, S., Dove, F., Vos, J. A., & Chavez, D. (2004). Participatory budgets in Europe between efficiency and growing local democracy. *Transnational Institute and the Centre for Democratic Policy-Making, No. 2004/5*, 1–24.

Birskyte, L. (2013). Involving citizens in public decision making: The case of participatory budgeting in Lithuania. *Financial Theory and Practice, 37*(4), 383–402. https://doi.org/10.3326/fintp.37.4.3

Gilman, H. R. (2016). *Participatory budgeting and civic tech: The revival of citizen engagement.* Georgetown University Press. https://www.jstor.org/stable/j.ctt1c6v8hr

International Budget Partnership (IBP). (2019). *Open Budget Survey Slovenia 2019.* https://www.internationalbudget.org/open-budget-survey/country-results/2019/slovenia

Klun, M., Benčina, J., & Umek, L. (2019). Online budget transparency index and its determinants in Slovenian municipalities. *Public Finance Quarterly, 64*(3), 393–413. https://ideas.repec.org/a/pfq/journl/v64y2019i3p393-413.html

Klun, M., & Stare, J. (2020). Participatory budgeting at local level in Slovenia. In: Hintea, C., Radu, B., Suciu, R. (eds.). *Collaborative governance, trust building and community development : conference proceedings.* Cluj-Napoca: Accent. pp. 174–185.

Memeti, M., & Kreci, V. (2016). Role of municipal council in increasing citizen participation at the local budget process. *Central European Public Administration Review, 14*(2–3), 53–73. https://doi.org/10.17573/ipar.2016.2-3.03

Municipality of Ajdovščina. (2020). *Moja pobuda—participativni proračun v Občini Ajdovščina.* https://www.ajdovscina.si/mojapobuda

Municipality of Komen. (2016). *Projekt "Jaz predlagam".* https://www.komen.si/projekt_jaz_predlagam

Petrovčič, T. (2018). *Kako bi pa vi porabili (svoj) občinski denar?* https://www.finance.si/8941346/Kako-bi-pa-vi-porabili-(svoj)-obcinski-denar?cctest&

Radu, B. (2019). The impact of transparency on the citizen participation in decision-making at the municipal level in Romania. *Central European Public Administration Review, 17*(1), 111–130. https://doi.org/10.17573/cepar.2019.1.06

Schneider, S.H. & Busse, S. (2019). Participatory budgeting in Germany – a review of empirical findings. *International Journal of Public Administration,* *42*(3), 259–73. https://doi.org/10.1080/01900692.2018.1426601

Shah, A. (Ed.). (2007). *Participatory budgeting.* The World Bank.

Vodušek, N., & Biefnost, A. (2011). *Legal framework and current practice in* *member states. Report on the CDLR survey of the role of central/regional* *Government in participatory budgeting at local level.* Council of Europe.

Wampler, B. (2007). A guide to participatory budgeting. In A. Shah (Ed.), *Participatory budgeting* (pp. 21–54). World Bank Publications.

World Bank. (2013). *Participatory budget formulation.* The World Bank.

CHAPTER 15

Unraveled Practices of Participatory Budgeting in European Democracies

Juraj Nemec, David Špaček, and Michiel S. de Vries

15.1   INTRODUCTION

The goal of this final chapter is to summarize lessons about the worst and best practices, causes, and effects of (successful or unsuccessful) participatory budgeting, delivered by the country case studies included in this

J. Nemec (✉) • D. Špaček
Faculty of Economics and Administration, Masaryk University,
Brno, Czech Republic
e-mail: juraj.nemec@umb.sk; david.spacek@econ.muni.cz

M. S. de Vries
Institute for Management Research, Radboud University Nijmegen,
Nijmegen, The Netherlands

Department of Public Administration, Kaunas Technological University,
Kaunas, Lithuania

Department of Public Administration, University of the Free State,
Bloemfontein, South Africa
e-mail: m.devries@fm.ru.nl

© The Author(s), under exclusive license to Springer Nature
Switzerland AG 2022
M. S. De Vries et al. (eds.), *International Trends in Participatory
Budgeting*, Governance and Public Management,
https://doi.org/10.1007/978-3-030-79930-4_15

book. As editors we asked the authors of the country chapters to address—at least in part—the following five questions:

1. First, about the developments in PB in the countries: Why and when PB started in the country and at what governmental level; how many municipalities/regional governments experimented with PB; whether PB processes were on-time only experiments or were repeated for several years?
2. Second, about the budget at stake, addressing especially the percentage of the municipal budget open for PB, whether it was about spending additional money or about austerity measures, whether it was already specified beforehand what policy areas were involved or whether the participants could opt for a destination of that budget?
3. Third, about the participation, addressing the rules/selection criteria used for being eligible as a participant; characteristics of the participants, how were they selected, and whether they were adequately informed/educated/trained, and how many residents did indeed participate?
4. Fourth, about the procedure, addressing whether and how ICT instruments were used, how the PB was organized and administered, whether deliberation and voting were involved, how decisions were made, and whether the outcomes were really implemented?
5. Fifth, about the outcomes, addressing whether the political representatives (councilors/aldermen) accepted the outcomes of the PB, whether the outcome did actually make a change in the contents of the budget, whether the participants were satisfied, and what lessons were learned?

Ultimately, the information collected serves to check to what extent participatory budgeting as practiced in the countries involved presents a real attempt to change municipal budgets toward addressing the needs of marginalized groups and to improve decision-making based on local democracy and participation, or whether these processes as such are to be judged to be more important than any output and outcomes. The core indicators for such judgment comprise the part of the budget about which citizens are allowed to have their say, the number of citizens involved in the process, and the extent to which their involvement has resulted in a real change in the public expenditures. For example, if municipalities opened only a very marginal percentage of their budget for participatory budgeting, this transforms it into a trivial pursuit with hardly anything at stake, but the process itself. If the process is more important than the outcomes, such participatory budgeting is not a significant phenomenon but just has become a hoax.

In theory, a distinction is made between policy diffusion, policy transfer, and policy mimesis (Massey, 2009). Diffusion was defined by Rogers (1983) as 'the process by which an innovation is communicated through certain channels over time among the members of a social system' (Rogers, 1983, p. 5). The probability of such policy diffusion is said to be determined by geographical proximity to the original actor implementing the innovation, the number of other actors who have already adopted the innovation, public pressure, learning, and the role of policy champions. Often, a distinction is made between leaders and laggards in such adoption processes, pointing to the extent to which actors are motivated to innovate and have the resources (Mohr, 1999, p. 14). The implicit assumption underneath theories on policy diffusion is that the innovation is copied in more or less the same way as the original. The question is only what determines the probability of adoption of such innovations by other actors. As mentioned in the introduction, such research has also been done on the spread of participatory budgeting (Röcke, 2014).

This book has taken another direction. It does not assume that the policies copied remained identical to the original, but asked instead to what extent deviations from the original are visible in the policy transfer and what this implies for the practices. This question better fits within theories on policy transfer in which policy transfer is defined as a process in which policies implemented elsewhere are examined by rational political actors for their potential utilization within another political system (Evans, 2004, p. 345). As Evans (2004, p. 246) argued, four types of policy transfers can be distinguished:

1. Copying, where a governmental organization adopts a policy, program, or institution without modification.
2. Emulation, where a governmental organization rejects copying in every detail, [but] accepts that a particular program elsewhere provides the best standard for designing legislation at home.
3. Hybridization, where a governmental organization combines elements of programs found in several settings to develop a policy that is culturally sensitive to the needs of the recipient and to develop a policy best suited to the emulator.
4. Inspiration, where an idea inspires fresh thinking about a policy problem, helps to facilitate policy change, expands ideas, and inspires fresh thinking about what is possible at home (Evans, 2004, p. 246 ff).

The question asked is what remains of the original goals and instruments when an innovative policy is transferred to other settings? Was there—in the words of (Hall, 1993) third-order change, that is, a change in the overarching goals that guide policy in a particular field; second-order change, that is, in the techniques or policy instruments used to attain these goals; or first-order change, that is, in the precise settings of these instruments? Dolowitz and Marsh (1996) developed a framework including policy diffusion, policy convergence, policy learning, and lesson-drawing.

In theories on policy mimesis, it is said that 'it may be that there is no such thing as a simple policy transfer, or indeed a transfer at all, rather there are levels of isomorphism' (Massey, 2009, p. 383) dependent on context, of people, and of place. As Andrew Massey argues, 'Everything in terms of policy decisions takes place in the way it does because of what has gone on before and what is going on around and nothing can be entirely replicated when it crosses geographical and cultural boundaries. All policy transfer is in reality policy mimesis' (Massey, 2009, p. 388).

The contents of those theories are reflected in the outcome of this volume. We started by giving a description and analysis of the original, that is, the process of participatory budgeting as it evolved in Porto Alegre, Brazil. In that municipality, participatory budgeting started after the country was democratized. PB involved a huge part of the municipal budget itself; the inclusion of marginalized groups was imperative; the process included deliberation as well as decision-making by the participants; the goal was to improve the position of the marginalized; and the process was repeated for several years.

As is summarized below, with the introduction of PB in European countries much of the original practice was lost. In the literature on PB, this is euphemistically described as "Porto Alegre adapted for Europe", "Proximity participation", or "Participation of organized interests". The fact is that PB as it emerged in Europe, often does not involve changes in the municipal budget but rather the granting of a small amount of money to proposals from neighborhood groups. Often, deliberation is not at all visible, but only a voting process on the grants for the best proposal. Also very often seen is that the process is a one-time-only process, not repeated and just seen as a one-time experiment to show goodwill or as something imposed and subsidized by NGOs. The effect is that only a few citizens actually participate, and the municipal budget is hardly affected.

15.2 Participatory Budgeting in Selected "Old Democracies"

The first three cases covered in this volume—Germany, Italy, and Sweden—serve as the benchmark for the evaluation of the PB practices in Central and Eastern European (CEE) countries that are the main focus of this book. The editors intentionally decided not to use countries, which were already evaluated by existing studies as countries of "best practices" in the area of participatory budgeting (like Portugal, Spain, and France), but selected countries with different administrative systems and traditions, facing potential problems connected with the implementation of PB. The understanding of factors enabling participatory budgeting but also of the weaknesses connected to the implementation of participatory budgeting in established democratic countries is critical for understanding the practices in the investigated CEE region.

Janina Apostolou and Martina Eckardt in Chap. 2 analyze the developments of participatory budgeting in Germany. Within the specific German conditions, where the decision-making power in regard to the municipal budget lies explicitly with the elected representatives of a municipality, Germany decided to adopt its own model of participatory budgeting. In 1998, the network "Kommunen der Zukunft" (Bertelsmann Foundation, the Hans Böckler Foundation, and the Kommunale Gemeinschaftsstelle für Verwaltungsmanagement) promoted the adoption of PB. The network offered to support the first-time adoption of PB processes and looked for municipalities interested in taking part in a pilot project introducing PB. In 2003, a nationwide PB network was launched by the "Service Agency Communities in One World". Following this, the number of PB processes increased over time, reaching a peak in 2013 with a total of 103 PB processes, followed by a drop of about 30% in the next two years. Thereafter the number stabilized at a slightly higher level.

The fact that in Germany 54% of PB processes enabled citizens to make proposals, another 32% to give both feedback and make proposals. Only in 4% of the PB processes citizens had the right to decide on the budget draft. This clearly demonstrates that German PB processes at the municipal level are mainly an instrument for consultation, not of direct democratic co-determination.

The empirical evidence about the impact of PB processes in Germany is relatively scarce. The available evidence suggests that some cities manage to reach quite a strong rate of participation by citizens, but even relatively high participation does not deliver large socio-political effects. Taking this into the account, the question remains why municipalities nevertheless adopt PB schemes. The authors of the German chapter argue that one explanation might be that the decision to adopt a PB process is to find legitimacy for upcoming austerity measures (many municipalities in financial distress have adopted PB and even a special type of PB called "Sparhaushalte", which means saving budgets).

The authors conclude that even if the actual impact of PB processes in Germany is small, they nevertheless meet the goal of increasing transparency regarding the financial situation of a municipality. Over time, this could create fiscal awareness about municipal finances and make citizens more educated in the field of public finances.

Francesco Badia in Chap. 3 argues for Italy that PB attracted considerable interest in the first decade of the current century and has been adopted in numerous cases by municipalities. In Italy, specific laws and rules regarding the promotion of PB were introduced after 2007, especially at the regional legislative level (like the Regions of Tuscany, Lazio, Emilia-Romagna, Umbria, Puglia, Sicily, and Marche). These regional laws promoted the participatory logic and tools, in some cases with the provision of specific funding for the implementation of PB practices. Italy recorded the first case in Europe of PB in 1994 in the municipality of Grottammare. Following this example and new legislation, in the last twenty years several municipalities embarked on the path of participation. The number of experiences with PB peaked in 2008, but then decreased, probably because of the financial crisis and also decreased political interest. The author focuses particularly on the period from 2015 to 2020, and through a survey, he identified 136 PB experiences between 2015 and 2020 that were active for at least one of these years. The results document the two growth peaks of the PB use in Italy, observed in 2008 and 2019, and also the fact that the political component of the municipality was decisive for the initiation of participatory processes. In the majority of cases, the patronage of the PB initiative is of political nature with the identification of the initiative in a party, or sometimes even in a single politician.

The dominant option realized in Italy is project-oriented PB, which gives the citizens the possibility to make proposals of any nature linked to possible intervention and funding from the municipality. The average sum of the municipal budget allocated to participatory projects from the sample researched was 0.76% and the average participation equaled 7.5% of the population.

The vast majority of municipalities researched reported no significant impacts resulting from PB, due to the limited number of resources allocated and small influence on the overall decision-making process of the municipality. However, the responses also provide significant concrete examples of the positive impacts of PB.

Iwona Sobis, the author of Chap. 4 about Sweden, argues that the aim of participatory budgeting in Sweden was to invite citizens into the local decision-making process by planning together how funds from municipal taxes ought to be allocated to different areas. The main promotor of participatory budgeting was the Swedish Association of Local Authorities and Regions (SALAR). In the starting phase, Sweden realized four pilot projects in Avesta, Haninge, Uddevalla, and Örebro, conducted during the period of 2007–2011.

Despite the fact that according to most evaluations the first pilot projects were successful, in their recognition by the public, and contribution to an increase in citizen participation, the continuation of such processes went on reluctantly in Sweden. According to the data collected from SALAR and the homepages of municipalities, only 12 out of 290 municipalities introduced a total of 33 projects of PB between 2007 and 2020.

The question is why Sweden, a country with a long tradition of cooperation between local government, trade and industry, civil society, NGOs, and inhabitants, where public participation in local matters is well established, is so reluctant to implement large scale participatory budgeting (despite the SALAR reports, the municipal websites, Facebook, and blogs from those municipalities conducting a PB project, confirming that citizens were positive about participatory budgeting projects in feeling engaged and satisfied in helping to improve their own community and that PB processes delivered interesting outcomes).

First, the conducted PB projects give the impression that they are introduced under pressure from the EU, the Swedish central government, and the Swedish Association of Local Authorities and Regions. Such top-down pressure imposing PB processes probably cause negative emotions among local politicians, public officials, and professional groups which have stunted its development.

Second, based on the existing experience, the conclusion cannot but be that the Swedish local authorities prefer a representative democracy with a citizen dialogue as sufficient support for decision-making on important local matters. Those in power at the local level are unwilling to share the real responsibility for the municipal budget, even if it only concerns a small fraction of that budget. In Sweden, local governance in which citizens are made (co-)responsible for decisions and the development of their community is absent.

The case of Sweden also indicates that having an organization promoting PB seems to be of the utmost importance. The existence of SALAR and its systematic work to motivate municipalities in their efforts to experiment with PB pilot projects helps to promote slow but growing interest in PB in Sweden. SALAR's latest effort to increase citizen participation in local decision-making has been to establish a network of municipalities for the period 2019–2022 to develop PB in line with the model of democratic- and social sustainability (Table 15.1).

15.3   Participatory Budgeting in Central and Eastern Europe

The editors of this book managed to put together ten country studies characterizing the developments of participatory budgeting in the CEE region. The selection tried to include all types of countries belonging to this group—EU member states, which accessed the EU in the first wave in 2004 (Czech Republic, Hungary, Poland, Slovakia, Slovenia), EU member states with later accession (Croatia, Romania) and non-EU countries (Belarus, Russia, and Serbia). The sample covers highly decentralized countries like the Czech Republic or Slovakia, but also countries where the decentralization is still in its very early phase (especially Belarus). The most important characteristics of countries included are summarized in Table 15.2.

15.3.1   Developments of Participatory Budgeting in the CEE Region

Yuri Krivorotko and Dmitriy Sokol in Chap. 5 argue that the only model of participatory budgeting that could be discovered in Belarus is so-called stakeholders PB because the more standard models of PB with direct or indirect participation in the local budgeting process are unacceptable in Belarus. According to them the working scheme of PB in Belarus is re-granting projects for local initiatives and the key drivers for the development of such a model of PB are international organizations and programs that propose granting money for local initiatives. Over the past 15 years,

Table 15.1 Summary of information of participatory budgeting in selected "old" democracies

Country	PB founded in law?	Diffusion	Main form	Proposals subjected to deliberation with residents?	Who finally decides on proposals? (citizens/council)	Were accepted proposals implemented?	Is PB a repetitive process?
Germany	No	Several municipalities	PB has mainly consultative character	Yes	Local councils	n.a. (consultative PB)	Usually yes, but some municipalities dropped.
Italy	Partly	Several municipalities	Project-based municipal funds are voted by the citizen, but in most cases below 1% of the budget is allocated to PB	Yes	Local councils	Yes	Usually yes, but some municipalities dropped.
Sweden	No	Few municipalities	Project-based municipal funds are voted by the citizen, but in most cases very small % of the budget is allocated to PB	Yes	Local councils	Yes	Usually yes, but some municipalities dropped.

Source: Authors

Table 15.2   Main characteristics of CEE countries covered by this book

Country	Population	Status	Index of decentralization[a]	Democracy Index 2019[b]
Belarus	9.4 mil.	Unitary presidential republic, member of the "Eastern Partnerships"	Very low	Authoritarian regime (2.5)
Croatia	4 mil.	Unitary parliamentary constitutional republic, EU Member from 2013	Medium (20.7)	Flawed democracy (6.6)
Czechia	10.7 mil.	Unitary parliamentary constitutional republic, EU Member from 2004	High (24.6)	Flawed democracy (7.9)
Hungary	9.8 mil.	Unitary dominant-party parliamentary constitutional republic, EU member from 2004	Low to medium (17.3)	Flawed democracy (6.6)
Poland	38.3 mil	Unitary semi-presidential constitutional republic, EU member from 2004	Very high (26.7)	Flawed democracy (6.6)
Romania	19.3 mil.	Unitary semi-presidential republic, EU member from 2007	Medium (20.0)	Flawed democracy (6.5)
Russia	146.7 mil.	Federal semi-presidential constitutional republic, BRICS country	Low	Authoritarian regime (3.1)
Serbia	6.9 mil.	Unitary parliamentary constitutional republic, candidate for EU memberships	High (25.2)	Flawed democracy (6.4)
Slovakia	5.5 mil.	Unitary parliamentary republic, EU member from 2004	Medium to high (22.0)	Flawed democracy (7.2)
Slovenia	2.1 mil.	Unitary parliamentary constitutional republic, EU member from 2004	Low to medium (17.3)	Flawed democracy (7.5)

Source: Authors

[a]Based on Ladner et al. (2016) and estimates for countries not included in this study

[b]Based on *The Economist*

many Belarusian organizations have implemented projects within the territory of Belarus, in which civil initiatives aimed at solving problems at the local level were selected and funded on a competitive basis. During 2006–2020 in total 110 projects were selected on a competitive basis and the total amount of (EU financed) funds raised to finance citizens' participation in local decision-making amounted to 558,000 euros.

Jasmina Džinić in Chap. 6 indicates that in Croatia the first formal projects of PB commenced in 2014, although some practices with characteristics of PB have been existing since the beginning of 2000. According to her findings, Croatia is lagging, both in the number of cities applying PB and in the elaboration of existing practices of PB. Nine towns used to have (Karlovac, Mali Lošinj), (Pazin, Trogir, Rijeka, Pula, Labin, Sisak) or are in the preparatory phase to introduce (Dubrovnik) some kind of PB—this represents only 1.62% of local units in Croatia. Croatian municipalities also apply different models of PB (like "Porto Alegre adapted for Europe", "Proximity participation", "Participation of organized interests"). Given the current situation, it is hard to expect broader diffusion of PB in the country and it is more probable that PB projects will be confined to a smaller number of more developed towns resulting in further disparities among Croatian citizens living in different local communities.

Lucie Sedmihradská, Soňa Kukučková, and Eduard Bakoš in Chap. 7 describe the developments of participatory budgeting in the Czech Republic, from its start in 2014 to its current magnitude. The first municipal participatory budgeting project was implemented in the city district Praha 7 in 2014. In 2019 PB was implemented in 48 towns and municipalities—a still relatively small number of municipalities (over 6200). However, because participatory budgeting is used especially by relatively large cities, the share of the total population involved is fairly high: in 2019 almost 20% of the country's population could participate in PB initiatives. In the Czech Republic, "Porto Alegre for Europe" project-oriented participatory budgeting prevails (suitable projects are selected for implementation according to predetermined rules within a given amount of funds). Additionally, some cases of consultation, where citizens do not vote for proposals and local governments freely and arbitrarily integrate some proposals in the public policy, are also implemented.

Péter Klotz in Chap. 8 argues that the practice of participatory budgeting in Hungary started relatively late (the first attempt was in Kispest in 2016) and is still very limited. The primary reason is political and stems from the different perceptions of the politicians regarding self-government and the involvement of citizens in public decisions. Although good practices in participatory budgeting (also from neighboring countries) were available for a long time, their real practical implementation in Hungary started only with the 2019 municipal election campaign, during which the active involvement of voters in municipal decision-making became an important message—but still, only a few of Hungary's 3155 settlements have practical experience in applying participatory budgeting. The information provided in this chapter presents and compares the practice of participatory budgeting in the most experienced Hungarian local governments: Kispest (District XIX of Budapest), Budafok-Tétény (District XXII of Budapest), and Budapest City. These municipalities use the same approach as most Czech self-governments: "Porto Alegre for Europe" (project-oriented) participatory budgeting. The interest of people to vote is relatively high and interesting projects were approved and realized. Because the national legal-regulatory environment does not support the application of participatory budgets, the use of this instrument is typical in Budapest City and the districts of Budapest under opposition control.

Artur Roland Kozłowski and Arnold Bernaciak provide in their chapter (Chap. 9) on Poland comprehensive information about participatory budgeting in this "regional forerunner". The first participatory budget in Poland was implemented in Sopot in 2011, a small city with 33,000 inhabitants, which is characterized by a high level of citizens' affluence and a high level of cultural, social, and professional activities. The specific factor enabling this start was a political impasse: the mayor and the majority of the City Council took opposite positions and local political forces were looking for new ideas to win the support and tip the balance to their favor during the next elections. The project in Sopot succeeded and became an impulse for other cities in Poland to follow this model. Since 1 January 2019, participatory budget is a statutory obligation for municipalities with county rights. Also, in Poland "Porto Alegre for Europe" (project-oriented) participatory budgeting is the dominant (if not sole) approach of implementing PB. The Polish Supreme Audit Office in its report from 2019 stated that the functioning of participatory budgeting has allowed inhabitants to participate directly in the decision-making process and has reinforced social participation. However, most academic evaluations are less positive and argue that this evaluation does not fully reflect reality and it refers rather to a smaller but active part of Polish society.

Emil Boc and Dan-Tudor Lazăr in Chap. 10 explain the very limited developments of participatory budgeting in Romania through two critical background elements. First, local authorities have limited funds at their disposal as compared to the needs. Second, the historical heritage from the communist era has kept citizens at a distance from any decision-making regarding public life. In Romania, the first public participation projects emerged in 2000 in those cities, which are also academic centers: Brașov, Timișoara, and Cluj-Napoca. The process, as it unfolded in Mănăștur, one of Cluj-Napoca's neighborhoods, in 2013, was the first PB process in the country—in the form of a consultative PB model. In 2015, in Cluj-Napoca, the first project-oriented participatory budgeting system started ("Porto Alegre for Europe" model). After being implemented in Cluj-Napoca, this approach has spread rapidly to other Romanian cities—as a relatively simple concept, easy to accept and apply by the administrations, regardless of their political spectrum and, last but not least, open to experimentation and improvement.

Mstislav Afanasiev and Nataliya Shash in Chap. 11 evaluate the functioning of so-called Initiative budgeting, which represents the concept used in Russian practice. It refers to several practices of involving citizens in the budgeting process, based on the ideology of citizen participation. "Initiative budgeting" is understood as the area of government regulation of public participation in determining and selecting projects, which are funded with budget revenues, and in the subsequent control of carrying out the chosen projects. The history of "Initiative budgeting" in Russia spans almost 15 years back. It started in 2007 with the World Bank launching the project "Local Initiatives Support Program" in the Stavropol region and gained active support from the Russian Ministry of Finance. The project was later extended to other regions. In July 2015 the Russian Ministry of Finance and the International Bank for Reconstruction and Development (IBRD) signed a memorandum calling for the further spread and development of similar practices. The "Initiative budgeting" received comprehensive support in subsequent years. In 2019, related projects covered 4.7 million participants from the country's population of 144 million people and almost 90,000 project ideas were put forward, covering 68 out of the 85 subjects of the Russian Federation. In the end, 18,700 winning projects were selected in 25 regional project centers for the amount of 19.3 billion rubles (or 233 million euros at an exchange rate of 83.5 rub/euro). Russia implements a "Porto Alegre for Europe" (project-oriented) participatory budgeting model, where citizens propose projects and play a critical role in selecting successful projects for financing. The executive practice differs, in some cases the whole process is administered by subnational governments, in other cases, this is completely or partially delegated to government (municipal) institutions or non-commercial organizations, the founders of which are municipal authorities or even outsourced to outside consulting organizations. "Initiative budgeting" in Russia, without doubt, generated growth in interest among citizens toward mechanisms for determining budget spending, primarily at the municipal level.

Miloš Milosavljević, Željko Spasenić, and Slađana Benković in Chap. 12 argue that participatory budgeting in Serbia developed through several externally financed projects centered around Local Finance Reform. The projects were initiated by civil society organizations that partnered with Serbian LGUs and were financed externally (EU funds, USAID, Norwegian, Swiss development agencies, and other donors). As the idea was not indigenous, the models implemented have been "imported" from West European local governments. PB was initiated in 2016 in ten municipalities, including the capital city of Belgrade, and included self-governments representing 11% of the total population in Serbia. Serbia uses the "Porto Alegre for Europe" (project-oriented) participatory budgeting model, where citizens propose a project, vote on alternative proposals, and the winning projects are implemented. The core problems connected with participatory budgeting in the country are the lack of interest and, consequently, the poor participation of citizens in the process of selection of projects, and the small amount of funds involved in the implementation of PB projects. The authors argue that the outcomes from participatory budgeting are below initial expectations although it contributed, to a limited extent, to the democratization and modernization of local government. Only in the city of Sabac the process is becoming popular among citizens as it addresses their needs and priorities.

Mária Murray Svidroňová and Daniel Klimovský in Chap. 13 characterize the situation in Slovakia where the first three municipalities starting with participatory budgeting were the city of Bratislava in 2011, followed in 2013 by the town of Ružomberok, and the city of Banská Bystrica in 2014. In all of these municipalities, the process was initiated by a local NGO initiative and the work of volunteers. The case of Bratislava was specific—in the first year (2011), the money for PB (€15,000) was obtained from sponsors, not from the public budget. The total number of local governments offering participatory budgeting to their citizens started to increase significantly after the realization of the first experiments as 53 local governments and 3 self-governing regions promoted the idea of a participatory budget at the beginning of 2020. However, given a total amount of 2900 municipalities and eight self-governing regions, this is still minor. Participatory budgeting is also realized at the school level, where pupils are enabled to co-decide on the spending of an allocated part of the school budget. A clear majority of projects belong to the so-called Porto Alegre for Europe (project-oriented) model of participatory budgeting, but other forms (like the consultative model) exist, too. The processes of project-oriented participatory budgeting vary over municipalities, but the main principle is similar—citizens propose projects, vote on them, and the winning proposals are approved and financed by municipalities. The authors argue that in Slovakia, PB is no longer understood as an experiment and is becoming an important part of modern democracy. However, the main challenge is to involve more citizens in PB processes since the share of participating citizens who voted on the projects is small, although it varies between 0.7% and 19.92%. The outcomes from participatory budgeting in Slovakia are not yet visible.

Maja Klun and Jože Benčina in Chap. 14 evaluate the situation in Slovenia. In this country, the first initiatives related to participatory budgeting started relatively late. The first, but failed, project started in Maribor in 2015, and the first successful participatory budget was initiated in 2016. In 2017 the GIFT network (Global Initiative for Fiscal Transparency) and the Court of Audit of the Republic of Slovenia initiated the start of a more comprehensive process. Subsequently, the country started to focus on participatory budgeting. Today, the legislation in Slovenia not only (as international standard) stipulates that municipalities are to submit a draft budget to citizens for public discussion and take a stand on the submitted proposals, but also (from 2018) requires that municipalities are to determine the amount of funds used to finance projects proposed by citizens in drawing up a municipal budget proposal. Despite the existing legal framework only a small share of Slovenian municipalities (26% or 12% of all Slovenian municipalities in the year 2020) has opted for the implementation of the "Porto Alegre for Europe" (project-oriented) model of participatory budgeting. The vast majority of them continue to merely inform the public about the draft budget, and few use specific models that allow citizens to submit initiatives. In Slovenia, only a small portion of the municipality's budget is used for participatory budgeting, providing only a weak ground for developing local participation. The low financial and administrative capacity of smaller municipalities is a vital obstacle to the process.

15.3.2   The Scale of Participatory Budgeting in the CEE Region

In all the examined countries the "Porto Alegre for Europe" (project-oriented) model of participatory budgeting (or its specific modifications in Belarus and Russia) dominates, but a common feature is a limited number

Table 15.3   The scale of participatory budgeting in selected countries

Country	PB founded in law?	Diffusion in municipalities	Main source of finance
Belarus	No	129 municipalities in total in different periods	EU funds (about 81%) + co-financing from local organizations
Croatia	No	Few, to several municipalities	Municipal funds (0.02–1.39% of the total budget), co-funding (contribution) from local community in one case
Czechia	No	Several municipalities	Municipal funds (0.02–1.94% of the total budget)
Hungary	No	Few municipalities	Municipal funds (from 0.25–1.5% of the total budget in cities covered by the chapter)
Poland	Partly	322 municipalities in 2017 (out of 2478)	Municipal funds (0.2–1.5% of the total budget)
Romania	No	Few municipalities (16 cities)	Municipal funds (about 1% of the total budget, in some cities even more)
Russia	No	Widespread on all subnational levels	Subnational funds plus co-financing (233 million EUR in 2019)
Serbia	No	Few municipalities	Municipal funds (from 0.04–8.50% of the total budget)
Slovakia	No	Few to several municipalities, three out of eight regions, few schools	On municipal level municipal funds (from 0.05–0.39% of the total budget)
Slovenia	Yes	12% of municipalities	Municipal funds (0.4% of the total budget in average)

Source: Authors

of participating public bodies and a small amount of funds allocated (Table 15.3).

In most countries, some form of participatory budgeting is realized at the municipal level. In Russia and Slovakia such processes also emerge at the regional level and in Slovakia also at the school level.

15.3.3 How Participatory Budgeting Is Organized and Administered in the CEE Region? How Many People Participate?

The country chapters indicate that the main form of participatory budgeting in CEE is the so-called Porto Alegre for Europe model—project-based participatory budgeting. The general picture of this type of participatory budgeting process in CEE is as follows:

1. announcement of a call for projects (in most cases total predetermined amount already approved in the budget is also announced),
2. collection of project proposals,
3. pre-selection of projects (dominantly by municipal bodies based on project feasibility or technical analysis),
4. voting on pre-selected projects, and
5. financial approval and implementation of successful projects.

Table 15.4 summarizes the main processual aspects of participatory budgeting in selected CEE countries.

The eligibility of a project can be fully open, but can also be somewhat restricted. For example, in Belarus there are three mandatory conditions to be met under submitting applications for funding from an extra-budgetary fund:

1. Mandatory participation of citizens in decision-making and problem-solving at the local level. Citizens should be active participants in the project implementation at the stages necessary and possible.
2. The project application must contain the creation or construction of a socially significant object (sports ground, recreational zone, bike path, ecological trail, etc.), or improvement of yards, parks, monuments of culture and nature, and so on.
3. EU funds submitted for financing shall be used to purchase building materials and equipment and may not be used to pay for works and

Table 15.4 Main processual aspects of participatory budgeting in selected CEE countries

Country	Proposals subjected to deliberation with residents?	Who finally decides on proposals? (citizens/council)	Were accepted proposals implemented?	Is PB a repetitive process?
Belarus	Yes, usually	Tender commission composed of representatives of two NGOs	Yes, usually	Yes, usually
Croatia	Yes, usually	Local councils	Probably yes	Usually yes, but few municipalities dropped
Czechia	Yes, usually	Local councils	Yes, usually	Usually yes, but some municipalities dropped
Hungary	Yes, usually	Co-decision (local council decides the total budget, citizens vote)	Probably yes	Usually yes
Poland	Yes	Co-decision	Normally yes, only in exceptional cases no	Normally yes, PB is now compulsory for certain types of municipalities
Romania	Yes, usually	Co-decision	Probably yes	In some cases yes
Russia	Yes	Co-decision	Yes	Usually yes
Serbia	Yes, usually	Co-decision	Probably yes	Usually yes
Slovakia	Yes, usually	Co-decision	Probably yes	Usually yes
Slovenia	Yes, usually	Co-decision mostly, sometimes only local bodies	Probably yes	Usually yes, but few municipalities dropped

Source: Authors

services that may be performed or provided for citizens free of charge.

The processes are far from perfect. Numerous organizational dilemmas pertain to the ways of project submission, organization of voting, economic efficiency of the process, and decisions about eligibility to vote. Social dilemmas pertain to the lack of well-developed, efficient systems of communication between local authorities and inhabitants and also to the open attitude and involvement of inhabitants in public affairs.

Illustrative are the problems in Polish participatory budgeting processes, even though PB is subject to legislation in this country. As the chapter on Poland mentions, there are:

1. no reporting on the implementation of participatory budgeting;
2. no national standards for the implementation and reporting on participatory budgeting;
3. no social control over the implementation of participatory budgeting;
4. a weak communication between administration offices and inhabitants;
5. a domination of strong lobbies;
6. no making decisions based on the current political needs.
7. the necessity of collecting inhabitants' signatures on the project submission forms;
8. the obligation of providing voters' PESEL personal identification numbers during the voting;
9. an introduction of age limits for people who wish to participate in consultations on participatory budgeting;
10. issues in the reliability of verifying project submission forms.

The level of participation in "Porto Alegre for Europe" (project based) model of participatory budgeting differs between CEE countries, but especially between involved self-governments. The most illustrative case is Poland, where an analysis by the Supreme Audit Office indicates a high differentiation in the interest displayed by the inhabitants. In 2017 the highest voter turnout was recorded in Kalisz (73%) and in 2016—in Pleszewo (71%). In 2016 the lowest voter turnout at the level of 3% was recorded in Piotrków Trybunalski and in 2017—in Aleksandrów Łódzki (NIK 2019, 44%). In Slovakia the participation in selected investigate projects was between 0.7% and 19.9% of inhabitants.

Limited participation, which prevails, is a critical obstacle for a successful implementation of participatory budgeting. If only 1–2% of inhabitants participate, it is obvious that only these are somehow linked to projects votes. In such a situation not the best projects, but those with the largest number of people supporting them (directly involved or invited to vote) win and receive financing.

The main reason for the very limited participation seems to be the limited amount of funds allocated. In such a situation, citizens do not feel that participatory budgeting is a significant tool to be involved in or to partake in decision-making processes about the most effective use of municipal (or other) resources.

15.3.4   What Are the Outcomes of Participatory Budgeting in the CEE Region?

The outcomes created by the use of participatory budgeting are rather mixed. It is interesting that in countries with the lowest "democracy score"—Belarus and Russia—the evaluations of such outcomes are the most positive. In Belarus respondents provide a set of important outcomes achieved, as follows:

1. PB promotes constructive interaction between citizens and local authorities and local problems become more visible and understandable; local and regional initiatives help to develop urban space, architecture to the extent which could not be achieved by unitary state action.
2. PB stimulates civic activism; citizens try to offer their idea, to be useful, to be heard, and are becoming more active.
3. PB is the support tool for local decisions initiated by residents and by this the public confidence in the authorities is increasing.
4. PB enables more efficient spending of budget funds to solve problems significant for citizens.

The chapter on Russia lists points to positive social effects—the involvement of citizens in the process of budget management, higher levels of trust in government; the engagement of citizens in the participation in the development of the region, reduced dependency of citizens, and increasing literacy of the population in matters of budget allocation.

The opinions of authors dealing with EU member or candidate countries vary and are in many cases less positive. The most optimistic expression could be found in chapters about Poland and Romania.

For example, the Polish Supreme Audit Office report about participatory budgeting is rather positive, concluding that participatory budgeting has allowed inhabitants to directly participate in the decision-making process and due to such social participation civil society is reinforced and the municipality inhabitants' trust toward self-government and its representatives increased. However, the authors are less positive and feel that such a positive evaluation only refers to a small, active part of Polish society. Numerous scientific publications on the efficiency of participatory budgeting implemented by Polish self-government units conclude that such processes have significantly affected the development of cities, as they have allowed numerous permanent projects to be implemented and have activated the involved citizens.

In Romania, the outcomes of those projects that were implemented are relevant for the communities. Even if the scale is small, for a former communist country like Romania, with a low level of decentralization, with a legislative environment that focuses solely on "citizen consultation", it is important to conduct such processes. Local administrations see these processes as a crucial element for developing local communities and as a support factor for local good governance.

Other opinions are more mixed. The chapter on Croatia argues that PB delivers some positive effects on citizen participation and mutual trust between citizens and local government. However, the effects are still very modest. The Czech chapter suggests that because PB mostly serves as an "extension" or "supplement" to existing financing by the municipality, it is disputable whether the PB expenses are high enough to motivate the Czech citizens to participate and to accomplish the goal of increased civic involvement. The Slovak chapter speaks about potential case effects, but not about positive systemic outcomes. The least positive is the Serbian case. The authors state that the outcomes that emerge from participatory budgeting in Serbia are below initial expectations and it cannot be concluded that the purpose and goals of this process are met.

15.4   Conclusions

All in all, the practices of PB as they evolved in European countries out of the innovative original as developed in Porto Alegre in the 1990s can neither be seen as a process of policy diffusion nor as a process of policy mimesis. At best they can be seen as an inferior form of policy transfer in which the original was inspirational, but nothing more. The terminology of Participatory Budgeting remained, but the goals and tools to achieve the goals resulted only in marginal changes in the status quo in municipalities in European countries practicing PB, instead of resulting in radical changes to increase spending in favor of marginalized groups.

The literature mentions factors at the macro, meso, and microlevel as key drivers or inhibitors of policy transfer. The chapters in this book show that Andrew Massey was completely right when he argued that 'Everything in terms of policy decisions takes place in the way it does because of what has gone on before and what is going on around and nothing can be entirely replicated when it crosses geographical and cultural boundaries' (Massey, 2009, p. 388).

Nonetheless, the contextual, macro, meso, and micro factors responsible for the unraveling of policy transfers are not easy to identify. The spread of PB in countries with a long tradition in representative democracy has been a process as tedious as it is in the European countries in transition, in our case the CEE countries. Longstanding traditions in shaping budgeting processes pose major obstacles for the actualization of innovative processes, no matter how influential the policy champions are and how intense the promotion of such novelties is.

Secondly, the chapters in this book suggest that the classic view in which micro, meso, and macrolevel factors are distinct factors promoting or inhibiting the adoption of innovations need revision. The microlevel actors are to be seen as mediators between the impact of meso and macrolevel factors on the dilution of novel practices. All country chapters point to the crucial role of local politicians in the way PB is organized and the outcomes thereof. In this case, explaining the appearance of unraveled policies during policy transfers is mainly explained by lacking political will to adopt a complete transfer. At the local level, this political will may well be due to institutional factors such as, lacking capacity of municipalities (Nemec & de Vries, 2015; Reddy et al., 2015); contextual factors, for example, the habits involved in longstanding representative democratic practices as seen in Sweden, Germany, and Italy blocking democratic innovations, or the backsliding of national democracy as seen in Poland, Hungary, and Slovenia, in which PB is a kind of compensation for the deterioration of national democratic practices.

The prerogative of elected politicians to decide on the budget, where to spend money on, how much money to spend on what, where, and how, relates to the classic political question already posed by Harold Lasswell in 1936, namely to see the question 'Who gets What, When, How' as the crucial question in politics. Local politicians in Europe in whatever macro-context, appear to be extremely reluctant to share the political power to decide on these questions with their residents. Partly this is due to their own meager influence on the local budget, that is, their own limited political power. Their budgeting is often restricted by national regulations determining not only the size of the local budgets as such, but the funding transferred from the national government to the local government often also predetermines in which policy area these grants are to be spent. All substantial decisions regarding local finances are to a large extent often already made by the national government. What remains for local elected officials is indicative of their minor power. They seem to be reluctant to experiment with PB, implying that if such experiments are initiated only a minor part of these minor amounts of money are subject to it, and preferably only once, and if possible, only with money from outside sources. From the local politicians' point of view, the municipal budget is theirs and theirs alone to decide upon as they are elected to represent the interests of their constituency.

The realistic conclusion cannot but be that this results in a vicious circle in which the absent political will of local politicians to initiate processes of PB degenerates such processes into reluctantly allocating only a very small sum of money in a one-time experimental setting. Residents are only being enabled to propose projects in predetermined policy areas on which hardly any deliberation takes place, after which the elected politicians decide on whether or not to spend money on successful proposals. The outcome is that only a few residents participate and many of them become disappointed. The politicians frame this as being indicative of the impossibility of PB and eagerly return to classic ways of budgeting.

The question is how to break through this circle. The results described in the previous chapters mention that separate steps to accomplish this have been taken in different countries. It involves external pressure as seen, for instance in Poland and Slovenia, in *national laws* stipulating municipalities to have some kind of PB. It also involves the sometimes successful but often also failing *persuasion* by external actors—policy champions—with their own funds to induce municipalities to experiment, and by the interest and pressure by local residents. Although such pressure is helpful in establishing PB, in none of the countries involved this resulted in a widespread diffusion of a form of PB similar to the original as developed in Porto Alegre.

The first part of this volume with three cases from "old democracies" indicates that participatory budgeting does not represent a "unique winning tool" from the perspective of improved local democracy, participation, and budgeting. In Sweden, normally ranked as a highly decentralized and democratic country with very strong local self-government, participatory budgeting is still unpopular, not welcomed by local officials, and only randomly supported and promoted by the citizen. Those in power at the local level are unwilling to share the real responsibility for the municipal budget, even if it only concerns a fraction of it. Local governance in which citizens are made (co-)responsible for decisions and the development of their community is not present in Sweden. In Germany, participatory budgeting processes at the municipal level are mainly an instrument for consultation, not of direct democratic co-determination. Moreover, in most municipalities, participatory budgeting is used only as a tool to show that municipal leaders want to cope with fiscal stress situations. The most positive picture is presented by Italy. This suggests that South European countries with their specific cultural features may be more open to participatory budgeting and more successful in its use (taking into account the fact that especially Portugal is frequently named as leader and pioneer in this area)?

This book revealed that in none of the countries the development of participatory budgeting is a natural bottom-up process, where local officials together with citizens apply an innovative instrument. This should not be so big a surprise for Russia and Belarus, because of the type of national regimes there. In both these countries (and also in Serbia) International organizations were the main source behind the development of participatory budgeting, which was welcomed and supported by local authorities as the resulting form of PB did not interfere with their decisions on the municipal budget.

The fact that political motives are determinative for the development of participatory budgeting is emphasized in several chapters. The patronage of the PB initiative is often political with the identification of the initiative with a party, or sometimes even with a single politician. In Romania, participatory budgeting has become a topic in election campaigns with opposition parties in several cities proposing the creation of such processes. The same picture is witnessed in the chapters on Poland and Hungary. In Hungary, their real practical implementation started only during the 2019 municipal election campaign, in which the active involvement of voters in municipal decision-making became an important message of opposition parties. The Polish chapter states that the implementation of PB in Poland has two aims:

1. involving local communities in co-management of the city through joint decisions about how to spend some part of public funds (as is reflected in the voter turnout) and
2. promoting the authority which originally comes from political rivalry.

The extreme form of the latter aim is judged to be a travesty, turning PB into an instrument used in political conflict.

The country chapters also show that different subjects serve as critical drivers of the development of participatory budgeting. Except for international organizations (already mentioned for Belarus, Russia but also Serbia), policy champions are found in NGOs in cooperation with central state organizations (Slovenia), NGOs and civic initiatives pushing local self-governments (Slovakia), NGOs pushing politicians (Czech Republic), and also in local leaders as part of their political marketing. It is clear that "a policy champion is needed" (most often an NGO), but that such an actor is not always available.

From the point of the process, it is clear that in CEE countries the "Porto Allegro for Europe" model of participatory budgeting dominates and the focus of its implementation is on the local self-government level. In most cases, citizens and/or NGOs propose projects and citizens vote for projects, which should be implemented (and in most cases also are implemented). The core problem for all countries is the relatively small sum of resources allocated for deliberate decisions by citizens—resulting in limited participation by citizens. With limited participation, participatory budgeting tends to become a "club good" and not a "common good" with all related negative impacts on expected positive outcomes (see de Vries, 2016).

PB in CEE has additional bottlenecks. Not only low amounts of money and a small number of people are involved, but also in many cases, participatory budgets are realized only once and are seldom repeated (as shown in country-cases, some municipalities join, others opt out—see Table 15.4). Participatory budgeting in most cases also does not serve as a tool for increased budget transparency and budget consultations. In too many cases it rather resembles a "fight" to get an additional project funded by the municipality.

To conclude, we may state that PB in European countries is far away from the level of "best practice" in which local democracy and participation are promoted. However, it is also not possible to conclude that all experiences are just "trivial pursuits". This would fail to appreciate its spread (at least in some countries) and the positive outcomes as perceived by the core stakeholders. This refers to the idea of PB promoting transparency, direct democracy, trust, and satisfaction among the citizenry. In reality, the level of satisfaction of people about processes of participatory budgeting is mixed. In some municipalities people are enthusiastic, in others, the participants are enthusiastic at first, but frustrated afterward, and in still others, the participation faces opposition from the start.

The CEE countries do not perform less than the old European democracies. The same evaluation as made above is equally applicable for the three benchmark countries as to CEE countries. In two of the three old democracies (Sweden and Germany) the situation compared to the "CEE average" is even worse. In these old democracies with strong traditions in representative democracy, local self-government leaders are not less reluctant to transfer decision-making power to the population than local politicians in the CEE countries.

The chapter in this book demonstrates that participatory budgeting in Europe is not yet a mature phenomenon, its potential is not fully utilized, and expected outcomes are only partly achieved. As to the future of participatory budgeting in Europe, it is not easy to predict if processes of PB are to improve in the near future. The COVID-19 pandemic not only critically affected the health status of inhabitants and damaged national economies and welfare but also blocked local participatory processes, including participatory budgeting. Most projects and initiatives were postponed to "better times". We assume local politicians will not be too upset by this finding.

REFERENCES

de Vries, P. (2016). The inconsistent city, participatory planning, and the part of no part in recife, Brazil. *Antipode, 48*(3), 790–808.

Dolowitz, D., & Marsh, D. (1996). Who learns what from whom: A review of the policy transfer literature. *Political Studies, 44*(2), 343–357. https://doi. org/10.1111/j.1467-9248.1996.tb00334.x

Evans, M. (2004). Understanding policy transfer. In *Policy transfer in global perspective* (pp. 10–42). Taylor and Francis. https://doi.org/10.432 4/9781315246574-2

Hall, P. A. (1993). Policy paradigms, social learning, and the state: The case of economic policymaking in Britain. *Comparative Politics, 25*(3), 275. https://doi.org/10.2307/422246

Ladner, A. N., Keuffer, N., & Baldersheim, H. (2016). Measuring local autonomy in 39 countries (1990–2014). *Regional & Federal Studies, 26*(3), 321–357.

Massey, A. (2009). Policy mimesis in the context of global governance. *Policy Studies, 30*(3), 383–395. https://doi.org/10.1080/01442870902888940

Mohr, L. B. (1999). One hundred theories of organizational change: The good, the bad, and the ugly. In H. G. Frederickson & J. M. Johnston (Eds.), *Public management reform and innovation: Research, theory, and application* (pp. 17–36). The University of Alabama Press.

Nemec, J., & de Vries, M. S. (2015). Local government structure and capacities in Europe. *Public Policy and Administration, 14*(3), 249–267. https://doi.org/10.5755/j01.ppaa.14.3.13434

Reddy, P., Nemec, J., & de Vries, M. S. (2015). The state of local government. *Public Policy and Administration, 14*(3), 160–176. https://doi.org/10.5755/j01.ppaa.14.3.13430

Röcke, A. (2014). Framing citizen participation: Participatory budgeting in France, Germany and the United Kingdom. In *Framing citizen participation: Participatory budgeting in France, Germany and the United Kingdom*. Palgrave Macmillan. https://doi.org/10.1057/9781137326669

Rogers, E. M. (1983). *Diffusion of innovations* (5th ed.). Free Press. https://www.amazon.com/Diffusion-Innovations-5th-Everett-Rogers/dp/0743222091

Index[1]

---

[1] Note: Page numbers followed by 'n' refer to notes.

Printed in Great Britain
by Amazon